after the Congress of Vienna

FINLAND

OF SWEDEN

Helsinki

St.Petersburg

Stockholm

Riga

Moscow

BALTIC SEA

RUSSIA

Tilsit

Königsberg

Danzig

RANIA

SIA

URG

Warsaw

POLAND

NY

SILESIA

Prague

Troppau

KRAKOW

AUSTRO HUNGARIAN

Vienna

Buda Pest

MOLDAVIA

Odessa

EMPIRE

CRIMEA

Laybach

WALLACHIA

DOBRUJA

BLACK SEA

Belgrade

Bucharest

Boundary of the German Confederation

DALMATIA

BOSNIA

SERBIA

BULGARIA

OTTOMAN

Sofia

MONTENEGRO

ALBANIA

THRACE

Constantinople

MACEDONIA

EMPIRE

Naples

KDM. OF THE TWO SICILIES

Messina

Athens

MOREA

Catania

SICILY

CRETE

The Sovereign Remedy

By the same author

The French Exiles 1789–1815
The Parvenu Princesses
Matters of Felony
The Empress Josephine
The Art of Cuisine (translation)
Napoleon and Paris (translation)

The Emperor Francis of Austria, the Czar Alexander
of Russia and King Frederick William III of Prussia

MARGERY WEINER

The Sovereign Remedy

EUROPE AFTER WATERLOO

CONSTABLE
LONDON

First published in 1971 by
Constable & Company Ltd
10 Orange Street London WC2H 7EG
Copyright © Margery Weiner 1971

ISBN 0 09 458100 2

Set in Monotype Ehrhardt
Printed in Great Britain by
Ebenezer Baylis and Son Ltd
The Trinity Press, Worcester, and London

In dedicating this book with great affection to Compton Mackenzie, I feel it an inadequate return for the many years in which his wit, his humour, his wisdom and his precious friendship have enriched my life.

Contents

Illustrations

1*

Illustrations

Foreword

The Sovereign Remedy is a study of the European congresses which followed the end of the Napoleonic Wars. As an attempt to settle disputes by international consultation they may be regarded, not perhaps without justice, as forerunners of the League of Nations and United Nations.

This book is concerned less with national policies than with the actual congresses and the friendships and enmities of statesmen and sovereigns, which made their meetings so rich in comedy and drama. To give the congresses 'the form and colour of their time', I have, wherever possible, allowed the characters to speak in their own words, derived from manuscript sources and their published correspondence. Except where absolutely essential I have deliberately avoided consulting modern secondary works.

The initial stages of writing were illumined for me by the invaluable advice and suggestions of the late Dr Thomas J. Wilson. I deeply regret that I did not throughout have the benefit of his wisdom and erudition.

Wherever I have worked, in record offices and archives both in England and on the Continent, I met with unfailing kindness and readiness to help. My very special thanks are due to Fraülein Elisabeth Janssen of the Stadtarchiv at Aachen. Her eager enthusiasm and willingness to assist me went far beyond the lines of duty.

I am particularly grateful to Major-General the Earl Cathcart, D.S.O., M.C., for allowing me to consult the relevant Cathcart Papers and personally demolishing the legend that his ancestor had any part in spiriting away from Russia Alexander I after his supposed death.

To the Marquess of Londonderry I am indebted for kind permission to quote from the Londonderry Papers in the Durham

County Record Office and to reproduce the portrait by Lawrence of the 3rd Marquess of Londonderry. I also want warmly to thank Dr Seaman and Mrs Christine Frame of that Office both for their generous help and loan of the block of that portrait.

Both at the Archives Diplomatiques of the Quai d'Orsay in Paris and the Public Record Office in London the staffs were extremely helpful. To them I should like to express my gratitude as well as to Mr Deryck Cooper of the British Broadcasting Corporation for information about Mozart's *Little German Cantata*.

Once again I should like to express my grateful thanks to the Vicomte Augustin de Rougé for the great interest he has shown in what I have written about his ancestor, the Comte Auguste de la Ferronays (and for taking so much trouble to unearth for me the original watercolours of Laybach which hung in the Comte's study).

Finally I am most grateful to Mr David Karmel, C.B.E., Q.C., and Mrs Karmel for drawing my attention to the gold snuff box presented at Aix-la-Chapelle to the Rev. Lewis Way and for much valuable information about it.

CHAPTER I

The Raft on the Niemen

THROUGHOUT the night of 24 June 1807, officers and men of the artillery of the French Imperial Guard had laboured feverishly to build the raft of boats which at sunrise floated gently on the swell of the broad river Niemen dividing Russia from Prussia. The bare planks of two pavilions, hastily knocked together on the raft, were masked by white drapery, fresh green branches and garlands of flowers, their entrances decorated with an intertwined A and N, the initials of Alexander I, Czar and Autocrat of All the Russias, and Napoleon, Emperor of the French and King of Italy.

For this rendezvous with Alexander Napoleon had travelled far in time and distance, exchanging on his thousand-mile and twenty-eight-year journey the threadbare uniform of a second lieutenant of artillery for the Imperial purple of France. In his stride he had taken the glorious victories of Austerlitz, Ulm, Jena and Auerstädt, the bloodier victory of Eylau and, on 14 June, anniversary of his triumph of Marengo in 1800, his victory of Friedland over the Russians and Prussians.

The march of Alexander, and his ally, Frederick William of Prussia, had been signposted only by the series of defeats which culminated at Friedland, and had now brought them to the old gabled city of Tilsit to sue for peace.

To the French troops, covetously eyeing the enemy's encampment across the Niemen, peace seemed premature. A final battle, another Friedland—a mere morning's work—would crush the Russians decisively. The French army would then have realised its passionate wish to re-establish an independent kingdom of Poland, scored and scarred off the map of Europe by the partitions of the 18th century, but it was now too late; the Emperor had decided otherwise. Alexander still had an army. Peace would be negotiated, not dictated.

The treaty between Russia, Prussia and France was already drafted and the raft on the Niemen designed as an ark of peace.

Precisely at noon on 25 June Napoleon galloped down the ranks of the Old Guard drawn up beside the Niemen to be rowed over to the raft. He was easily recognizable to watchers on the further shore by the dark blue uniform of his Imperial Guard, slashed with the broad red ribbon of the Legion of Honour, and the familiar black beaver hat with its tricolour cockade.

Cheers of *Vive l'Empereur* floated across the water to Alexander as he embarked in his turn, wearing the sombre black tunic, collared and cuffed in red laced with gold, of the Preobrazhensky regiment of the Imperial Russian Guard, and the pale blue sash of the Order of St Andrew.

Alone on the Russian bank the disconsolate figure of Frederick William, King of Prussia, huddled in a Russian cloak to hide his Prussian uniform, watched the boats draw away from the shore while cannon boomed in salute from both banks of the Niemen. The King saw Napoleon spring aboard the raft a few seconds before Alexander landed on it, saw the two Emperors embrace and then disappear into the theatrical setting Napoleon had devised for the meeting.

When Napoleon and Alexander emerged from the pavilion two hours later not only the weathercocks on the roof, in the shape of Imperial Russian and French eagles, and changed direction. Napoleon, despite his confidence in remaining unmoved by the Czar's charm, had felt its impact, while Alexander was bewitched by the man whose powers of seduction were as irresistible as his military genius.

Each man, however unwillingly, was fascinated by the other so that, however far their policies diverged in the future, however cruel the wounds each inflicted on the other, the electric current sparked off between them on the raft on the Niemen never wholly lost its potency. To the end of his life Napoleon held to his belief in Alexander's affection for him, while of Napoleon the Czar said,

'I never loved anything as much as I loved that man.'

Natural grace, courtesy and amiability, the frank expression and smile of a handsome, rather boyish face, combined with fastidious elegance, were elements of Alexander's charm. Especially attractive in so powerful a monarch was his love of simplicity, as genuine as his dislike of the pomp and circumstance imposed by his rank.

Alexander's education and upbringing had been submitted to two incompatible influences, the liberalism of his grandmother, Catherine the Great, and the autocracy of her son, Paul. As a shuttlecock between them the boy maintained his precarious position as ultimate heir to the Russian throne only by acquiring habits of dissimulation, foreign to his nature but which with time became ingrained.

Catherine, patron of the enlightened philosophers of the 18th century, gave Alexander as tutor the Swiss republican, Frédéric-César de La Harpe, who fed his eager pupil on ideas of social equality and human welfare, while his father subjected him to a régime of fear and strict military discipline.

Marriage to a young princess of Baden at the age of sixteen emancipated Alexander too early, but the couple did not enjoy much happiness together. They became wholly estranged when their two children died in infancy, a loss which made Alexander more passionately devoted to his two daughters by his adored *maîtresse en titre*, Princess Narischkin. Although not as promiscuous as his grandmother, Alexander flitted from one love affair to another, benefiting by the convention that mistresses were as essential an attribute of monarchy as the regalia.

Under La Harpe's influence Alexander hesitated between two dreams; to abandon his claim to the throne for the quiet and detached life of a contemplative, or to seize his opportunity to free Russia from servitude and obscurantism.

The moment of decision came prematurely with the murder in 1801 of Paul I whose progressive insanity in a reign of five years had brought Russia to the verge of disruption. Paul's violent death cast the shadow of parricide over Alexander, but his life-long remorse stemmed from his connivance in the plot to force Paul's abdication, not from complicity in the assassination.

With his father's death Alexander assumed the formidable responsibilities of an autocrat, but he determined to wear his powers with a difference. He would be a liberal autocrat, although La Harpe's admirable concepts were of little practical application to a vast country as yet barely emerged from the dark ages.

The ambivalence of the Czar's character showed itself first in his foreign policy. In the course of six years he attached himself to France, then to England and finally, by joining with Austria and Prussia against France, brought disaster on himself.

Alexander was thirty when he came to Tilsit, but his susceptibility to external influence, his sudden violent enthusiasms, succeeded by equally sudden revulsions, suggested a protracted adolescence and the strong feminine streak frequently found in men attractive to and greatly attracted by women. These rapid changes in mood, responsible for startling reversals in policy, indicated a basic insecurity and inner conflict between the philosopher Alexander was by education and inclination, the despot by inheritance and the antagonistic genes of his mixed Russian and German ancestry. In time he became apparently so schizophrenic as to lead some of his contemporaries to suspect traces of his father's madness.

This then was the man, Tom Moore's 'half Caesar and half dandy', who at Tilsit made another *volte-face* when he fell under the influence of Napoleon's magnetism.

After the meeting on the raft Alexander transferred his headquarters to Tilsit for a fortnight's inseparable companionship with Napoleon while their armies fraternized by signs and the universal language of meat, beer and brandy.

Only two discordant notes marred the general harmony, the deplorable weather and the anguish of Frederick William of Prussia, finally summoned by his conqueror to Tilsit for a *Diktat* and a welcome as icy and contemptuous as Alexander's had been warm and friendly. While the Czar was treated more as an ally than as an enemy Frederick William felt himself to be a trophy of conquest rather than a fellow-sovereign. Napoleon lost no opportunity of turning the knife in the still unhealed wound he had inflicted on the Prussians at Jena in 1806.

As Frederick William trotted behind the two Emperors with the awkward gait and manner which embarrassed Alexander and irritated Napoleon his face was so dejected that even the French pitied him. Only in letters to his wife, Luise, could the King reveal his bitterness and the snubs he suffered at the hands of 'the beast and his infernal suite'. He was paying heavily for his worship of Frederick the Great, which had led him to emulate his great-uncle's military exploits without his genius and ruthless drive.

Napoleon believed that, although Frederick William relied heavily on his wife's superior intelligence, his jealousy of Alexander kept Queen Luise away from Tilsit. The three monarchs were firm friends. Common German blood, mutual eagerness to further their subjects' well-being, similar high-mindedness and benevolence had drawn them together at their first meeting in 1802. Thereafter their friendship was strengthened by an affectionate correspondence. Whether or not Alexander's susceptibility to Luise's beauty sustained their intimacy it was Frederick William who clung to it most tenaciously.

Of the trio the King of Prussia was the least attractive. He was reserved and taciturn, the habitual expression of his pale blue eyes one of melancholy. Even Luise's belated arrival at Tilsit failed to enliven his spirits.

Queen Luise of Prussia had envisaged the momentous meeting of three crowned heads as having some noble end in view, some manifestation of greatness and clemency. As well as a treaty lenient to Prussia she hoped for a peace guaranteed by all the European powers, a premature ideal she shared with Alexander. Her disappointment was thus the keener when all she met with from Napoleon was his usual clumsy gallantry to beautiful women and a bland disregard of her plea for moderation. Prussia's future now depended only on Alexander's friendship.

At their daily conferences Napoleon was dazzling the Czar with the prospect of perpetual peace, a vision to which La Harpe's pupil, genuinely concerned about the welfare of humanity, could not fail to respond, but Catherine's grandson listened greedily to the suggestion of a world divided between the two Emperors, of which his share would be the Ottoman Empire.

From the conferences a little news leaked out to the waiting armies—the Emperors had reached agreement, the terms of a peace treaty had been settled. The Grande Armée began to murmur,
'We've well and truly done with wars now'
and to dream of a triumphal return to France and the garlands of peace.

On 7 July 1807 the Emperor of the French and the Czar of All the Russias signed a treaty of peace and perfect friendship, preparatory to a general peace, to which the first step would be Alexander's mediation between France and England. Should he fail, a secret treaty of alliance, annexed to the Treaty of Tilsit, required him to declare war on England.

If the axiom that all alliances spring from common hatreds is true then the Franco–Russian agreement stood a good chance of success. English failure to lend him adequate support against Napoleon had turned Alexander's earlier cordiality to hatred, but it was still only reluctantly that he submitted to Russia's participation in the

Continental System and, in common with French-dominated Europe, denied his ports to British ships.

In his turn Napoleon made what he regarded as a handsome gesture. 'To prove his sincere desire to unite France and Russia by ties of unalterable confidence and amity', and because of the Czar's personal friendship with Frederick William, the French Emperor agreed to modify his demands on Prussia, but the hand he held out was empty. A trivial restitution of territory was poor compensation for the amount he seized, leaving Prussia dismembered as once Frederick the Great had carved up Poland, and a breeding-ground for revenge. Yet another peace treaty carried within it the seeds of new wars.

Frederick William's bitter silences and Luise's disdainful glances were witnesses that Alexander's failure to press Prussia's case showed him to have fallen short of his almost antique idea of chivalry. After the meeting at Tilsit the friendship between the sovereigns cooled and their correspondence was not resumed.

The Treaty of Tilsit was a diplomatic triumph for Napoleon as great as any of his victories in the field, but his grandiose scheme of a world divided into an Empire of the West and an Empire of the East was a bluff. While Alexander, with unwavering faith in the Emperor's dream, waited only for his word of command to launch his own eastern ventures, the French ambassador to Russia was instructed to discourage the Czar from forays into Turkish territory. He was encouraged to declare war on England.

When Alexander re-crossed the Niemen to return to St Petersburg Napoleon from the river bank waved to him in friendship and farewell. The Emperors had exchanged promises to visit each other's capitals and Alexander was already planning enthusiastically for his guest. Before Napoleon came to Russia the Czar intended to visit Paris, see the French Emperor at home, talk to him again and inspect the great institutions he had created.

Alexander was mistaken. Napoleon came to Russia first and when, seven years after the meeting at Tilsit, Alexander kept *his* promise, the French Emperor was not in Paris to welcome him.

In the following year the two Emperors met again at Erfurt but, although their friendship was apparently still as warm, their ambitions and policies were beginning to diverge. Napoleon, intent on building his castles in Spain, now needed Alexander's co-operation to secure his rear while he took personal charge of military operations in the Peninsula.

This altered relationship enabled Talleyrand, no longer French Foreign Minister but still an adviser, to begin sapping his master's interests. He undermined the Czar's confidence in Napoleon and suggested that Alexander's true alliance was with the French people rather than with their Emperor. Luise of Prussia, fearful of fresh humiliations in store, resumed her correspondence to warn Alexander not to be inveigled into action against Austria, pointedly omitted from the galaxy of sovereigns invited to Erfurt.

This concerted pressure encouraged Alexander to show unusual resolution in resisting Napoleon's blandishments. Where the French Emperor hoped for steel he found lather. Alexander offered nothing but vague promises of support should Austria declare war, but he stood aloof when Austria again rashly challenged France, to meet the defeat at Wagram in July 1809, which raised Napoleon's empire to its apogee.

Alexander had returned an evasive answer to Napoleon's proposal of marrying his sister but illogically he felt slighted when Napoleon, impatient for an heir, married the Austrian Archduchess, Marie Louise. The Czar's allegiance to Napoleon was being eroded less by the personal rebuff than by the realization of his fears that the Continental System would ruin the Russian economy. At the end of 1811 he finally renounced Russian participation in the blockade of the British Isles to conclude a secret agreement with England. Tilsit was remote when he could write to his sister, the Grand Duchess Catherine of Oldenburg,

> These devilish politics go from bad to worse, and the infernal being who is the curse of the human race becomes from day to day more abominable.

The infernal being was about to show himself more abominable still. Napoleon wilfully refused to admit that rigid adherence to the blockade was economic suicide for Russia; he seized on Alexander's relaxation of import controls as a *casus belli*. When the French Emperor, mounted on the horse ominously named *Friedland*, crossed the Niemen on 24 June 1812, the river bore not even a spar from the ark of peace. It had sunk with all hands since Prussia and Austria were now his reluctant allies in the invasion of Russia.

As Napoleon rode into Moscow on 14 September 1812, the Czar's plans for his reception had long since gone by the board. He was grimly retreating into the interior, loudly accused of the misfortunes of his empire, of public and private ruin, of having forfeited his country's honour and his own. Military disaster could easily result in personal disaster for the son of Paul I.

For a month Napoleon lingered in the blazing city, hoping that Alexander would, as after Friedland, fall into his arms. Finally, as he gazed into the sour face of failure, he realized that he had to deal not with his friend, Alexander Romanoff, but with a determined enemy, the Czar of All the Russias, who had acquired a powerful ally.

When Napoleon turned his back on the gaudy domes and barbaric steeples of the Kremlin to stumble across the interminable plains, rapidly blanketed in snow and ice, Alexander, hot in pursuit, now rode with the sword in one hand and the Bible in the other. Holy Russia's deliverance from the invader had converted him from a man of no religious faith into one convinced that national and personal salvation lay only in religion. Alexander believed that divine providence had saved Russia and in all humility attributed victory to the Supreme Being. From this moment he became absorbed in the quest for salvation which progressively influenced his own conduct and policies.

On 16 October 1813, at Leipzig, the Russians, once again allied with the Prussians, the Austrians, the Swedes, a motley collection of German states, including the Saxons, who changed sides in the course of the fighting, broke Napoleon in the Battle of the Nations. Two months later the Allies were on the Rhine while Wellington with the British was pushing up into the south of France from Spain where Napoleon's castles had been built on sand.

The Allies celebrated the New Year of 1814 by crossing the French frontier, but this invasion seemed full of hazard. Informed circles in England, after twenty years of French victories, were sceptical of the Allies' chances of success. Bonaparte would play his games better at Paris than in Russia and would again be felt in English blood and pockets; though clipped, his wings and nails would grow again. All would depend on how the French nation answered the call Bonaparte made to them.

As he began the rearguard action of the Battle of France and rallied the peasants into irregular bands of 'blue blouses' there were no signs of the nation's failure to respond.

Behind the waggon-trains, the camp followers and the commissaries hurried the diplomatists to engage in manœuvres as intricate as Napoleon's feints, withdrawals, defeats and victories, in this, his most brilliant campaign. In rhythm with the armies' advance or retreat the Foreign Ministers and Chancellors shifted their ground from Bâle to Langres, from Langres to Châtillon, from Châtillon to Troyes and from Troyes to Chaumont in a dizzy see-saw as at one moment Bonaparte was up and the Allies down and the next he was down and they were up. Only three men held doggedly to their set course—Alexander of Russia to fulfil the promise made at Tilsit, Marshal Blücher to avenge Jena and Napoleon Bonaparte to keep his throne at all costs.

Congresses, conferences, projects of armistice and treaties had proliferated since the Russian campaign revealed the vulnerability of Napoleon and his Grande Armée. Alliances had been renewed, broken and re-aligned. Disunion was the Allies' greatest danger; their solidarity was in urgent need of reinforcement.

Lord Grenville, the former Prime Minister, was pessimistic about their having learned, even with the experience of thirty years, the wisdom of the old fable of the bundle of sticks; if they had not, then Bonaparte might repair by negotiation in the winter all he had lost by defeat during the campaign.

Viscount Castlereagh, the British Foreign Secretary, decided that, while the fighting continued with unabated severity and Napoleon's defeat was still problematical, his personal intervention was essential to weld the Allies into an inflexible offensive treaty of alliance against France.

Castlereagh's arrival on the Continent was doubly interesting to his Continental colleagues. Alone among the European diplomatists he was the unknown quantity. The other Allied representatives were all well acquainted, either because as young men they had served *en poste* at the same Courts or because more recently they had attended the same conferences. Although England had been France's most persistent enemy, her naval victories, colonial conquests and even her intervention in the Peninsula were remote from the Continental main stream of the war, nor had she previously sent a senior representative to Allied councils.

Was Castlereagh's presence at the Allied green table now to be taken as an indication that England was moving away from her traditional aloofness from the Continent?

Two contingencies faced the Allies, the victory or defeat of Napoleon. If he was victorious they would, as on so many previous occasions, have to make the best terms possible with him. If he was defeated then Castlereagh for one realized that the confusion of Allied aims must be clarified. Mediation would be necessary to resolve the clash of ambitions, particularly those of Austria and Russia, rival claimants to the supremacy in Europe which Napoleon's collapse would leave to let.

Between the two empires the main issue was Poland. Metternich, the Austrian Chancellor, who governed the Emperor Francis and Austrian policy, wanted to dismember Poland yet again. The Czar was bent on establishing her as an independent kingdom under his own rule, there to carry out those essays in liberal government impracticable in Russia.

The Grenadiers of the Guard at Tilsit showed greater foresight than their Emperor. Had they in 1807 been allowed to show their admiration for their comrades in arms, the Polish Lancers, by making the kingdom of Poland, her independence would have been assured and they perhaps not now fighting on their own soil.

While the outcome of the war was still in doubt and Napoleon's dominion of arrogance, although diminishing, still intact, the complex Polish problem was shelved although it continued to be a latent irritant between Austria and Russia. Political hostility between the two countries was further embittered by personal antagonism between Alexander and Metternich, who in public professed admiration for the Czar's noble character while privately distrusting his liberalism.

A less avowable cause of antipathy between the two men was the undercurrent of boudoir rivalry. In Vienna at this moment the Russian Princess Bagration, favoured by them both, was flaunting her liaison with the Austrian Chancellor and throwing 'her Metternich' in everyone's teeth.

Alexander's anger was further roused by Metternich's consent to Allied violation of Swiss territory, whose independence he had been taught to respect by La Harpe, still one of his most trusted advisers. The resignation and humility before God the Czar counselled in

private were not shown to Metternich, whom he roundly accused to
his face of conduct disgraceful in itself and damaging to Alexander's
own reputation. To mark his displeasure, and to frustrate Metternich's wish to curtail military operations in the hope of reaching
agreement with Napoleon on peace terms, the Czar transferred his
headquarters to Langres.

Count Nesselrode, one of the principal Russian foreign secretaries,
shared Metternich's views about the inadvisability of further fighting. He fell into disgrace with Alexander because he wanted to push
on, not to Paris, but with negotiations for the good and even glorious
peace he believed to be in the offing and which would be jeopardized
by intensified hostilities. Nesselrode, however, was inured to 'the
cracked ideas which germinate in certain heads' and bore his august
master's vagaries with resignation, waiting hopefully for him to veer
on another tack.

While the Czar sulked at Langres the Allied discussions began at
Bâle. Austria was represented by Prince von Metternich, in uneasy
harness with Count von Stadion, his predecessor as Foreign
Minister, Prussia by the elderly and deaf Prince von Hardenberg,
Russia by the Corsican Count Pozzo di Borgo, another of the Czar's
hybrid troupe of advisers, and Great Britain by her Foreign
Secretary, Robert Stewart, Viscount Castlereagh, accompanied by
his private secretary, Joseph Planta, Jr.

To Castlereagh's earlier career, to the stigma he carried at home
of repressive policies in Ireland the Continental statesmen were
indifferent. He was, and had been since 1812, the Foreign Secretary
of Great Britain, their most powerful ally. To his 'sort of Irish
eloquence which often excited the hilarity of Parliament and amused
the public' they were prepared to listen indefinitely; the pleasant
sound of guineas for subsidies jingling in his pocket drowned the
'weak, washy, everlasting flood' of his oratory.

Castlereagh's impassivity, hauteur and icy demeanour were
deceptive; for his family alone he kept the warmth of an affectionate
heart. In Lawrence's portrait the eyes of Castlereagh seem fixed dis-
dainfully on a remote object but careful study of the painting reveals
a boyish diffidence about the mouth. Had his contemporaries
observed it they might have tempered the abuse and dislike his conduct of public affairs attracted.

William Hazlitt was perceptive enough to glimpse the 'gallant
spirit that shone through his appearance'; his pen picture of

Castlereagh 'whom nature seemed to have meant for something better than he was' is as revealing as Lawrence's oils.

'It might be said of Lord Castlereagh, with disparagement, that he looks more like a lord than a gentleman; we see nothing petty or finical, assuredly . . . but a flowing outline, a broad, free style. He sits in the House of Commons, with his hat slouched over his forehead, and a sort of stoop in his shoulders, as if he cowered over his antagonists, like a bird of prey over its quarry—"hatching vain empire".

'There is an irregular grandeur about him, an unwieldy power, loose, disjoined, "voluminous and vast"—coiled up in folds of its own purposes, cold, deathlike, smooth and smiling—that is neither quite at ease with itself nor safe for others to approach.'

The spontaneous sympathy which sprang up at this first meeting between Castlereagh and Prince Clement von Metternich can only be attributed to the attraction of opposites. In common they had the aristocracy which supersedes nationality, their early success, distinguished careers, conservatism and suspicion of the mass. There the similarities ended. Far more than three years in age separated the two men.

Although German by birth, Metternich was French by education and Austrian by adoption. When his native Rhineland was overrun by the French he went to Vienna and in the Austrian diplomatic service was *en poste* at Dresden and Berlin and finally as ambassador in Paris.

Except in height Castlereagh did not appear to advantage against Metternich's more obvious good looks and decidedly more graceful manners. Metternich, too, had the manner, which Castlereagh lacked. One was a natural cosmopolitan, the other insular. Metternich was fluent in many languages; Castlereagh grappled, not always successfully, with French alone.

Metternich's intelligence was exceptional but he was naturally a born dilettante. While he clung to the policies and outlook of the 18th century, in the universality of his knowledge and interests he was a man of the Renaissance. His fascinated absorption in the sciences was brushed by German pedantry, he was a magpie collector of anything and everything, his taste in literature was sensitive but, perhaps first and foremost, he was a musician. An accomplished violinist, he adored listening to music and playing it himself. Beethoven's grandeur was beyond him; his preference was for virtuoso singing, especially of Italian opera.

Where Castlereagh never showed his feelings, Metternich was expansive. Where Castlereagh was an indefatigable worker, Metternich at this period of his life dissipated his enormous vitality. Where Castlereagh was a faithful, even uxorious, husband, Metternich's liaisons were legion.

Metternich's chief fault was the overweening conceit which increased with age and success. His fatuity led him to regard himself as equal in stature with Napoleon; he preened himself on being a great moral force and indispensable in Europe but Talleyrand, his equal if not his superior in professional finesse, called him the great liar who never deceived.

Although a devout Catholic Metternich was not overburdened with principles. His guiding light was the same as Sir Robert Walpole's—*quieta non movere*. In his best of all possible worlds everything was for the best, therefore change did not indicate progress.

How far removed was this hedonist, cultured to his fingertips, this *galantuomo* with the saving grace of a sense of humour and a mordant wit, from Castlereagh, austere in character and conduct. Few people did not succumb to Metternich's charm and gaiety but perhaps Castlereagh was more susceptible to the Prince's absolute certainty, about himself, his talents and his policies. As Hazlitt suggested, in Castlereagh there was something not 'quite at ease with itself', some wound to the spirit inflicted by the contumely he inwardly suffered while outwardly apparently impervious.

The friendship which developed between Castlereagh and Metternich facilitated an early understanding of their national objectives. Austria wanted only the restitution of her Italian possessions. Since she was not a maritime power Metternich readily fell in with Castlereagh's wish to exclude discussion of British jealously guarded maritime rights from the peace conference, inevitable whichever side proved victorious. Metternich was also ready to concede the union of the former Austrian provinces in Belgium with Holland in a kingdom of the Netherlands. The port of Antwerp, vital to British security, would then be held by hands friendly to Great Britain, essential since others beside Lord Grenville believed that, if Napoleon kept his throne, his temperament would scarcely suffer him to keep the peace.

As an additional precaution against any future aggression towards

Great Britain based on the Low Countries Castlereagh, on his way to
Bâle, had arranged a dynastic alliance between Prince William of
Orange and Princess Charlotte of Wales, heirs to their respective
thrones.

Castlereagh, now assured of Metternich's valuable support, bent
all his efforts to securing the Allied unity demanded for Allied victory. When the two ministers, armed with their own basic agreement,
met Alexander at Langres they were relieved to find him in a more
amenable frame of mind. The Four Powers were thus able on 29
January 1814 to sign a Protocol providing for the continuance of the
war under the supreme command of the Austrian Field-Marshal von
Schwarzenberg, for armistice negotiations to be held simultaneously
with peace talks at Châtillon and, when peace had been made, for a
congress to meet at Vienna to settle any matters left outstanding.

The preliminary conference opened at Châtillon at the beginning
of February. Napoleon was represented by his Foreign Minister,
Caulaincourt, Duc de Vicence. Alexander's esteem for the former
French ambassador to Russia seemed a good augury for success had
the terms offered by the Allies not hardened considerably since the
conference held at Frankfort in November 1813.

Then Napoleon, still confident of defeating the Allies in the field,
had scorned their offer of France's 'natural frontiers', the Alps, the
Rhine and the Pyrenees. Now all the Allies were willing to concede
to France was her 'old limits', her frontiers as they stood in 1791.
Caulaincourt was desperately anxious to persuade his master to accept these terms, but could he be brought to agree to this amputation
of his empire?

Napoleon himself had no illusions about the compatibility of the
Allied ultimatum and his own future as Emperor of the French. Only
personal disaster could result from the sacrifice of what France herself had gained by the exertions of her ragged revolutionary armies
before his own advent. At Dresden in June 1813, he had stormed at
Metternich,

'Your sovereigns born upon the throne can allow themselves to
be beaten twenty times and will always return to their capitals. I am
only a self-made man who will cease to reign the day I cease to be
strong and therefore fail to command respect.'

Napoleon's future was not a matter of concern for himself alone;
the Allies also were involved. Metternich, Castlereagh and Hardenberg were all equally anxious to quash Alexander's latest enthusiasm,

to replace Napoleon by Bernadotte, once Marshal of France and now Prince Royal of Sweden.

At this point Castlereagh was ready to subscribe to Metternich's policy, to which the Chancellor clung for two months of negotiation —an early peace to save the Bonaparte dynasty before irreparable disaster overwhelmed Napoleon. Austria wanted to keep him on the throne but cut down to size with a truncated empire; his family alliance with the Hapsburgs would add France to Austria as counter-weights to increasing Russian influence in Europe.

Castlereagh made it plain that any change in England's attitude to France's future régime was more apparent than real. While personally he favoured a Bourbon restoration as a more likely guarantee of lasting peace the principles laid down by Pitt in 1792 were still those of the British cabinet in 1814—abandonment of French conquests in return for British non-interference in the internal affairs of France or her choice of government.

As General Bonaparte the soldier was trying to save Napoleon the sovereign the Allies finally realized that their hesitations and dissensions were imperilling their victory. At Castlereagh's insistence the Allies, supported by the incentive of further British subsidies, on 9 March 1814 at Chaumont signed a treaty of defensive alliance against Napoleon to be maintained for twenty years after the end of the war.

This treaty was reinforced by a solidarity pact, guaranteeing their mutual security to the four signatory Powers. At some future date these guarantees might be extended to the rest of Europe, especially to those states which peace might liberate from French domination. These states the Powers proposed to erect as bulwarks against any attack by the revolution they believed Napoleon to personify. The Allies further bound themselves to maintain their solidarity by periodical meetings, the first of these, as mooted at Langres, to be held at Vienna.

Caulaincourt at Châtillon was fighting as doggedly in conference as Napoleon in the field, but all his desperate concessions were now confidently rejected by the Powers since it was apparent that, short of a miracle, Napoleon was fighting his final campaign.

In their lengthy course the Allied discussions had often seemed idle and frustrating, but at last agreement had been reached on immediate policy and some national aspirations revealed. The most valuable outcome of the talks was the Treaty of Chaumont, the matrix of European relations for a number of years and begetter in the future of remarkable progeny.

Through the hail of words, proposals and counter-proposals Castlereagh had held firmly to his line, the conclusion of a satisfactory peace founded on the old principle of the balance of power.

'It is something', wrote Lord Grenville, 'to have lived to see the moment when one may without ridicule talk again in the British parliament of the balance of power.'

For once Nesselrode was justified in putting on his rose-coloured spectacles. He had been confident that, with the aid of a few sensible men, the ship could be brought to port. In this category Alexander was not included since the 'personage' was still at variance with his ministers, but Castlereagh merited a place. Nesselrode did not think him at all brilliant but conceded that he was eminently distinguished for the conduct of affairs, nor did the Russian deny that the success of the discussions was largely due to Castlereagh's patience and persistence.

Neither France nor Napoleon had gained anything from the negotiations. Napoleon consistently refused all Caulaincourt's appeals to make peace while it was still possible. The Allies, therefore, had no qualms about outlining a new settlement for Europe which included the future government of France but, although the French people were promised a free choice, it was already clear that this choice would be limited.

Austrian horror of a new French republic was shared by the English Tories who were convinced that security in Europe would remain in jeopardy until the revolutionary taint had been washed away. The Allies were hesitant about a regency under Marie Louise for the King of Rome as Napoleon II. Even Metternich was now inclined to the recall of the Bourbons although everyone but the ultra-royalists knew that France did not want them.

Public opinion in England reacted violently against retaining Napoleon or his son. When Lord Liverpool, the Prime Minister, learned that Bordeaux had declared for the Bourbons he instructed Castlereagh to make no peace with Bonaparte. The British were opening immediate negotiations with Monsieur, the Comte d'Artois, brother of Louis XVIII, who was poised in hopeful expectancy of an end to his long English exile.

As Schwarzenberg and Alexander closed in on Paris the Czar's enthusiasm for Bernadotte was waning, but he felt no desire for a Bourbon restoration. Towards Louis XVIII his feelings were of the coldest. Almost in defiance of all that had occurred since the meeting on the raft on the Niemen, Alexander was still reluctant to dispose finally of Napoleon.

CHAPTER II

The Great Congress

GUNFIRE had ceased on the heights of Montmartre. Paris, 'the proud city, the city of philosophy, Babylon the great', had capitulated to her enemies. The sudden silence seemed to the anxious crowds a divine malediction as they waited to know their fate. Tension rose when, punctually at eleven o'clock, a troop of red-coated Cossacks, riding fifteen abreast, swept through the Barrière de Pantin towards the centre of the city, the vanguard of an endless cavalcade of Russian, Austrian and Prussian Lancers, Cuirassiers and Hussars.

Behind his Cossacks Alexander, mounted on a grey charger, rode among a jingling group of aides-de-camp jacketed in dark green, their massive silver epaulettes embroidered with the letter 'A' surmounted by an Imperial crown. The presence at the Czar's left of Frederick William of Prussia was proof of a friendship more enduring than the infatuation of Tilsit. On Alexander's right Field-Marshal Prince von Schwarzenberg represented the Emperor Francis of Austria, scarcely able with propriety to enter his daughter's capital at the head of an army which had defeated her husband.

From Pantin the procession, bands playing and colours flying, wound its way to the Porte St Denis and along the boulevards to the Champs-Elysées for a grand review. Even as the Parisians watched the interminable column with despair and winced at the foreign words of command they were forced to admire Alexander's good looks and elegant seat on his horse.

At this moment when the Czar seemed singled out to be the arbiter of France's future he gave no sign of elation. He looked calm, even a little sad and humble, as for the first time he, the barbarian Muscovite, faced those Parisians whom he regarded as the personification of culture and civilization.

The aspect of Paris itself was not unknown to him. For years Napoleon's chief architects, Percier and Fontaine, had sent him descriptions and illustrations of the Emperor's embellishments to palaces, monuments and buildings of public utility, markets, fountains and abattoirs. Alexander would be 'inconsolable if any violence were committed on the magnificent city'.

As the Czar rode by he called out to the people that he came not as a conqueror but as a liberator, not as an enemy but as a friend. These words he repeated in his proclamation to the French nation; he was drawn to France neither by thirst of conquest nor desire for revenge; he and his Allies were engaged not in a war of reprisals, not a war against France but against Napoleon and the enemies of French liberty. He added that France should be perfectly free in her choice of government, uninfluenced by the Allies.

Alexander's honest intentions were doubly checkmated. Because the troops wore a white armband as a sign of victory, and white was the Bourbon colour, the Parisians mistakenly believed that the Allies were committed to a Bourbon restoration. And Talleyrand was swiftly at work to consummate the treachery initiated at Erfurt. In him Napoleon at Fontainebleau, feverishly trying first to rally his army and then to win the war of words, found an enemy more formidable than any he had encountered in the field.

Almost within hours of the Allies' arrival in Paris Talleyrand had engineered Napoleon's formal overthrow by the Senate, instituted himself as head of a provisional government, and confused Alexander by his arguments in favour of the principle of 'legitimacy', his formula for a Bourbon restoration.

The Czar, still haunted by the old friendship, was not yet convinced. His emotional conflict was shown in his talks with Bourrienne, Napoleon's schoolfellow and former secretary, now an ardent royalist, and the Duchesse d'Abrantès, still devoted to the Emperor.

To Bourrienne Alexander said,

'You have been the friend of Napoleon and so have I. I was his sincere friend, but there is no possibility of remaining at peace with a man of such bad faith. We must have done with him.'

Yet to the Duchesse d'Abrantès Alexander spoke wistfully of the fraternity of arms and heart which had existed between him and

Napoleon, and how together they would have made Europe the finest part of the universe.

Had the Duchesse d'Abrantès succeeded in her plan for a secret confrontation between the two Emperors would Alexander again have been subjugated by Napoleon? He was given no opportunity. His Allies had compromised themselves irrevocably in the Bourbon cause and, however reluctantly, Alexander submitted to the majority decision.

> 'Friendship's the privilege of private men; For wretched greatness knows no blessing So substantial. . . .'

The British were ready to kill and eat Napoleon but Alexander's chivalry demanded for him a more reasonable fate and provision worthy of the rank he had occupied. He sent a message to Fontaine-bleau to assure the Emperor that, if he wished to reside in his states, he would be well received, though he brought desolation there; Alexander would always remember the friendship which had united them. Napoleon should have the island of Elba or something else. It was Elba.

On 6 April 1814 Napoleon signed his formal act of abdication and the Treaty of Fontainebleau which, on paper, assured his own and his family's future. The Allies, breaking their promise to respect the wishes of the French nation, had by virtue of adept royalist propa-ganda been hoodwinked into believing that the Bourbons would be welcome. If they had visited the popular quarters of Paris they would have realized their mistake; it was a reluctant nation which let a reluctant Napoleon go. The people of his 'good city of Paris' mourned their Emperor.

Lord Grenville decided that the dénouement of the island of Elba and a pension changed the tragedy into something approaching pretty nearly to a farce. Napoleon's future was, however, of less importance than that Britain could now brace herself to repair the breaches made by her war effort in her economy. After twenty difficult and distressing years, made crippling to the taxpayer by Allied subsidies, the counting houses could at last begin to calculate profits instead of losses.

When an armistice had been signed by the Comte d'Artois, Louis XVIII returned to his kingdom on 23 April. The autocrat Alexander had insisted that Louis' restoration was contingent on the grant of

The meeting between Napoleon and Alexander on the raft on the Niemen,
June 25th, 1807

Alexander I in undress uniform

a constitution to his people. Thus he underlined his declaration that war had been waged not against France but against Napoleon and the enemies of French liberty. The King gilded the unwelcome pill with the formula that his Charter was 'freely granted to his people in the nineteenth year of his reign'.

Now the way was clear for the diplomatists who worked so diligently that, only two months after the Allied occupation of the capital, the Peace of Paris was signed on 30 May. The preamble to the Treaty was couched according to the traditional formula 'In the name of the Most Holy and Undivided Trinity'. It expressed the contracting parties' 'equal desire to terminate the long agitations of Europe, and the sufferings of mankind, by a permanent peace, founded upon a just repartition of force between its States, and containing in its stipulations the pledge of its durability'.

'His Britannic Majesty (or His Imperial and Apostolic Majesty the Emperor of Austria, or His Imperial Majesty the Czar and Autocrat of All the Russias, or His Majesty the King of Prussia), together with his Allies, being unwilling to require of France, now that, replaced under the paternal government of her Kings, she offers the assurance of security and stability to Europe, the conditions and guarantees which they had with regret demanded from her former Government,'

made generous terms with His Majesty the King of France and Navarre.

The integrity of 'old France' as it had existed under her legitimate sovereign was respected but of the Great Empire only minor territorial additions remained. France was saved from war indemnity by the Allied declaration that, for the happiness of Europe, she must be great and strong; she was required only to repay debts contracted to private individuals.

In their anxiety to have done with war the Allies undertook to withdraw their troops from France, a premature sign of confidence in the restored Bourbon régime. All questions left unsettled by the Peace of Paris were referred to the Congress to be held at Vienna where France, when her own interests were involved, was assured of representation on an equal footing with the other Powers.

Before leaving Paris Alexander staged a piece of theatre more impressive than Napoleon's raft on the Niemen. On the spot in the Place de la Concorde where Louis XVI was guillotined Mass was celebrated in his memory according to the Greek Orthodox rite. This act of piety expressed the Czar's increasing occupation with religion not goodwill to Louis XVIII to whom he felt none. Louis reciprocated the Czar's antipathy. He looked down his high Bourbon nose at the upstart Romanoff and persisted in attributing his restoration to the Prince Regent and England alone.

Alexander, his duty done to God and man, crossed the Channel with Frederick William in close attendance to enjoy the sweets of peace and an enthusiastic welcome from the English.

The Emperor of Austria excused himself from accepting the Prince Regent's invitation on the grounds that he must return to Vienna to prepare for the Congress. In reality Francis shared Alexander's dislike of ceremonial and the public appearances at which he made an awkward showing.

To avoid involvement in the intrigues leading to Napoleon's downfall Francis had lurked near Dijon until it was an accomplished fact. Only on arrival in Paris did he seem to recollect that Allied policy had deprived his daughter and grandson of a throne. Just as the Emperor had arbitrarily disposed of his daughter in marriage to the Corsican parvenu so now he ordered Marie Louise to return to Vienna until she took possession of the duchy of Parma, assigned to her by the Treaty of Fontainebleau. To ensure that the Empress made no attempt to join Napoleon her father instructed her escort, Count Neipperg, to wean her from allegiance to her husband, if necessary by seduction. Francis' instructions were punctually obeyed.

Metternich was commended for signing the Treaty of Fontainebleau on behalf of the Emperor who, nevertheless, deplored the proximity of Elba to France and Europe. The island as part of the Hapsburg domain of the Grand Duchy of Tuscany should not have been ceded to a stranger, even though still falsely addressed by Francis as his 'good brother and dear son-in-law'.

Francis of Austria, apparently so worthy of the respect and confidence shown in him by Europe, was not innocent of duplicity where his paramount interests were involved. This most bourgeois of monarchs had a profound sense of the prestige of his own family, the oldest reigning house in Europe, of having been the Holy Roman Emperor, of being His Imperial and Apostolic Majesty, of majesty *tout court*.

Training for monarchy was not an 18th-century concept. Like Alexander and Frederick William, Francis was brought up under the

shadow of a great ancestor. Maria Theresa's example was considered
adequate preparation for the Imperial responsibilities he assumed in
1792 at the age of twenty-four.

Although not uncultured Francis was not receptive to ideas, but
if his intellect was limited his piety was not; the primary influence in
his life was religious. So fervent was his belief in the direct intervention of divine Providence in human affairs that he almost courted the
defeats and progressive erosion of his empire which were the net
result of his wars against France.

After the crushing defeat of Austerlitz Francis was too cautious
again to risk undermining by personal appearance on the battlefield
the Imperial prestige of which he was so jealous. War he now preferred to leave to his generals and government to men who shared his
horror of the faintest smell of revolution. Since Austria, untouched
by 'Jacobin' ideas, was the last bastion of conservatism in Europe
the Emperor commanded a wide choice of counsellors among the
enemies of revolution who had taken refuge in his states.

Francis had much in common with Louis XVI; he enjoyed his
hobbies more than his duties, trivialities rather than weighty matters
of state; content to reign, he found in Metternich the ideal minister
of outlook similar to his own, both willing and competent to rule his
empire for him.

Metternich's was by no means a primrose path; it was strewn with
the obstacles put in his way by Francis' narrowness and dogmatism,
his doubts and scruples, his self-justification and the malicious
gossip of his insignificant entourage. In Francis' Court they were 'a
little fond of secret information and plots', remarked Lord Stewart,
British minister in Vienna.

Of these traits Francis' subjects were ignorant; they enjoyed his
informal contacts with them and repaid with considerable affection
his affability and paternal concern. The only fault they admitted in
their Emperor was excess of benevolence and his tendency to be too
easily guided, especially by Metternich. Him they regarded as a deep
politician who, like a famous French actor, cried with one eye and
laughed with the other.

Although Francis was only a year older than his son-in-law,
Napoleon, his somewhat vacuous face was prematurely aged, partly
as a result of his wartime trials but also of his exaggerated uxoriousness; he had taken keenly to heart the old saying, *tu felix Austria,
nubes*. His consorts were obliged to support the burden of his intense

sexuality without help since piety forbade his taking a mistress. By 1814 he had already worn out two wives, the second succumbing to her seventeenth pregnancy in seventeen years of marriage. Francis was now busily wearing out his third wife in uneasy gloom that she would not stay the course.

When Francis became a widower for the second time the Grand Duchess Catherine of Russia, Alexander's sister, would willingly have overlooked his personal unattractiveness for the dignities of reigning as Empress of Austria and Queen of Hungary. The Emperor, however, decided on a Hapsburg princess and the Grand Duchess had to make do with a minor German prince, George of Oldenburg. This second dynastic rebuff was not without effect on the Czar's attitude to Austria.

When Alexander with Frederick William, Marshal Blücher and the Ataman of Cossacks, Platoff, arrived in England to be lionized he was delighted to find his sister in London. The Grand Duchess, now widowed, was busily hunting in the Courts of Europe for a second husband. She scorned the English royal dukes to set her heart on the Prince of Orange who was betrothed to Princess Charlotte of Wales. The Grand Duchess contrived to have the engagement broken off and so ruin Castlereagh's scheme for a dynastic union between Great Britain and the Netherlands. That the Grand Duchess did not get the Prince for herself was no more than she deserved.

To the Grand Duchess's meddling there was no end and she involved her brother in the numerous scandals she created. Together they succeeded in affronting the Tory government by their ostentatious preference for the Whig opposition and antagonizing the Prince Regent by their championship of his estranged wife.

But for the work of the ministers in attendance Alexander's visit would have been a political disaster. He threw away his chance of reaching agreement with Castlereagh and the cabinet who had been amenable to the idea of a Polish state under the Czar's rule. He failed to overcome Metternich's opposition. On the contrary, the Austrian Chancellor, progressively more hostile to Russia, cultivated the Prince Regent and worked on Hardenberg to bring Prussia round to his own views on Poland. Given Frederick William's reluctance to take any action capable of prejudicing his friendship with Alexander Metternich had set himself no easy task nor was it surprising that he failed to achieve his objective.

The solid results of the ministers' conference in London were the ratification of the Peace of Paris, the signing of a Convention, which confirmed and supplemented the Treaty of Chaumont, and agreement on the establishment of a kingdom of the Netherlands. The future of Poland and Saxony was deferred to the Congress of Vienna.

After nearly twenty-five years of war the roads of Europe no longer echoed to the tramp of armies marching and counter-marching to battle. Their place was taken by the eager feet of troops returning to their own countries from the victorious campaign in France, and homeward-bound prisoners of war. Most agonizing among the criss-cross of hopes and fears was the question asked themselves by the remnants of the Grande Armée on their long trek westward. What kind of France would they find without the Emperor and with King Louis at the Tuileries?

Only briefly were the highways solitary. Soon they were jammed by an endless cortège of diplomatists which snaked its way across the Continent, overwhelming the postmasters with demands for relays of horses. This massive drift towards Vienna did not begin until September. As Castlereagh was needed at home for Parliamentary business, and Alexander was anxious to sandwich in a visit to Russia, the formal opening of the Congress was deferred until November.

Between an international conference and a congress the distinction lies generally in the rank of the delegates. Resident ambassadors and ministers are usually considered sufficiently senior to negotiate at conferences. Congresses require the authority of Foreign Secretaries and Chancellors. Enhanced dignity was given to the Congress of Vienna by the presence of Francis, Alexander, Frederick William and other German sovereigns.

An international congress depends for its success on thorough advance preparation and decisions already reached in principle on the most important subjects to come up for discussion. Failure to solve the Polish-Saxon question before the Vienna Congress met suggested that it would see a battle of interests rather than formal ratification of agreements already concluded.

The gathering at Vienna was the largest in Europe since the Peace of Westphalia in 1648 ended the Thirty Years War. Present by right were the signatories of the Peace of Paris—the Four Powers, Austria, Great Britain, Prussia and Russia—together with Spain, Portugal and Sweden and, of course, France.

Invitations to attend had also been sent to those sovereign states which had not signed the Peace together with a number of former monarchs, pretenders and mediatized German princes. An uninvited tail was made up of a hotch-potch of unofficial communities and private individuals who in this influential gathering saw an opportunity to promote their own individual interests.

From the Peace of Westphalia the sovereign state had emerged as the European political unit. This concept gave birth to the theory of the balance of power, adopted as the guiding principle of British foreign policy. Inevitably this principle had gone by the board during the long years of revolutionary and Napoleonic wars. Would Castlereagh now be able to restore it and, in so doing, endow the Congress of Vienna with the permanent lustre shining on the Peace of Westphalia?

The diplomatists assembled at Vienna enjoyed an advantage denied their predecessors. From the numerous international gatherings since 1813 an invaluable by-product had resulted. Old acquaintanceships had been renewed and new friendships formed. Personal standpoints, habits, manners of speech, idiosyncrasies and even the handwriting of the plenipotentiaries were now so mutually familiar that their reactions were predictable. Moreover, during the protracted negotiations national policies had been largely exposed.

Among those whose friendship was confirmed at Vienna were Castlereagh and Metternich, but Russian suspicion of the Prince had not abated. Nesselrode in particular was influenced by his wife's violent attack on Metternich—he was a wicked intriguer who did not merit confidence, who had ingratiated himself with Nesselrode the better to dupe him. As Countess Nesselrode begged her husband to beware of every line written and every word spoken by the Prince she became almost hysterical. Nesselrode, however, had little opportunity to follow her bidding to search out the man behind the mask.

The Czar acted virtually as his own Foreign Minister, largely ignoring the advice of his formidable entourage kept firmly in the background. To Nesselrode he was especially hostile because the Minister did not think the world well lost in order to keep one or two more Polish hovels.

Although Frederick William was always ready to play the sedulous ape to Alexander he had no ambition to assume an active role. The King was content to let his Chancellor, Prince Hardenberg, act for him; he intervened personally only when any clash of interest with the Czar was involved.

Francis was merely the host to his multitude of guests. Vienna had been chosen as the site of the Congress both for its central position in Europe and as a tribute to his unremitting sacrifices in the common cause. When the moment came to foot the staggering bill for the lavish entertainment he provided Francis may well have ruefully decided that the compliment was a dubious one and that his pecuniary sacrifices at least were not ended.

Castlereagh's position and authority at the Congress were almost those of a sovereign since the distance between London and Vienna precluded frequent consultation of the cabinet. The British courier system was admirably organized but the return journey of some two thousand miles could not be done in much under four weeks. Even this speed was possible only if the circumstances were favourable which, in winter especially, was not always the case.

When the weather was too rough for the regular packets to cross the Channel the courier or King's messenger was required to hire an open boat, risking seasickness at best, shipwreck at worst, but risk and danger were words which found no place in the courier's vocabulary. His motto was, 'If anybody goes, I must; if nobody goes, I must.'

Once in his carriage, piled with Foreign Office bags five feet high containing smaller bags of white leather, the courier had to face hazards no less serious than at sea. His vehicle, drawn by the regulation three horses—four were allowed only for extraordinary speed— was sturdily built to withstand rough roads but not highway robbery and even murder.

Most dangerous was the three week journey to St Petersburg when, in winter, the courier was exposed to ice and frostbite, to temperatures of twenty degrees of frost and frozen rivers. Bribery was sometimes necessary to get help to remove the wheels and mount the carriage on a sleigh to cross frozen rivers otherwise impassable. Even then the carriage might overturn in a snowdrift and the hungry howling of wolves menaced a terrible fate. Not surprising that one messenger collapsed on arrival at St Petersburg and died as the result of his fatigue and the series of accidents he had suffered.

Weather hazards were common to all travellers but the rich at least could endure them with the maximum of comfort. Their carriages were exceedingly well sprung and drawn by four or six horses. To make the long hours cooped up in a carriage less wearisome every amenity possible was fitted into the small space available. Few other travellers aped the luxury of Napoleon's travelling-carriage with its canteen of silver-gilt cutlery and ingenious combined chair and writing table of rare woods and ormolu designed by a famous Florentine cabinet maker, but their necessities were choice. Reading and writing desks were converted into travelling bookcases, leather toilet cases were lined with silver and velvet, china was delicate and cutlery silver. Means of heating food were not neglected.

When much night travel was necessary a *dormeuse* was used in preference to an orthodox carriage. To enable the traveller to lie at full length the coachman's seat was removed and the horses' postillion ridden. In either carriage or *dormeuse* a well under the floor contained a safe with money for posting charges and expenses of the journey.

So much travel was involved in the golden age of international consultation to safeguard the peace of Europe, initiated at Vienna and followed by congresses with little pause until 1822, that Friedrich von Gentz, their perpetual secretary, dubbed it 'diplomacy of the highway', while Metternich sighed,

'Few lives are so fatiguing.'

Metternich, as the constant factor in all negotiations with Napoleon, had been on the road almost continuously since the summer of 1813, but at last his travels had ceased. The new carriage he had ordered during his stay in London stood idle in his coach house.

As principal delegate of the host country the Prince enjoyed the dominant position as President of the Congress. He had at his disposal a large and efficient diplomatic machine for the preparation, printing and distribution of documents but his greatest asset was Friedrich von Gentz, the foremost publicist in Europe and without a rival in drafting Notes and protocols.

Gentz was born in Breslau in 1764 and, as a young man, joined the Prussian civil service. Like so many other young men he was devoted to the principles of the Enlightenment and a warm supporter of the French Revolution. His allegiance changed after translating into German Burke's *Reflections on the French Revolution:* henceforward he was an avowed opponent first of the revolution and then of Bonaparte. Progressively he became as great a believer in the established order as Metternich himself.

As Napoleon's armies overran the Continent Gentz was forced

into various periods of exile in London and Bohemia but the celebrity he already enjoyed, his excellent knowledge of languages, his extensive acquaintance with European literature and his acute political intelligence attracted the attention of Stadion who, in 1802, invited him to Vienna where he at last found his niche.

Although Gentz ingratiated himself with Metternich so successfully that he became the Prince's close collaborator he never overcame Francis' hostility. He was too much a hedonist, too great a libertine, to win the Emperor's favour. All his life he remained the Chevalier, or Freiherr, of a minor Swedish Order since Francis denied him the title he coveted.

Gentz was a man of many loves, not all avowable, although he remained constantly attached to Rahel Varnhagen von Ense whose celebrated salon he had frequented in his youth. His overriding passion, however, was to be 'in the secret', to have his opinion sought by everyone who mattered in European circles. Gentz' vanity was almost as great as Metternich's.

The Congress of Vienna finally established his indispensability in the councils of Europe. Since Gentz was far from scrupulous as to how he obtained the money to maintain his luxurious living standard, he used his position to make himself the pensioner of anyone who would pay him for confidential information and support in negotiation.

In Gentz Metternich was assured not only of first-class practical assistance but of a shrewd adviser capable of manipulating the course of discussions and documents in the Austrian interest.

At his villa on the Rennweg Metternich disposed the orchestra to which he intended that the other plenipotentiaries should dance to tunes of his own choice. He was chagrined to find a rival virtuoso in Talleyrand, again Foreign Minister and principal French delegate to the Congress, who was convinced that harmony in Europe required that France play in the major key.

Talleyrand had prepared the ground in a fawning letter to Alexander, saluting him as the saviour of France and reminding him that the provinces, not Paris, were the true French nation; they had acclaimed his victory and blessed the return of the Bourbons.

Any contrary opinion the Czar might have formed was anticipated by Talleyrand's warning that France needed a long time to become accustomed to her new government, but the Prince was confident that the King's sagacity would end by winning the people over.

No great sagacity was needed on Talleyrand's part to realize the appeal to Alexander of a monarchy walking hand in hand with liberty. Shrewdly he left the crux of his argument implicit only; France must henceforward take her legitimate place in the councils of Europe.

By the time Talleyrand and Alexander reached Vienna their relationship was distinctly cooler although no immediate clash of interests existed between France and Russia. The Czar was still resentful of being jockeyed into acceptance of the Bourbons, whom he continued to despise, and uneasy about the part he was forced to play in Napoleon's overthrow; he had been shown as less chivalrous than he believed himself to be.

Pozzo di Borgo, now Russian ambassador in Paris, saw no change in Talleyrand's character or methods. He was immovable as marble and his anxiety to maintain good relations with Russia would last only so long as it served his own interests.

Pozzo's assessment was proved accurate when, in the early stages of the Congress, Talleyrand neatly called the Allies' bluff. They had intended that France should take part only in discussions involving her own direct interests. Talleyrand reminded them of their repeated assertion that they had waged war not against France but against Napoleon. Logic demanded that France without Napoleon be restored to her rightful place among the Powers—and France had for so long overawed Europe that this thesis was meekly accepted. Henceforward the Congress, which never in fact met in plenary session but was governed by a series of committees, was directed by five not four Powers.

The committees worked harmoniously and with despatch to reach decisions which long survived the Congress of Vienna. No difficulty was found in the formal verification of the plenipotentiaries' *pleins-pouvoirs*, elegantly inscribed in Latin on parchment. Other tasks of minor importance were carried out with almost equal ease—confirming Swiss independence, determining the free navigation of international waterways, regulating diplomatic status and protocol and investigating problems of demography, to which a special committee was assigned.

Less harmony was in evidence in the Five Power directorate where personalities influenced policies. While some friendships were strengthened so were some antagonisms. Daily Bible reading and growing spiritual fervour did not cause the Czar to abjure the pleasures of a man of the world. Between him and Metternich existing acrimony was still further soured by the presence in Vienna of their chosen ladies, whose theme song might have been borrowed from John Gay, 'How happy could I be with either, were t'other dear charmer away.'

Rivalry between Alexander and Metternich was a staple of the gossip which was the favourite diet of the idlers at Vienna and the Emperor of Austria. He shared with Louis XVIII an appetite for the salacious titbits lavishly served up to him in police reports and the correspondence intercepted by the black cabinet, the name given to the murky officials of the secret service.

Even Frederick William forsook the melancholy intensified by Luise's death in 1810. He succumbed to the hothouse atmosphere of Vienna in the winter of 1814 to show himself a not inconsolable widower. The King of Prussia's fancies, like those of everyone else, what they said, to whom they whispered it, with whom they slept, were all sifted through the highly efficient Austrian espionage system. If all the information so painstakingly collected served no other purpose, to Francis it was some slight compensation for the deep inroads made on his purse by the dragging on of the Congress.

Only from the British delegation was there little leakage because Castlereagh had issued strict orders to his staff to avoid dangerous loose talk and lax security.

Security was the more essential because Castlereagh was progressively drawn to Metternich's ambition to re-establish Austrian domination on the mainland of Europe, a design which ran counter to Alexander's determination that Russia should occupy the place left vacant by Napoleon. Since the trial of strength would be made over Poland Alexander's preference for dancing the polonaise at the many balls which enlivened the Congress should have been noted as a pointer to his stance about the still intractable Polish-Saxon problem.

On his arrival in Vienna Nesselrode wrote to Pozzo di Borgo in Paris, advising him to deny any rumour that the Congress could lead to anything but a durable peace. When the Congress crept through the last months of 1814 and into the spring of 1815 not only was Nesselrode once again proved over-optimistic but the existing peace itself fragile.

Because Castlereagh believed in strengthening Prussia he was willing to countenance her large claims on Saxony, ripe for plunder since her King had remained obstinately faithful to Napoleon. With greater prescience and political intelligence Talleyrand foresaw the formidable threat to Europe presented by a powerful Prussian state.

Frederick William, although no less covetous of 'souls' and territory than Frederick the Great, hesitated to thwart Alexander. Continued refusal on the part of Great Britain and Austria to admit the Czar's demand for Poland and part of Saxony, could lead the Congress to waltz into war. Everyone realized that such a war would be impossible to localize and would inevitably provoke further calamitous revolutions.

Russia, with half a million men under arms and supported by a re-arming Prussia, constituted a serious threat to the peace of Europe. Castlereagh saw the only deterrent to war in a defensive alliance with France and Austria. Even Alexander would hesitate to take on three Powers so formidable. Although the treaty was intended to be kept secret its existence was known to the Czar and did effectively prevent his making any hostile move. Nevertheless, after complicated bargaining, Alexander succeeded in securing his kingdom of Poland, largely at the expense of Saxony.

Finally the inevitability of gradualness produced further decisions. Saxony suffered more loss of territory to Prussia, which also acquired parts of Westphalia, formerly Austrian, and Pomerania. Austria, as provided for in the Peace of Paris, regained Lombardy and Venetia, with additional Italian states along the Adriatic. Further prestige and power came to her with the formation of some thirty-nine German states into a loose German Confederation, of which the Austrian Emperors would be perpetual presidents. Most pregnant with consequences for the future was the restoration of the legitimate dynasties in Spain, Portugal, Naples, Piedmont, Tuscany and Modena.

The Powers at Vienna might be said to have learned little and forgotten much. If Lloyd George at Versailles 'forgot Teschen' they forgot the French revolution. Only the decisions of the minor committees constituted an innovation. In their determination to wipe out any vestiges of revolutionary feeling the sovereigns decided everything among themselves. Gentz noted that, in parcelling out 'souls' and acres in the manner of 18th-century partitions, not even a cursory glance was thrown at the civil and political rights of peoples, many of whom now 'with wail passed to new lords'.

Unhappiest perhaps were those satellite states which had been integrated in the French empire and were faced with formidable problems of re-organization now that the French proconsuls were withdrawn. Their state of shock was akin to that of a family which has suffered the loss of a tyrannical wealthy relative. Relief at their deliverance quickly gives way to anxiety about their own position and their future means of support.

Nations were not alone in feeling grievous disappointment that their aspirations were neglected at Vienna. Little real progress was made with the abolition of the slave trade which seemed a matter of greater concern to the British than the redrawing of the map of Europe.

His Most Christian Majesty, Louis XVIII, busily seeking friends, paid lip service to this British obsession by 'concurring without reserve in the sentiments of His Britannic Majesty with respect to a traffic repugnant to the principles of natural justice and the enlightened age in which we live'.

Despite strenuous efforts Castlereagh met with little delight elsewhere.

A further 'principle of natural justice and enlightenment' achieved only a partial success, the emancipation of the Jews. The British cabinet was in a position too delicate with regard to the emancipation of her own Catholic population to risk involvement with any other religious minority. The British Jews, fearful of unpleasant repercussions, allowed the German Jews to plead the cause of all.

Metternich, Hardenberg, Alexander and Gentz, his pockets lined with English guineas for services rendered on the slave trade question and weighted down with Jewish thalers, lent their support. Their concerted aid succeeded in the insertion of a clause in the Final Act of the Congress, providing for the gradual extension of civil rights to the Jews of Germany. This was only half a loaf and cut up still further by the alteration of a vital word in that clause which left the German Jews in the same position as before Napoleon's Great Sanhedrin.

Concessions and compromises had at last so stabilized the situation that Castlereagh, whose presence was urgently needed in London to deal with a turbulent House of Commons, was able to leave Vienna in February with an easy mind.

His place as first British plenipotentiary was taken by the Duke of Wellington, since the peace British ambassador in Paris, and another new face made a brief appearance in Vienna. The Duc de Richelieu was homeward bound from twenty-five years of exile in Russia to pay his duty to Louis XVIII.

Wellington's stay in Vienna was short. Vienna and the whole

world was startled by the news of Napoleon's escape from Elba and
his landing in France on 1 March. As the Emperor advanced towards
Paris Louis XVIII fled to Ghent in Belgium; the Congress hastily
declared Napoleon an outlaw; the Allies renewed to each other
the assurances given at Chaumont and Wellington hurried to the
Netherlands to prepare for certain war. Lord Clancarty was left in
Vienna to conclude the business of the Congress with the other
plenipotentiaries and, on 9 June 1815, to sign the Final Act of the
Congress of Vienna.

The major share of responsibility for Napoleon's return fell
squarely on Francis of Austria for preventing Marie Louise and the
King of Rome from joining their husband and father at Elba. With
his wife and child beside him Napoleon might well have become
reconciled to dwindling into the King of Elba, particularly since he
was already conscious of waning physical powers. In 1811, before
the taxing Russian campaign, he had asked his architects, when
planning the vast Palace of the King of Rome to be built on the
heights of Chaillot, to consider it as a home for a man growing old.

Louis XVIII's failure to fulfil the conditions of the Treaty of
Fontainebleau may have been less reprehensible than Francis'
cynical indifference to marital ties, but his conduct was no less impolitic. To deprive Napoleon of his promised income and to hound
his family from one European country to another was a virtual
invitation to him to end a state of affairs which had become intolerable.

On the part of Francis and Louis XVIII these were personal
lapses of decency and good faith. The Allies had made a political
blunder in treating the restoration too optimistically. They had shut
their eyes to the indifference of the French nation at large to the
Bourbons yet, with an astonishing lack of political intelligence, hoped
that the desperate longing for peace in France would reconcile even a
reluctant nation to the restoration.

When Pozzo di Borgo wrote to Nesselrode, assuring him that the
French saw the only guarantee of peace, an end to revolution and
civil disorders, in the principle of legitimacy represented by the
Bourbons, he was the victim of wishful thinking. Pozzo's judgment
was blinded by his personal Corsican vendetta against the Bonapartes
which had converted him into an ardent Bourbon partisan. All he
now succeeded in doing was to call down on his aggrieved head
reproof for being too crudely *bourbonnique* and advice that less
vehemence in their cause would serve the Bourbons better. As war

and the dangers of war receded the French were progressively more hostile to the Bourbons.

Long exile from France had alienated Louis XVIII from her aspirations. He could feel no sympathy with her revolutionary conquests nor mourn with her the loss of her empire. His most urgent task was to eradicate from the hearts, minds and institutions of the nation twenty-five years of glory, but this could not be done overnight. The King needed time, time to create a climate of confidence, time for France to recover from its shock at Napoleon's sudden eclipse, time to refashion the administration, time for the Chambers to acquire much needed discipline and experience of constitutional government.

Whatever Louis' impatience to see foreign bayonets marched off the soil of France, without them he lacked security. The Allies had gambled too heavily on the King's vaunted political acumen when they wrote into the Peace of Paris that France 'replaced under the paternal government of her kings, offers the assurance of security and stability to Europe'. Genuine security and stability demanded an allied army occupying France. Only after the event did the Allies learn this wisdom.

Louis' greatest mistake was his treatment of the French army. He imperiously dismissed on half-pay hundreds of thousands of soldiers who had fought so long and so brilliantly for France. In their stead he filled the ranks of his recreated *Maison du Roi* with returned émigrés who had seen service only against their native country.

The Imperial army, stunned by the loss of its idol, was wounded in its pride, disorganized, helpless and adrift with no leadership. Promotion for the higher cadres was blocked, for the junior no prospect but a bleak and poverty-stricken future. The contrast between their present humiliation and their recent glory was bitter but not more so than their realization that only the Emperor could restore their prestige and that now there was no Emperor. These half-pay officers, the *demi-soldes*, their clothes increasingly threadbare but the ribbon of the Legion of Honour flaunting in their buttonholes, found relief from their grief and frustration only in gibes at the royal family and provoking duels and quarrels with the royal household troops.

On Elba Napoleon shared the nation's discontents. Was it then surprising that he staked everything on a return to France? His ecstatic welcome from the army and the country encouraged him to believe in the success of his gamble, but his dice broke on the immovable hostility of the deputies. In face of the Chambers' arrogant consciousness of their power the Emperor's attempt to conciliate the liberal element by substituting constitutional monarchy for personal rule failed.

Time for Napoleon as much as for Louis XVIII was the vital factor. Most of all he needed time to reorganize his army, particularly the cavalry; armed men might spring out of the ground but not horses. Time was not on Napoleon's side yet, despite the opposition of the Chambers, he might have beaten time had Alexander so willed it.

The Czar hesitated about joining the new attack preparing on Napoleon. He was still incensed about the secret tripartite treaty and the British were showing marked reluctance to pay out fresh subsidies. Nesselrode felt that Castlereagh owed Russia some reparation for the fine piece of work he had made of his treaty aimed against Alexander; another couple of million sterling would not kill Great Britain.

In the end the Treaty of Chaumont prevailed over the secret treaty of Vienna. As Napoleon advanced towards the Belgian frontier Alexander marched forward towards the west not eastwards to Russia.

There was no campaign, only a battle, but that battle was Waterloo. The Vicomte de Chateaubriand, who had accompanied Louis XVIII to Ghent as Minister of the Interior *ad interim*, listened to the distant sound of gunfire, torn between his feelings as a royalist and as a Frenchman. Would Wellington triumph? Would legitimacy reenter Paris in the wake of those redcoats tinged a deeper scarlet with French blood? Would royalty have for its coronation coaches the ambulance carts filled with wounded French grenadiers? The final question Chateaubriand put to himself with less bravura and more sincerity. What would be the future of a restoration made under such auspices?

Chateaubriand's answers came from Fouché who, in Talleyrand's absence, dominated the Parisian scene. He now manipulated the Chambers to force Napoleon's second abdication and hound him out of Paris with no decision taken about his future.

Again the Allies entered Paris and again a peace treaty had to be concluded with France but now the pretence of 1814 was abandoned. The response of the French nation to Napoleon's hundred-day adventure had been too enthusiastic for it to be regarded as the innocent victim of Corsican tyranny. By violating the most sacred treaties the French had put themselves at the mercy of the Allies, who now felt themselves fully entitled to indemnity and extreme measures to preserve their own security.

The Peace of Paris was a dead letter. The Second Peace of Paris, less hastily and blindly negotiated than the First, was inevitably much harsher in its terms.

CHAPTER III

The Year of the Three Treaties

LAMENTABLY the brave hopes expressed in the preamble to the First Peace of Paris had been dashed. Stability in France was essential to tranquillity in Europe but the British were sceptical of Louis XVIII's capacity to maintain himself, indeed that any French government would prove itself able to assure European security. Committed as they were to the final elimination of the Bonapartes and destruction of the revolutionary spirit in France they could see no viable alternative to the King's reinstatement. The difficulty was how to enforce the authority of a monarch twice prodded back on his throne by foreign bayonets.

Alexander, while contemptuous of a king who fled without attempting to defend himself, hesitated to act unilaterally in seeking a substitute. He could only hope that, if the peace made no inroads on French power and territorial integrity, a strong ministry might yet reconcile the nation to the dynasty. Francis of Austria likewise preferred allied unity to pressing the claims of his grandson, the former King of Rome. Frederick William cared for nothing but squeezing France until the pips squeaked.

Only the ultra-royalists and Pozzo di Borgo, who was convinced that the Bourbons were not a family but an institution, deluded themselves that the French wanted Louis' return.

To fill a dangerous vacuum Louis' early return from Ghent was vital but, to give credence to the fiction that his second restoration was the nation's spontaneous wish, he must govern and his armies operate at some distance from the Allies.

'Get the King to go back to France, south, north or west, wherever you like, provided he is *in his own country*, removed from foreign bayonets and foreign support,' Metternich wrote imperatively to Talleyrand a week after Waterloo.

On 8 July the King, whom the fishwives of the Halles derisively called *Notre Père de Gand*, crept back to Paris; on his way he proclaimed that he hastened for a second time to stand between the Allies and France, a typically arrogant statement which must have caused great amusement to those Allies.

As a preliminary to their peacemaking they demanded from the King three guarantees—for Napoleon, for the French army and for the tranquillity of Europe. Lord Liverpool regretted that Louis XVIII had not hanged or shot Napoleon but, since the Emperor had thrown himself on the mercy of the British people, this course was no longer practicable. The awkward personage must be disposed of in some other manner but not, the Prime Minister shrewdly decided, in England. Here in a few months he would possibly become an object of compassion although his presence anywhere in Europe could contribute to the persistence of a certain degree of ferment in France. St Helena was from all points of view the ideal place for his incarceration.

Lord Liverpool was confident that Napoleon, being withdrawn from the European world, would very soon be forgotten—a gross miscalculation.

Once Napoleon was disposed of, the Allies turned to the more recalcitrant problems of securing the tranquillity of Europe and clipping the wings of the French army. With the Emperor irrevocably a prisoner of war tempers among the *demi-soldes* were even more exacerbated than in 1814, jests coarser, caricatures of the King more scurrilous. The royalists in their turn were more clamorous for reprisals and extermination of *la canaille*. Civil war was averted only by the revolting behaviour of some of the occupying troops which welded all parties into sinking their mutual rancour in common defence of France.

Lord Liverpool quaintly believed that to make his throne secure Louis XVIII must dare to spill traitors' blood; the rolling of even a few heads would be sufficient. After the sanguinary scenes of the French revolution the Prime Minister failed to understand the apparently universal repugnance to shedding blood. He concluded that it must be ascribed to fear of retaliation rather than to feelings of mercy. No doubt Liverpool and the cabinet were responsible for the Duke of Wellington's refusal to intervene to prevent the execution of Marshal Ney.

Initially the tranquillity of Europe might be secured by an army occupying France which would further act as a deterrent to any resurgence of French militarism. Even this safeguard did not allay Lord Liverpool's fears—for the future of France after the evacuation of the Allied forces and for the future of Europe if, notwithstanding their presence, the Bourbon régime was overthrown in favour of a Jacobin or Bonapartist system.

In equating the Bonapartist régime with 'Jacobinism' Lord Liverpool was again mistaken. Napoleon constantly emphasized that he was a product not a maker of revolution. Although aware during the Hundred Days that his donning of the red bonnet would entail disaster for the kings of the coalition he scorned to become 'Emperor of the Jacobins'. In domestic affairs the Emperor's watchwords were always law and order, now ironically Liverpool's guiding principle for France.

How secure law and order in a country in a state of turbulence, where partisan war raged in the west and a sanguinary White Terror in the south, where the King's writ ran in only twenty-seven departments of his kingdom? How subdue an army still hostile, although hopelessly conscious that its Emperor would not again come with the violets in another spring?

So threatening was the French army's attitude that the Allies seriously considered denouncing the armistice concluded in July. Once the nation recovered from its first panic long nights and wet or cold weather would facilitate resistance. As a precaution against any military revolt, a possible hazard because of the clumsy and dilatory methods of the French government in disbanding the army, Wellington's army of occupation was reinforced with regiments opportunely returned from America. The Duke was instructed to make the Allied armies ready to take the field if the need arose.

In this uneasy atmosphere the peace talks opened in great secrecy in July. The British, the Russians and the Austrians were all anxious to make a peace which would not inflame the French to risk a new war by demanding from her such considerable sacrifices for European security as would lower the character of the government they all wished to uphold.

Security in Europe was the obsessional British policy to which indemnity took second place; the British had fought not to recoup the millions spent on war but to win a lasting peace. Yet an enduring peace would be jeopardized if France were left with all her plunder intact. A final difficulty was the ambivalent position of the French themselves, at one and the same time allies and enemies.

Lord Liverpool's insistence that only serious inconvenience could arise from delay in reaching a settlement was only partially due to the unknown complexion of the Chamber to be returned by the elections in August. The British were in haste to have done with the Continent.

Alexander also was anxious for a quick agreement to avoid a winter march for his armies returning to Russia. The French were naturally apprehensive as to the extent of their humiliation and liabilities. Only the minor Courts, the *sous-alliés*, were content with the sluggish pace of the early talks; they were feeding, housing and supplying their troops at French expense and were further assured of British subsidies until the conclusion of the peace treaty.

That there would be no repetition of the speed of 1814 soon became clear. The negotiations Metternich had calculated would last six weeks dragged on for five months. Napoleon was well established on St Helena before agreement was finally reached in Paris.

The Prussians were the great stumbling block to a prompt and judicious peace. Only a week after Waterloo Marshal Blücher voiced to Frederick William the perennial complaint of soldiers when he urged that the diplomats should not lose what the soldiers had won with their blood. He warned the King that this was the final and only moment to buttress Germany against France.

Victory at Waterloo had not reconciled the Prussians to the French. Hard pounding at Waterloo was followed by hard bargaining in Paris for Alsace and Lorraine. Although Hardenberg tried to curb the Prussian generals' cannibal appetite for French territory he shared their anxiety to avenge French depredations in Prussia.

Blücher especially, puffing acrid pipe smoke through the salons of St Cloud while his soldiers placidly fished the goldfish from the lake, was determined to expunge from French memories any recollection of victory over the Prussians and to plunder the plunderers. Without waiting for a peace treaty he arbitrarily sent troops to remove by force the trophies of conquest accumulated in the Louvre.

Idle for the Duke of Wellington to say that French fury at the spoliation of the Louvre was mere vanity, that it taught the nation a great moral lesson. The works of art were visible signs of French conquests and, irrationally, their loss was a humiliation greater even than the presence in the French capital of enemy armies.

Although Wellington lent British troops to guard the men making further removals from the museum Great Britain herself demanded no spoils of war. She wanted only the return of flags taken in her wars against the French, particularly those of the Coldstream Guards captured at Fontenoy in 1745 and laid up in the Ecole Militaire.

Such moderation was popular neither with the Prince Regent nor the British public. Like the Prussians they clamoured for more stringent peace terms than those of the First Peace of Paris. Castlereagh and Wellington, even with Metternich inclining to their viewpoint, found it hard to maintain their stance that France should neither be crushed nor irremediably humiliated.

By the time Gentz arrived in Paris in August the pace of the talks had quickened. Metternich immediately took him on a tour of the city, to dine at the *Rocher de Cancale*, to the Louvre, to see the hermaphrodite and, to crown his enthusiastic impressions of Paris, to marvel at the rhinoceros.

Gentz did not agree with Pozzo di Borgo that 'war is a state of tranquillity compared with the intrigues of this Babylon'. Paris was the most beautiful city on which the sun ever shone; it was a great error in creation that here the day had only the same twenty-four hours as in a village.

The Freiherr quickly became an accomplished Parisian. When not attending the peace talks or busy nursing an arm exhausted by his endless correspondence with his patrons, the Hospodars of Wallachia, and his protégé Pilat, editor of the *Oesterrischer Beobachter*, he slipped away to indulge his passion for gambling at the *Salon des Etrangers* or the halls of the Palais Royal. Between a diplomatic dinner at Talleyrand's and a decorous soirée and ball at Lady Castlereagh's he sandwiched in a visit to a brothel but there was less time for 'all kinds of libertinage' when at last the peace talks gathered momentum.

The Court was in no position to entertain the peacemakers so that social life fell far below the brilliant standard set at Vienna but Paris was bursting with hordes of sightseers and troops bivouacked all over the city.

French politicians and diplomatists did not share the royal family's inhibitions. They wined and dined freely with their conquerors, ready to open their hearts to anyone who would listen, always eager to make capital out of inevitable leakages of Allied disagreements. At his princely banquets Talleyrand dropped broad hints that, while the King and his government were prepared for pecuniary sacrifices, neither would ever yield an inch of French territory. The Duc de Dalberg did better. By offering hospitality to Gentz he had a key figure within his own four walls.

The plenipotentiaries were those who had negotiated the first Peace of Paris—Metternich and Wesenberg for Austria, Hardenberg and Humboldt for Prussia, Nesselrode, Capo d'Istrias, Razumoffski and Pozzo di Borgo for Russia. Castlereagh was reinforced by the Duke of Wellington, Commander in Chief of the Allied armies. Labrador, the Spanish envoy, and Palmella, the Portuguese, were mere walkers-on in the scene dominated by the delegates of the Four Courts. Talleyrand and Dalberg, the French ministers, were not invited to take part in the talks. They waited in the wings to enter the stage only before the final curtain fell.

All the delegates were housed within easy reach of each other in the Faubourg St Honoré which facilitated informal talks and meetings. The delegates met every morning at the British embassy, where Castlereagh was housed with the chancery and archives. A few doors away the Czar was at the Elysée-Bourbon with Wellington close by at the Hotel de la Reyniére. Metternich in the Rue Richepanse was a near neighbour of Talleyrand in the Rue St Florentin, off the Place de la Concorde. Frederick William had the hotel of Eugène de Beauharnais and Francis of Austria Berthier's mansion.

A surprise feature of the talks, and one most gratifying to Castlereagh and Liverpool, was the new conciliatory spirit shown by Alexander. Not only did he take great pains 'to show attention to the Duke of Wellington and the British army' but in his anxiety to act in concert with the Prince Regent to consolidate the peace of Europe, he even made a handsome gesture towards healing the breach of 1814. No less magnanimous, the Prince Regent subdued his dislike of the Czar to make an equally gracious response.

Alexander, his St Petersburg palaces intact, was lukewarm about restitution of the captured art treasures but disapproved hotly of Prussian rapacity. He refused to countenance any further truncation of French territory and, with Great Britain and Austria, insisted that France should not be humbled beyond endurance.

Liverpool was cautiously pleased with this favourable development in Anglo-Russian relations but he warned Castlereagh to curb the Czar's disposition to act as protector of the French nation. Although Alexander's desire was intelligible he must not be permitted to sacrifice his allies' security to the unfounded claims of the

French nation. Suspicious of Prussia and Austria though Liverpool was he still felt that Great Britain's true interests in the present crisis were more closely identified with those nations than with Russia; British policy must always be to avoid involvement when she had no principle of common concern with her allies.

Castlereagh was finally able to report his belief that, by dint of hard work, he had succeeded in weaning Alexander from his inclination to act as the exclusive protector of the King of France, a position which for Europe's general politics it was most important that he should *not* occupy.

In congratulating themselves that Alexander's change of heart had been effected by the pressures they had brought to bear on him Liverpool and Castlereagh were mistaken. Other influences had been at work. The Czar was now neither victor nor liberator as in 1814. Although his army was the most formidable in Europe (far too formidable in the general opinion) it had come up too late to share the prestige of Waterloo, not that its absence from the battle weighed with the French. Their general bitterness was extended to all their conquerors without discrimination.

Alexander's vanity was wounded by his loss of popularity and cold reception from a nation for whose liberty he had made such great exertions. His confidence in the French was still further shaken by a threat of assassination, signed by 'The Captain of the Regicides', as a reprisal for his failure to promote the cause of the King of Rome. The Bonapartists believed, and obstinately continued to believe, that Alexander's influence could restore the dynasty.

Although the Czar's chivalry asserted itself in face of the universal desire to batten on France and the passion for vengeance he sovereignly despised, he was disillusioned with the weathercock nation, apparently guided neither by reason nor gratitude. To the Grand Duchess Catherine he confided that he found alleviation for his cares only in the sublime consolations which flow from the Supreme Being. Disenchanted with the contrast between his present standing in France and last year's adulation, Alexander lived almost in isolation.

The Czar's allies felt little surprise that he constituted himself the champion of France but they were startled when he suddenly stood forth as the Eighth Champion of Christendom, an unexpected démarche from a man known as much for his libertine as for his liberal tendencies. In Vienna Alexander had doubled the roles of international arbiter and roué whose paraded flirtations titillated the Congress. In Paris he no longer sought out the most beautiful women at a ball, bent his one good ear for scandalous *on-dits*, indulged in languishing glances or passionate hand-kissing.

The Czar's brother sovereigns and their entourages noted with amused dismay that Alexander's leisure hours were spent not in amorous pursuit but in bible readings and prayer meetings. They did not guess how far his leanings towards religion had been accelerated by the final break made with Princess Narischkin. At Vienna he found himself unable any longer to tolerate her flagrant infidelities which inflicted wounds on his self-esteem as man and monarch. No new Narischkin had entered his life; the vacuum she left was increasingly filled by concern with his own spiritual salvation.

Of all the European sovereigns Alexander was possibly the only one to consider seriously the letter addressed to them by Napoleon on his return from Elba. The Emperor expressed the hope that the re-establishment of his throne might secure repose for the whole of Europe. Henceforward, rather than present the world with the spectacle of great battles, it would be gratifying to recognize only the rivalries of peace and a holy struggle for the happiness of peoples.

Napoleon's sincerity was now immaterial, but not Alexander's response. From La Harpe he had imbibed Rousseau's doctrine that religion is essential in a civil society and for the survival of a nation. It was also Rousseau who declared that the sole hope for the future lay in a federation of Europe.

Rousseau's ideas had gained wide currency in Europe. Even Wolfgang Amadeus Mozart was affected by them through his freemasonry which brought him in touch with liberal thinking. He was therefore the natural choice to compose a musical supplement to a prospectus for the Utopian way of life sponsored by an industrialist, Ziegenhagen, the founder of a naturist colony near Strasbourg. His hearers were to be stimulated not only by Mozart's music for the *Little German Cantata* but also by its libretto in praise of 'non-violence, universal brotherhood and the unity of all religions'.

Since 1804 Alexander had been groping towards this ideal. In that year he sent his ambassador, Novosiltsoff, to England to expand the existing Anglo-Russian alliance into one founded on the sacred rights of humanity and the union of Europe based on a new code of international law.

While Napoleon continued to be the decisive force in Europe

Alexander's vision remained shadowy but at last the climate seemed favourable to giving it substance. After twenty-five years of living on its nerves in alternating states of fear or exaltation Europe was plunged into post-victory depression and ready for a revelation.

'Will no great idea, no judicious project', urged a confidential British agent in Paris, 'come from your side of the Channel? Will Great Britain not use her ascendancy in the public councils of Europe to cause the other Powers to take a new view of things and of men, and their own situation, and make them do what is wise and right?'

The great idea came from Russia not Britain but, before Alexander made his allies a party to the project he had in mind, by a demonstration of Russian power, he gave further evidence of the duality of his nature. Whatever the Czar's personal doubts about his spiritual worthiness, about his temporal position as Autocrat of All the Russias he had none. While the diplomatists were working at top speed to finalize the bases of the peace treaty Alexander staged a mammoth review on 10 September of 150,000 Russian troops and 600 guns on the plain of Vertus in Champagne.

Suitable lodging was conjured up from nowhere for Francis, Frederick William, the Duke of Wellington and a host of invited guests for whom lavish banquets were provided on three successive days. In a country denuded of resources by the occupying troops, where the local officials were unco-operative and marauding Cossacks showed scant respect for their Czar's property this was an almost superhuman achievement.

The architect of these miracles was the great *chef de cuisine*, Marie-Antoine Carême. From Paris he imported hundreds of kitchen utensils, table linen, plate and glass. A whole troop of oxen, calves and sheep were driven to Vertus by a butcher to be slaughtered on the spot. Forty assistant chefs aided Carême to prepare the banquets.

To the strains of martial music the guests were served in the Russian style in marquees elegantly decorated by Fontaine, once Napoleon's coadjutor in the embellishment of Paris, and now the royal architect. They consumed 300 plates of oysters, garnished with 150 lemons; three soups, 28 dishes of hors d'oeuvres, 28 cold entrées, 28 roasts, 112 hot entrées, 28 dishes of quails, poultry and loins of veal, and 56 desserts, including the fantastic *pièces montées* of spun sugar work for which Carême was especially famous.

Unlike the Prussians, for whom France was one vast area to be looted, Alexander settled his accounts a few days after the return to the Elysée of Carême and his *marmitons*.

The guests were suitably impressed by the Czar's magnificent hospitality and the splendid bearing of his troops but they felt some discomfiture when the military review and celebration of Alexander's name day ended as a revivalist meeting. Popes in barbaric pearl and gold said Mass at seven altars simultaneously in thanksgiving to God for the end of Europe's sorrows. Alexander himself, his heart 'filled with love of his enemies', prayed for the salvation of France.

In reaching this apotheosis Alexander had been influenced by a curious mentor. Julie Barbe, Baronne de Krüdener, 'Saint Theresa without divine grace', was a classic example of the woman who seeks compensation in religious mysticism for the follies her age no longer permits. She claimed that the Almighty had personally revealed to her His choice of Alexander to liberate the oppressed and to lead all Christians who had found salvation. The Baroness had long been hovering in the Czar's wake to inform him of his election until, on his way from Vienna to the Belgian front, her skilful intelligence work and manœuvre led their paths to cross. To Alexander, in particularly troubled mood after Vienna and seeking revelation ever more urgently, her arrival seemed the intervention of divine Providence.

For a time the Czar became Madame de Krüdener's ardent, although never wholly committed disciple. However deep his belief in the power of prayer and the Christian way of life, he was too conscious of his own shortcomings to regard himself as a new Messiah. To Madame de Krüdener's chagrin Alexander, at the nightly prayer meetings in her apartments next door to his own, showed far greater animation in discussing his personal spiritual problems than a disposition to fall in with her plans for moral rearmament and regeneration of the Church.

Ultimately, by pushing too far with her religious propaganda and dogmatism, the Baroness overreached herself. Alexander wearied of her efforts to dominate him and the faint air of mothballs which clung to her, but not before this interlude had served to crystallize ideas so long lacking a shape.

Many people claimed a share in the authorship of the Holy Alliance, not least Madame de Krüdener herself, but in its final form the treaty was unquestionably Alexander's own work. Nevertheless, as Castlereagh wrote with some embarrassment to Liverpool, he was surprised to find that this flight of fancy traced back to a proposal he himself had made before leaving Vienna—that the Congress should close with a declaration from the sovereigns. The draft, couched in Gentz' most grandiloquent language, moved Alexander to tears. In Paris he told Castlereagh that the ideas the declaration enshrined were constantly before him.

A new era in world history had opened, read the manifesto, recognition that the true foundation, security and strength of states lay in the wisdom of governments, that without justice and moderation the most solemn treaties were powerless. The sovereigns' simple, sacred and only undertaking would be to subordinate all other considerations to the inviolable maintenance of peace and the suppression of any enterprise which might lead to the overthrow of the established order. Religious feelings and respect for established authority must again become the unbreakable links of civil and political society, and homage be paid to the eternal principle that, for nations as for individuals, true happiness lay only in the prosperity of all.

In the confusion of the closing stages of the Vienna Congress the declaration was forgotten by all except Alexander who, on his return from Vertus, ignored protocol to bring his revised version in person to Castlereagh.

The Foreign Secretary was nonplussed to find that the sovereigns' declaration now read that 'The Christian world has in reality no other Sovereign than Him to whom alone power really belongs' and that

> 'The precepts of . . . Justice, Christian charity and Peace, must have an immediate influence on the councils of Princes, and guide all their steps, as being the only means of consolidating human institutions and remedying their imperfections.'

Castlereagh, poles apart from the mysticism of Alexander's *âme slave*, eagerly seconded Francis' and Metternich's belief that the Czar's mind was affected. He did, while ridiculing the proposals, grudgingly concede that the objection to 'protecting Religion, Peace and Justice' lay in the excessive excellence of the project.

Scepticism was to be expected from Charles-Maurice de Talleyrand-Périgord, ex-Bishop of Autun and married priest, and the older statesmen, grown to manhood under Voltairean influence. Less obvious was the reluctance of the pious Francis of Austria to admit this unexceptionable truth, corroborated in a dozen places in the Holy Writ which was the Czar's daily reading.

Did Francis overlook the fact that the core of Christianity is the establishment of the kingdom of God on earth or that for centuries that Church, whose devoted son he was, had constituted itself the *respublica Christiana*? Was it envy that the revelation came from Greek Orthodox Alexander which caused Francis to dismiss the Holy Alliance as a 'wild conception'? Even the infatuated Frederick William echoed Francis' sneers.

After some initial hesitation Francis and Metternich decided to humour the slightly deranged Czar. Lately he had been so friendly and reasonable on all points that they were unwilling to thwart him. So long as it lasted his plan might save him and the rest of the world much trouble but it was obvious to them that it would not last long.

On 26 September 1815, the Emperor Francis of Austria, the Czar Alexander of Russia and King Frederick William of Prussia signed the Treaty of the Holy Alliance, for once justified in being drawn in 'the name of the Most Holy and Indivisible Trinity'. The final clause announced that all the Powers 'who choose solemnly to avow the sacred principles which have dictated the present Act' would be received with 'equal ardour and affection into this Holy Alliance'.

Louis XVIII was an early and enthusiastic signatory. The Holy Alliance seemed to offer France some guarantee against the threats implicit in the other alliances being worked out by the plenipotentiaries of the Four Courts. Accession to the Holy Alliance both raised Louis' personal stature and offered him possible compensation for his inability to modify the terms of the peace treaty which threatened to be onerous.

Ultimately all the European Powers acceded to the Holy Alliance with the exception of the infidel Turk, who saw in it the menace of a new crusade, the Catholic Pope, indignant that a Greek Orthodox monarch should usurp his sovereignty over the Christian ethic, and the Protestant Prince Regent.

Castlereagh had been obliged to forward to London the text of the Holy Alliance, together with a wistful letter in which the three sovereigns expressed their regret at the Prince Regent's absence at the important moment of signature. They invited him as their most intimate ally to declare his adherence to the pact.

This the Defender of the Faith *ad interim* found himself unable to do. In elegant phrases and 'with the most invariable sentiments of friendship and affection', the Prince Regent retreated behind the letter of the British constitution which precluded his formal accession to any treaty without the consent of Parliament. (The British were not even sure what to call the embarrassing document; they labelled their copy 'the Sacred Alliance'.)

With his customary empty graciousness, the Prince, anxious not to disturb the harmony now subsisting between himself and his allies, informed the August Sovereigns of his entire concurrence in the principles they laid down. Farther he did not go and with this sop they had to be content.

Castlereagh remarked later that the British were a practical people who cared little for theoretical discussion—still less, apparently, for poetry in politics. Great Britain rejected the high moral ideal of the Holy Alliance in favour of the severely utilitarian renewal of the Quadruple Alliance on which Castlereagh's energies were now bent.

On the day of the review at Vertus Gentz and Capo d'Istrias were instructed to draft the peace treaty which had its first reading a week later at Lord Castlereagh's. Gentz considered it would be a diplomatic miracle to have the treaty ready by the end of September and was equally sceptical of its passive acceptance by the French.

The first conference with the French ministers, Talleyrand, Dalberg and the Finance Minister, Baron Louis, was held on 20 September, but prospects of an early settlement were frustrated by a sudden cabinet crisis, precipitated by Fouché's dismissal. Both the planned departure of the sovereigns and the meeting of the new ultra-royalists and reactionary Chamber were postponed, to the great irritation of the delegates. By now they were heartily tired of their protracted stay in Paris. Even Gentz petulantly complained that the lack of calm and the noise made Paris a city impossible in which to live.

Following Fouché's dismissal Talleyrand resigned, alleging that he could not sign a treaty so humiliating to France. Since he believed himself to be indispensable, he was surprised and mortified to find that Louis XVIII blandly accepted his resignation. Talleyrand never again held office under the Bourbon régime.

The wits, erroneously crediting Alexander with manœuvring the change in the government, sneered that he was to be appointed President of the Council; they were only a little wide of the mark. The new Prime Minister and Foreign Secretary was Alexander's trusted friend and servant, Governor of the Crimea, the Duc de Richelieu.

When Richelieu returned to France in 1814 he intended to remain only long enough to arrange his family affairs, pay his duty to the King and then return to Russia which he regarded as his home. France was now to him a foreign country; he had been absent so long that he had forgotten her social usages and even his French was tinged with a slight accent.

Richelieu's appointment to the office of First Gentleman of the Bedchamber, once held by his grandfather, the Marshal-Duc, annoyed him but did not shake his purpose.

'No human power,' he wrote to his cousin and confidant, the Comte de Rochechouart, 'can make me live with the people whom I have unhappily learnt to know so well.'

In this instance Richelieu, of whom Wellington said that his word was as good as a treaty, was destined not to keep it. His objections were all waved aside when Louis XVIII invited him to succeed Talleyrand. Possibly the King was as much influenced by his commanding height, stern, handsome face and air of a *grand seigneur* as by his name, borne by the great Cardinal Richelieu, in itself a guarantee of devoted loyalty.

Richelieu could withstand the King but not Alexander to whom he was deeply attached. When the Czar insisted that he placed confidence only in Richelieu, with misgiving and reluctance the Duc was obliged to accept the office he so greatly dreaded.

Russia already had one powerful advocate in France in Pozzo di Borgo in the anomalous position of Russian ambassador while still a French citizen. To give the government an even deeper Russian complexion Pozzo was offered the post of Minister of Police which he wisely refused.

Castlereagh showed comparable wisdom in acquiescing in the preponderant Russian influence in the new cabinet. Nothing must be allowed to weaken Louis XVIII's position since Great Britain's prime object was to support him under any conditions. Privately Castlereagh believed that, if the nation could be brought to submit for five or even three years to Louis, the government would have become habitual and unlikely to be overturned except by the folly of his successors.

Strict adherence to the Constitutional Charter and maintenance of the royal authority could secure to France the confidence and good-will of her neighbours. The tranquillity of Europe would be assured by the Second Peace of Paris. Five months of stiff negotiation to satisfy all Allied claims while preserving French integrity and dignity culminated on 20 November 1815 with the signature at the Duc de Richelieu's home of the Treaty between the Four Powers and France.

The most important of the twelve articles of the Treaty concerned the French frontiers which were restored to those of 1790; placed the French fortresses at the disposal of the Allied Powers; decided the strength and duration of the military occupation along the north-eastern frontiers and fixed French pecuniary indemnity at 700,000,000 francs. A special Convention regulated methods and dates of payment. The French may have taken some small comfort for this swingeing penalty from Marshal Blücher's loss of a million and a half francs in the gambling hells of Paris.

Great emphasis was placed on the precautionary rather than the punitive nature of the military occupation, whose utmost extent was to be seven years. This period the Allies considered justified by the precariousness of Louis' rule and the difficulties ahead of him. Not-withstanding his paternal intentions, 'the state of uneasiness and fermentation, which after so many violent convulsions, and par-ticularly after the last catastrophe, France must still experience', made the occupation indispensable.

Annexed to the Treaty was a minatory Note to Richelieu from the Allied ministers, stressing their hope that France would succeed in maintaining the public repose and in re-establishing universal union and confidence. Should she fail to do so then the Allies would be under the painful necessity of using force.

However brave their words the Allies were still gloomy about the Bourbons' ability to re-establish themselves successfully. They con-tinued to be haunted by fears of a new 'Jacobinical' uprising, which influenced them to reinforce the Second Peace of Paris with a renewal of the Quadruple Alliance. Here Castlereagh found himself on ground firmer than the quicksands of Alexander's Holy Alliance.

An enduring peace was the urgent need of all the Powers. To recoup her finances and her forces Great Britain required a mini-mum period of seven years of peace, the longest Castlereagh believed peace could be preserved. Whatever might be suspected of

The Grand Entry of the Allies into Paris,
March 31st, 1814

Soirée at the Tuileries, July, 1815—*Nous avons notre Père de Gand—*

Alexander's intentions in the east, he showed no immediate signs of wishing to engage in wars of conquest; internal affairs in Russia, neglected during his long absences abroad, demanded his attention. Prussia needed time to absorb the gains she had made at Vienna; even though her claims had not been met in the Peace of Paris she was in no position to risk a new war. Austria had no warlike intentions. All the Powers were beginning to understand that even limited aggression could lead to a general conflict.

Although there was no immediate or foreseeable *casus belli*, Great Britain, Austria, Russia and Prussia decided to form a defensive association should war nevertheless break out. Their Quadruple Alliance was signed simultaneously with the Second Peace of Paris. They pledged themselves both to maintain that Peace and to redouble their watchfulness lest 'the same revolutionary principles which upheld the last criminal usurpation of Napoleon Bonaparte, might again, under other forms, convulse France'.

The military engagements of the Treaty of Chaumont were renewed, to continue during the occupation of France and to remain in full force and vigour thereafter. By banishing the Bonaparte family from France the Allies hoped to ensure their impotence to foment a rising.

Castlereagh's riposte to the Holy Alliance was the sixth article, which resumed one of the proposals made in the Protocol of Langres. The Czar and his brother sovereigns had pledged themselves to maintain the peace of Europe by Christian principles. Castlereagh found a more practical formula:

'To facilitate and to secure the execution of the present Treaty, and to consolidate the connections which at the present moment so closely unite the Four Sovereigns for the happiness of the world, the High Contracting Parties have agreed to renew their meetings at fixed periods, either under the immediate auspices of the Sovereigns themselves, or by their respective Ministers, for the purpose of consulting upon their common interests, and for the consideration of the measures which at each of these periods shall be considered most salutary for the repose and prosperity of Nations, and for the maintenance of the Peace of Europe'.

This Article VI provided the basis for the four congresses of the Quadruple Alliance which were held in the seven successive years. It established

3

'A European tetrarchy in place of French hegemony but, since their joint jurisdiction was wider even than that of Napoleon, never before had Europe been reduced so nearly to a unitary state as by the Quadruple Alliance.'*

Although the Quadruple Alliance could not maintain itself even for the twenty years' term laid down in the Treaty of Chaumont, the principle determined in Paris in November 1815 was never abandoned. Meetings for the purpose of consultation upon common interests and considering measures 'most salutary for the repose and prosperity of nations' became a commonplace in the 19th century.

Now, in 1815, what originated as a complimentary jest to Gentz might have inaugurated a united states of Europe. The suggestion was made that he be appointed Secretary-General of Europe—with suitable emoluments. What had been put forward idly was then considered in all seriousness. Just before the signature of the Peace Treaty and the Quadruple Alliance the idea was again scouted but was allowed to lapse into oblivion. The opportunity was lost for a radical change in the relationship of the European states.

In its stead, and until the next international meeting, a 'kind of permanent congress for swift and united action' was set up in Paris. Its members were the ambassadors of the Four Courts—Sir Charles Stuart for Britain, Count Pozzo di Borgo for Russia, Baron Vincent for Austria and Graf von der Goltz for Prussia. Their function was to sustain the impotent King on his throne and to ensure that the terms of the Peace of Paris were carried out.

This kennel of ambassadorial watchdogs was there to warn, to comfort but most of all to command since, as Gentz wrote to the Hospodars of Wallachia,

'Were France to be abandoned to-day to herself, it is indubitable that, in less than six months, we should see reproduced in this country the most distressing scenes, and in all probability, a complete upheaval. As the government has no military force at its disposal, it is obvious that a mere serious shock could overthrow it.'

The fault lay in those who in 1814 had thought it possible to re-establish the *ancien régime* pure and simple, thereby doing as much harm as Robespierre and Bonaparte. How lamentable was the situa-

* F. J. C. Hearnshaw: *European Coalitions, Alliances and Ententes since 1792.*

tion of a government whose sole guarantee of existence was the presence of a foreign army of 150,000 men and the terror they inspired! So tormented and harassed were the wretched ministers by the country's internal discontents and the intrigues of the dominant reactionary faction at Court that the Duc de Richelieu, disgusted with his office, would long ago have resigned but for his feelings of honour and duty.

The depth of Richelieu's disgust was revealed by him to Rochechouart:

'The life I lead is every day more and more intolerable; it clashes with all my tastes and habits, so that my whole being is on the rack—unhappy country where there is no choice between fanaticism and crime, and where the voice of reason is the only voice to which no one will listen!'

While Gentz shared something of Richelieu's pessimism about France he did not believe that she would be mad enough once again to provoke Europe. So long as the Quadruple Alliance existed a long and profound peace would prevail; there would be neither war nor revolution in Europe. Neither the King's own worth nor his people's love would preserve Louis XVIII on his throne, but he would remain because any attempt to unseat him would attract few partisans since France's final ruin would be the inevitable result.

Pozzo di Borgo was more cheerful about France's future. The Holy Alliance, by bringing about a return to religion, would give France her much-needed tranquillity. The Holy Alliance should be engraved on the heart of every Frenchman. How diplomatists delude themselves! The French were thinking not in platitudes but in practicalities—their obligation to feed and supply 150,000 men under arms and somehow to find the staggering sum of 700,000,000 francs to pay their war indemnity.

Gentz' thoughts also were now turned to money while the final details of the peace treaty and the alliance were being settled. He was highly pleased with his own achievements and looked for the rewards he had undoubtedly merited. Nothing had been left undone, no question unresolved; he had drafted more than a hundred protocols and seven treaties in all since each of the Allies made a separate treaty with France.

For signing a peace treaty there were recognized perquisites. A

British Foreign Secretary received £6000 from his own government while a similar amount was shared out among his subordinates. By the French government Castlereagh was given a Sèvres porcelain service and diamond snuff boxes rained on all who had taken part in the negotiations. Sir Charles Stuart demurred when the Duc de Richelieu called on him to present the statutory snuff box but neither his colleagues nor Gentz showed the same delicacy.

Gentz could scarcely be blamed; he had no fixed emoluments and was obliged to run round Paris from one delegation to another to discover the extent of his gratifications. He was delighted with British generosity, had high hopes of good presents from the Spaniards and Portuguese and that his delicate approaches to Hardenberg were likely to produce suitable recognition. Unexpected largesse from the French was, Gentz admitted, the result of his own clever manœuvres—a snuff box valued at 3000 francs, filled with bank notes for 12,000 francs, presented to him in the King's name by the Duc de Richelieu in person.

Only the Austrian government lagged behind the others. Francis gave no sign of particular appreciation of Gentz' services in Paris. As avid for status as for money, Gentz began a complicated negotiation on his own account, using Nesselrode as his intermediary. Francis might be sufficiently impressed to bestow on him the title of State Councillor he coveted if Alexander gave him the First Class of the Order of St Anne. Gentz warned Nesselrode that Metternich must not meddle in the transaction; he would do more harm than good.

In spite of this implied criticism Gentz was happy to tell Nesselrode that Metternich was now applying himself to his work with a zeal and energy which would startle the Russian minister who had known him otherwise. He was showing unprecedented firmness and courage, had never been so vigorous or industrious nor enjoyed so much of Francis' favour. Had he but been like this at the Congress of Vienna many things would have turned out differently.

Metternich had left Paris with Francis for a tour of the Austrian provinces in Italy. Gradually the other diplomatists drifted away. Finally Gentz remained alone to sum up his impressions and to conclude that his stay in Paris had been one of the most satisfying periods of his life; he had been loaded with praise and with gifts and looked forward to enjoying the fruits of this decisive epoch.

'*Finita la commedia!*' was the last entry, written with a flourish, in

Gentz' diary. Then, followed by his new *fourgon*, loaded to the axles with his expensive purchases, Gentz set out for Vienna.

Under the watchful eyes of the Conference of Ambassadors the French nation was left to endure the consequences of the peace.

CHAPTER IV

The Tranquillity of Europe

THE Most Illustrious and Most Noble Arthur, Duke, Marquess and Earl of Wellington, bore innumerable other honorific titles; he could flaunt on his plain blue frock coat a zoo and aviary of orders and decorations, nestling within the circlet of the Garter. With the sovereigns of Europe he was on terms of equality. They showed him the most gratifying attentions, praised his energy in deed and prudence in counsel, honoured him with their confidence and flattered him that in the hands of Providence he was a great instrument for peace.

By general assent the Duke was the most important personage of his times, of which no one, said the spiteful, was more aware than Wellington himself.

After Waterloo the Duke's official title was Commander-in-Chief of the Allied Armies of Occupation although some dubbed him disrespectfully the *postillon de la Sainte Canaille*, an anagram of *Alliance*. In Brussels a 'seditious and revolutionary journal' spluttered that 'an English general to-day governs France with 150,000 bayonets', an allegation the Duke at times denied, but at others he admitted that the French government frequently sought his advice.

Castlereagh had indeed patronizingly assured Louis XVIII, whose prestige in Europe was negligible compared with Wellington's, that the Duke would uphold him with all his influence. This promise Wellington on occasion interpreted as freedom to admonish the King for tolerating unruliness in the Chamber, to urge him to support his ministers and to warn him of the dangers of his family's opposition to the government and intrigues with the ultra-royalists.

Before Gentz left Paris at the end of 1815 he optimistically decided that matters in France were going remarkably well and that, even in the National Assembly, moderate views were prevailing. Had he remained a little longer he would have seen his error. France, in common with the rest of Europe, was in the throes of peace. Far from being as insipid and boring as Gentz feared, peace had its storms and catastrophes no less than war.

Economic causes were only partially responsible for the unrest which spread over Europe after Waterloo. Depression invariably follows the cessation of inflated manufactures for war, unemployment the disbanding of armies, difficulties of credit and high prices falling markets. When a succession of bad harvests coincided with the end of a long war weather as much as policy influenced the fate of nations.

Clamour for political reform stirred up almost universal effervescence. Gentz had remarked how signally the Congress of Vienna failed to further democratic and national aspirations; the principle of dynastic property in 'souls', regardless of language or nationality, had retained its virginity intact but, if dynasties could be frozen into the *status quo ante* Napoleon, ideas of national entity and political liberty resisted refrigeration.

Ingratitude to victorious war leaders is not a recent innovation in Great Britain; the government's achievements in winning the war were either ignored or discounted. Hungry men were driven by a series of bad harvests to demonstrations of protest, which culminated in a particularly ugly riot at Spa Fields in London and an assault on the Prince Regent. Suspension of the Habeas Corpus Act and further retaliatory measures failed to check the disturbances although greater apparent calm followed the better harvest of 1817.

From his detached vantage point at army headquarters at Cambrai the Duke of Wellington conceded that a principal cause of unrest in England was the reduction of war establishments. Understandably the man who accused his soldiery of enlisting for drink decided that basically disorder was due to the idleness, dissipation and improvidence of all the middling and lower classes of England. The gentry also were not innocent; their rage for travel deprived some people of employment.

A London weekly journal, *The Champion*, was of the same opinion; foreign travel had all the fury of a contagious fever. The intrigues and conspiracy of some Englishmen on behalf of the Bonapartes had consequences even graver than the others' hauteur, pretension and affected scorn of the French.

The hapless traveller was assailed on all sides. Pozzo di Borgo had little to say in favour of the English in Paris; some sneered, others conspired and believed themselves to be something more than they were at home, but his criticisms did not deter Pozzo from opening his house to the friends he had made in England during his periods of exile. His pious intention was to disrupt the machinations of the fools and the intriguers.

George Canning was neither fool, intriguer nor Bonapartist. He was a member of a government gravely embarrassed by the series of irresponsible speeches he made during his visit to Paris in 1816, although no one who knew the enmity existing between him and Castlereagh believed that the Foreign Secretary approved Canning's ill-founded and imprudent behaviour.

To borrow Hazlitt's sneer, Canning lavished 'the faded flowers of his oratory, like the faint smell of a perfumer's shop' on jealous attacks on Russia and declarations that France ought to be made incapable of stirring for a century. Canning's vanity and frivolity kept Paris in a state of agitation as he 'played off the tricks of a political rope-dancer on the nerves of humanity'. His sole success was inflaming French bitterness and suspicion of English policy, impeding the British and French governments' efforts to maintain a climate of goodwill and dividing the two nations more widely.

Whatever the ill-will engendered by British travellers abroad they alone were not responsible for giving the lie to Milton's words, arrogantly carried beneath *The Champion*'s masthead, 'Let not England forget her precedence in teaching nations how to live.' The example England set to be copied by other nations was one of domestic disorder.

Dissatisfaction in Austria was as widespread as exasperation at the government's apathy in dealing with the nation's discontents, yet Metternich would have made some concessions to the spirit of the age had Francis not forbidden even a toe-hold in his empire to 'Jacobinism'.

'You cannot conceive,' wrote Gentz, 'how for some time we have been agitated and tormented by the bad spirit abroad with us, by the unrestrained licence of the press and by the ever-growing audacity of the trouble-makers.'

Chief trouble-maker was the press. In England the seditious *Black Dwarf* was suppressed but its vari-coloured counterpart in France, *Le Nain Jaune*, flourished unchecked since freedom of the press was a benefit Alexander insisted that Louis XVIII incorporate in his Charter.

From the Netherlands Lord Clancarty, the British ambassador, wrote wistfully that, were Gentz less of a voluptuary and less spoiled than he was in Vienna, he would have made an excellent director of an official paper, similar to the *Moniteur* in France, to counteract an unrestrained press.

Although press and public opinion were less vocal in Russia she did not escape the general malaise. Alexander faced a ruined commerce, a deteriorating financial situation and administrative problems with which he was personally disinclined to cope. His whole attention was concentrated on the achievements in foreign policy which had won him universal praise at home.

Absence of restraint of constitutional forms or influence of public opinion on his authority led Alexander to an impulsive decision, contrary to his agreement with Austria and Prussia not to make the content of the Holy Alliance public except by mutual assent. The Czar was reluctant to forego the applause he was confident this great declaration would win him, happily unaware that half the world sneered at his religious zeal while the other half accused him of hypocrisy.

The British did not share the opinion of informed international circles that Alexander's religious fanaticism was less dangerous than a thirst for conquest or similar anti-social passion. His unilateral publication of the text of the Holy Alliance in the Russian press gravely embarrassed the cabinet. Although Great Britain was not a party to the treaty it was used as a stick with which to beat the government.

Tom Moore inveighed against the 'Grand conspiracy of Kings, the High Legitimates, the Holy Band', those eagles 'handsomely provided with double heads for double dealings'.

The House of Commons vented its sour and discontented temper on the innocuous principles of the Holy Alliance. Members of Parliament saw in them something more sinister than Gentz' mere embroidery on the solid treaties signed by Alexander. They scorned the Freiherr's dismissal of the Alliance as 'a political nothing, without a real object and leading to no positive result—a farce, a mere exemplar of the Czar's vanity'.

Henry Brougham for one read in the text something written in invisible ink, which led him to denounce the Holy Alliance as a

3*

'convention by the despotic monarchs for the purpose of enslaving mankind, veiled under the cloak of a zeal for the interest of the Christian religion and universal philanthropy'.

Ironically Castlereagh, who had poured such scorn on the treaty, found himself obliged to constitute himself Alexander's champion.

> 'Posterity will do justice to his noble determination. Having already done so much for mankind by his arms, to what better purpose can he apply his great influence in the counsels of Europe than by securing for it a long and beneficial peace?'

The maintenance of peace was Castlereagh's chief preoccupation. 'Diabolical Jacobinical elements' might precipitate a new war, therefore the Allies must stand firmly together to prevent any change in the social order which no Power could leave with impunity. On a bad day in Norfolk when he decided to spare the pheasants, Castlereagh drew up a blue-print for British policy:

> 'The immediate object to be kept in view is to inspire the States of Europe, as long as we can, with a sense of the dangers they have surmounted by their union, of the hazards they will incur by a relaxation of vigilance, to make them feel that the existing concert is their only perfect security against the revolutionary embers more or less existing in Europe . . . Their true wisdom would be to keep down the petty contentions of ordinary times and to stand together in support of the established order.'

The great exertions which would be required of Great Britain were both her duty and her interest yet Castlereagh instructed his ambassadors abroad that, while Great Britain's insular position enabled her to pursue a generous policy, her influence would be greater if she stood aloof from separate alliances with other Courts.

This proposal to return to virtual isolationism, apart from British commitments to the Quadruple Alliance, was not a practical possibility in the opinion of Continental statesmen. They believed that, not only must Great Britain remain the pivot of the European Federation which she, not Alexander, had created in full consciousness of the dangers inherent in any new general conflict, but she must remain on a very friendly footing with Russia. The need was the more obvious because the United States, fast becoming a formidable rival, had entered into a close alliance with the Czar, who assured the Americans of his support 'as to any consequences which might occur in Europe'.

Whatever the complexion of the British government in power, its permanent policy must in the interests of peace be the maintenance of good relations with Russia.

However urgently the world needed peace the Powers as yet had to learn to live with peace and its problems. With the exception of Hardenberg all the statesmen had grown to manhood in years of war, still too close for them not to fear the fragility of peace and the danger to the tranquillity of Europe. Few shared Gentz' hopeful view that peace would be of indefinite duration—not perpetual since nothing lasts for ever—but stability was easier to envisage than its overthrow. He could not foresee that a new war would set Europe aflame, basing his conviction largely on the 'frank and noble declarations coming from St Petersburg, especially from the adorable Alexander'.

'The Czar wants peace.' So Capo d'Istrias, his Corfiote Greek adviser now superseding Nesselrode, wrote to Pozzo di Borgo. 'Therefore he wants the most meticulous attention to the engagements from which this peace must result.'

So long as Alexander intended to maintain the Quadruple Alliance, which was the sole guarantee of security in Europe, and work in close harmony with his partners, no one cared whether he called the alliance the glory of the century and the salvation of the world, nor that from it he awaited his immortality. Important only was that Alexander did not intend to make Russia an offensive and conquering state. Of this no one was more confident than Richelieu who pinned his faith to the Czar as a model of chivalry, honour and wise policy.

Those who rated the Duke of Wellington as Europe's most important personage overlooked its most powerful, intelligent and capable monarch, Alexander of Russia. In military authority there was no comparison between them. The Duke's derived from the temporary command of 150,000 men, while the Czar disposed of an army nearly a million strong.

Alexander's practical difficulties in disbanding so large a force in so vast a country were recognized by his allies who were progressively disarming. No one believed that, after the stupendous sacrifices he had made for peace, he would be so foolish as to use this force to destroy his own work. Everyone, moreover, was tolerably aware of the Czar's pride and pleasure in his frequent mammoth reviews of his troops which stood in the way of his carrying out a very necessary measure of economy.

Although familiar with the Czar's vanity Castlereagh was naturally too cautious to take him at his face value. Despite his recent consistency his past record of unpredictability in foreign policy must always render him suspect. At any moment a whim might make him alter course or put forward some idea as irrational as the Holy Alliance. Castlereagh could at least be thankful that Alexander continued 'to manifest the most cordial disposition to act in concert and confidence with the British government'.

Alexander was professing more affection than he felt; his antipathy to the British government was increasing in spite of his declared partiality for Great Britain and his desire to revisit the country. In common with his fellow sovereigns he hated the British tone of superiority which he was obliged to tolerate because policy demanded respect and consideration for England.

From St Petersburg Lord Cathcart, the British ambassador, issued a warning not without contemporary application. Preference for English opinions, produce and inventions was visible in innumerable instances in Russia, but:

'All Russians are peculiarly alive to unfavourable comparisons. They are hurt at any apparent superiority. Perhaps it hardly amounts to the definition of envy, but they hate us for doing what they cannot do; and, without any particular object of immediate advantage, will always feel inclined to abate rather than increase our power, and to join in any measure to curb our dominion over the sea or to check our commerce ... I am convinced that there exists a jealousy of our influence with the kingdom of the Netherlands, and with Persia, and of the extent and importance of our Indian Empire.'

More encouraging was Lord Cathcart's report of Alexander's apparently greater stability, self-confidence and reliance on his own judgment. This satisfaction was, however, tempered by a warning that want of control and advice sometimes led to hasty actions which cool reflection would have avoided. In general the Czar's improved spirits, the absence of any declared favourites or secret influence, his greater attentions to his wife and continued absorption in religion were gratifying.

Gentz confirmed Lord Cathcart's opinions. From Nesselrode he had learned that Alexander's weaknesses were less obvious and his great qualities had developed astonishingly, but consciousness of his superiority over his fellow monarchs had enlarged his ambition to play the dominant role in Europe.

Within the framework of the general alliance Alexander's personal relationships were undergoing a significant change; he was now convinced that only an entente between Austria and Russia could guarantee the tranquillity of Europe. Although with no greater love for Metternich he set out to woo the coy Francis to a personal alliance as the only sovereign of impeccable loyalty in Europe.

This change of heart indicated no weakening of Alexander's personal friendship with Frederick William, whose daughter had recently married the Czar's brother, the Grand Duke Nicholas. He was, however, swivelling round from his previous stance, protection of Sweden, great friendship with England and intimate links with Prussia.

Prussian rapacity at the Paris peace talks was only partially responsible for the divergence between Russia and Prussia. What infuriated the Czar even more, after all he had done or believed himself to have done for the Prussian nation, was its present hostility and jealousy. Had Alexander not realized that isolated conflicts were now impracticable he might have been tempted to declare war on Prussia.

The Concert of Europe had ears cocked only for rumblings in France, potentially explosive because of the possible resurgence of those 'elements of disorder who had engendered, produced and fed the spirit of revolution'. Yet Prussia might also develop into a power house since the civil authority was incapable of controlling the rampaging military faction.

With all Castlereagh's partiality for Prussia and conviction that she must preserve her Great Power status to keep France in check, he was alarmed by exaggerated Prussian patriotism, kept at fever pitch by a press oozing poison.

Prussia had wasted no time in bemoaning the depredations of war but with habitual energy and efficiency set about repairing them. Her malaise was neither economic nor military but political. Frederick William had failed to keep his promise to grant a constitution, that mirage which beckoned the peoples of the Continent, only to vanish the nearer they approached it.

'Liberal ideas and representative institutions are the idols of our age,' wrote Gentz. 'Alexander's ideas inspire those who continue to deplore their governments' dilatoriness in reforms and changes.'

The Czar, in granting a constitution to Poland, had incurred general disapproval, intensified when Prussian disappointment at lack of this placebo inspired a demonstration by students and professors in Luther's Wartburg at Eisenach. This outburst alarmed no one more than Castlereagh, ever on the alert for echoes of subversion in Europe. What would be the end of this impulse towards very free notions of government if the Prussians secured a representative system of government in which they might develop themselves? The Leader of the House of Commons apparently regarded the system of parliamentary government as the brightest jewel in the British crown and therefore definitely not for export.

For any warning that representative government should not be equated with the millennium the nations of Europe needed only to look at France. Pozzo di Borgo raged at the 'matadors of the Chamber' as a handful of egoists ready to quarrel with the whole world and, from purely selfish motives, delay the destiny of nations; they were good for nothing because they had done nothing but antagonize the nation and the Powers, instead of making an honourable appearance on the stage of human actions.

The Allies might think such antagonism and divergence between a nation and its elected representatives misplaced; they failed to take into account that no government could in so short a time change the whole generation which Capo d'Istrias called completely demoralized—if twenty years of glory as the dominant power in Europe can demoralize a nation.

Richelieu was even more exasperated than Pozzo di Borgo with the National Assembly which he was impotent to control, but it was the state of France herself, humiliated, crushed by taxes, with neither commerce nor industry, which reduced him to near despair and increased his natural nervousness and irritability.

'France,' he wrote to Rochechouart, 'is literally expiring under the weight of Europe which is crushing her . . . No one shows any energy here except in hatred. Society is intolerable and passions as violent as in 1792.'

Richelieu's own energy was almost entirely concentrated on persuading the Duke of Wellington to reduce the armies of occupation. This the Duke, pointing to the bad spirit abroad in France and the antics of the Chamber, categorically refused to do. He went farther and warned Louis XVIII that he might have to put the army into a state of readiness for war.

Both Pozzo di Borgo and Capo d'Istrias believed that Europe might well be on the brink of a new war. This peace, founded on a general alliance, might turn out to be one of those fine ideas that human perversity relegated to the sphere of abstractions. Happily the Duke of Wellington had no truck with abstractions. He dealt not with ideas but with men and guns and horses.

The Duke's energy was inexhaustible. He constantly flitted from his headquarters at Cambrai and Paris to act as supreme watchdog over the Conference of Ambassadors, all instructed by their governments in case of dissent among themselves to be guided by the Duke. Wellington's good humour and common sense which kept the Allied machine running well justified his opinion that his interventions frequently benefited the common cause. Not least was his effective quashing of the ambassadors' pretensions to act as a European parliament and to elevate themselves into a super-Power.

Two of the four ambassadors were required to show little initiative. Graf von der Goltz, the Prussian, was merely Hardenberg's mouthpiece and as colourless as the Austrian Baron Vincent who, in accordance with Metternich's instructions, followed the line taken by the British. The trouble, according to Wellington, was that Sir Charles Stuart, the British ambassador, seemed reluctant to take the lead which England's position demanded.

The British were highly conscious of alone having saved Europe by their exertions, and that they had coalesced and subsidized the sovereigns who individually could not 'have done the thing'. Were British moral force removed from the Continental political machine Europe would once again be at the mercy of private passions. Only Great Britain, with no common frontiers with any country, was sufficiently detached to play the dominant role with the least danger to others.

Sir Charles Stuart was in constant hot water both with Wellington and Castlereagh for showing too little and too much independence at the wrong times. The Duke's chief complaint was that in conference Stuart frequently 'allowed his colleagues to go on, said nothing, and signed with the majority'.

As Wellington's only rival in ability and energy Pozzo di Borgo dominated the conference in his absence. Happily the two men were on the best possible terms. Wellington honoured Pozzo with his confidence while Pozzo showered praise for his wisdom and impeccable conduct on the Duke, under whom he had served at Waterloo. Particularly laudable was Wellington's high-mindedness and aloofness from British political intrigues; from him nothing but good would result.

In the early stages of the Conference of Ambassadors Pozzo was also on good terms with his colleagues, but this honeymoon was not destined to last long.

Charles-André Pozzo di Borgo was the stormy petrel among the Allied ambassadors, but his had been the most stormy career. Divergent political opinions and a family quarrel estranged him from his distant cousin, Napoleon Bonaparte, who for twenty years pursued him ruthlessly. While one Corsican dazzled the world with his genius the other was forced to fritter away his talents as he was hounded in turn to England, Italy and Austria. Yet, despite Pozzo's reciprocal hatred of Napoleon, he was compelled to admire the phenomenon whose like would never again be seen.

Pozzo shared with Bonaparte many of the temperamental characteristics of their native Corsica—tenacity, obstinacy, pride, violence, intrigue, ambition and irritability. In both their bad qualities were redeemed by irresistible charm and in Pozzo by scintillating wit and easy manners.

During his Viennese exile Pozzo sharpened his mind against Metternich's and absorbed many of Gentz' ideas on the importance and feasibility of European unity. At last the Czar noticed Pozzo's gifts and experience and appointed him as Russian ambassador to France, where his unrivalled knowledge of the ground, men and matters kept him for twenty years.

Alexander rated Pozzo highly although he was frequently irritated by his devotion to lost causes and his habit of forgetting that he was the Russian ambassador remembering only that he was a Frenchman. Nesselrode was frequently obliged to beg Pozzo to be impartial to the point of pedantry in his reports and particularly to tone down the expression of his hysterical attachment to the Bourbons.

Alexander did not allow his personal aversion to Louis XVIII to prejudice his desire to draw Russia closer to France, once again by a dynastic alliance. Pozzo worked hard to bring about a marriage between the Grand Duchess Anne and the Duc de Berri who, when a penniless émigré, had scoured the Courts of Europe in vain for a bride. Now, as Louis XVIII's ultimate heir, he was the most eligible of royal bachelors.

Pozzo was keenly disappointed when the project came to grief on the religious difference. The Grand Duchess Anne finally married her sister's 'day-dream', Prince William of Orange, to strengthen Russian rather than British influence in the Netherlands.

Frustrated of a great diplomatic triumph, Pozzo used his surplus energy to pursue Sir Charles Stuart with venomed darts; his outlook was mediocre and his principles uncertain; he was devious, jealous, haughty and antagonized everyone. More damaging to Sir Charles's reputation than Pozzo's dislike and suspicion was his accusation that when the British ambassador did take the initiative in conference, it seemed always to be in perverse opposition to his cabinet's policy.

As Pozzo took no pains to keep his opinions confidential his allegations were heard in London. Castlereagh sharply reproved Stuart who was at the same time warned not to expose himself and his government to the prejudicial notion that they were secretly caballing to upset the Duc de Richelieu, the best minister France could now furnish.

The close friendship existing between Richelieu and Pozzo di Borgo may well have inspired Stuart's hostility to the Duc. They were drawn together by common nationality, long exile from France and devotion to Russia and Alexander. Richelieu had need of friends since he was repudiated by his own caste for caring more about liberating France from her burdens than putting the clock back to 1789. The 'noble' Faubourg St Germain incited the reactionary Chamber to restore the aristocratic privileges of the *ancien régime* which the renegade Richelieu refused to do. The Duc would have found small consolation in the remark once made by Fouché to Napoleon,

'It is traditional; the Seine flows, the Faubourg intrigues, demands and calumniates; it is in the nature of things.'

Richelieu's depression and disillusion were mitigated only by Alexander's support; his vigilance and beneficent authority were vital to the welfare of France. Pozzo's real influence on Richelieu derived precisely from this special relationship between France and Russia. Despite Alexander's emphatic denial of any unilateral understanding with France, Richelieu in a letter hinted at an entente which he regretted must not be suspected but which he hoped would not always remain secret.

In the hotbed of a Paris where the government was subservient to the Conference of Ambassadors secrets were hard to keep especially since jealousy and suspicion were increasing among the ambassadors beneath a film of harmony.

Stuart, driven into a corner, accused Pozzo di Borgo of undue influence on the Duc de Richelieu and interference in French affairs. The hit was palpable. The French, who viewed their foreign watchdogs with a sardonic eye, murmured,

'Are we still governed by a Corsican?'

Pozzo retaliated by expressing indignation at Stuart's encouragement of the 'permanent conspiracy of revolutionary English in France', engaged in Bonapartist plots. These intrigues and those of the opposition in England exacerbated the rivalry between France and England which 'neither reason nor policy nor even the force of circumstances would ever diminish'. British newspapers were 'infected by alarming and libellous information reaching them through diplomatic couriers and correspondence of the British embassy'.

If Pozzo's ideas were frequently prejudiced his information was always accurate. Wellington himself wrote to Castlereagh that the diplomatic bag was used by unauthorized people, thereby creating unwarranted suspicion of the British government. He maintained that 'the means by which base intrigues are carried on with the sole view of overturning the King of France's government is by the ambassador's messengers'.

Wellington's accusation was not levelled at the couriers and messengers themselves, chosen with scrupulous care for their excellent character, good health and knowledge of foreign languages. Couriers were frequently of foreign origin but the King's messengers were invariably British; theirs was a long-established service and their distinguishing badge of a silver greyhound and the royal arms encased in crystal had been worn for over a hundred years.

Such great importance attached to the reliability of messengers that Castlereagh himself swore them in with a most solemn oath. 'On the Holy Evangelists and by the faith they bore to Almighty God' the messengers bound themselves to be 'true servants to their Sovereign Lord George the Third and to serve the King most truly and faithfully in the place whereunto they were called as Messengers in Ordinary to His Majesty'.

A messenger was required not to know anything 'that shall in anyways be hurtful or prejudicial to the King's Majesty's Royal Person, State, Crown and Dignity, but you shall for as much as whatever may lie in your power under it or else with all possible speed reveal the same to the King's Majesty or to some of His Most Honourable Privy Council'.

This oath was reinforced by every possible precaution to ensure the virtual impossibility of leakage in the transmission of British despatches. Strict rules and regulations were drawn up both for the guidance of the messengers themselves and ministers to foreign Courts.

No messenger was allowed to canvass for any preference or in any other way prejudice the rest of the Corps; he must take his allotted turn on the rota, unless health or some domestic calamity prevented his so doing.

When in London he received the boxes with an ingenious spring label to change the name of the addressee the messenger was provided with a special passport and one or more printed 'Way Bills', which he was required to keep clean—an obligation faithfully carried out as the state of those Way Bills which have survived testifies.

Whenever he delivered a Foreign Office bag to one of His Majesty's ministers or ambassadors the messenger had to note the date, time and place and obtain an official counter-signature. In his turn the minister or ambassador acknowledging despatches invariably noted the date of receipt, the name of the messenger and the time he was sent forward to his next destination.

Any extraordinary accident or other cause of delay occurring on the journey must be stated on the back of the Way Bill and subscribed by an authorized person—a post master or packet agent. Difficulties must have arisen in lonely places in obtaining such certification but, without it, vouchers for extra expenses and allowances could not be presented. This was a matter of great importance to the messenger who was allowed extra board wages for the period when he was under the orders of, or in attendance upon, ambassadors, nor were his wages excessive.

Wages were some £50 a year, plus a dress allowance of some £12.10.0. Board wages of one William Hunter, Junior, Messenger in Ordinary to His Majesty in the Foreign Department, for 110 days in attendance on Sir Charles Stuart on the Paris station were £73.6.8, with an extra expense allowance of £11.0.0 for passing through fortified towns during the night on eleven journeys on the Cambrai road.

With so much vigilance surrounding a messenger any delinquency on his part was unthinkable. The fault could lie only with Sir Charles Stuart's laxity in permitting the abuse of the official facilities provided both for maximum security and greater economy than utilizing the French postal service.

Now from Baron Vincent came a warning of intrigue, weakness and mistaken policy of the French, all contributing to arouse the dread spirit of revolution. Of this Wellington needed no reminder. With a want of his normal common sense he, like Castlereagh, was always inclined with a delicious shudder to see a plotting *demi-solde* or *sansculotte* lurking under every bed.

The Duke was deeply convinced that the French Revolution had left in the world 'heaps of dangerous and unquiet characters, kept down for a while by the force of Bonaparte's character and the vigour and strength of his government'. Bonaparte now being thrown aside, these men, without an object and uncontrolled by their respective governments, had become 'a focus of mischief, of conspiracy and rebellion in every country in Europe'.

Was Wellington's reluctant admiration of Bonaparte's ability to keep revolution in check responsible for the opinion he expressed shortly before the Emperor's death in 1821, that the Allies made a tremendous mistake in getting rid of him, that Napoleon was the man they ought to have had?

The man they had was Louis XVIII and it was the British government's main objective to keep him where he had been put. Since the French were making the royal family the scapegoat for their sufferings this was not an easy task. Wellington had to hammer home to Louis and the Comte d'Artois that the principle of legitimacy was not the prime motive in restoring the Bourbon dynasty. France was not to be kept quiet because 150,000 bayonets spoke in favour of legitimacy, but to enable legitimacy to dispense with them. The foreign troops were the King's allies, there to help him strengthen his throne and give him time to establish himself securely. A tranquil France was vital to enduring peace among the nations and so far as possible to ensure the tranquillity of the world.

Pozzo di Borgo naturally exceeded the Duke's efforts to bring the King to a just appreciation of his position; he was intent on promoting French interests and attempting to secure France's reinstatement in the European family. As he paid court to Wellington and in his turn sermonized the King—how tired Louis must have been of his allies' constant admonition, 'Louis, be a king!'—Pozzo di Borgo likened himself to a dog running round in circles to rid himself of pestering fleas. He made no mealy mouth in his forthright warning to the Comte d'Artois that only his family's ruin would result from his intrigues. Finally Pozzo had to counter the scoundrelly 'Jacobins'.

Putative 'Jacobins' frightened Richelieu less than bad harvests, war debts and French hostility towards the Allies. Particularly resentful were the inhabitants of the areas occupied by the Prussians, the Austrians and the Bavarians, who vied with one another in using and abusing the fruits of victory; only the British and the Russians behaved with decorum. Life in France was generally intolerable because of the obligation to support the army of occupation and at the same time pay the indemnities. The Allies might understand French animosity but its existence made them reluctant to grant any concessions or alleviations.

Richelieu felt increasingly incapable of struggling against his difficulties. But for his sense of duty and conviction that he alone could secure the liberation of France he would have resigned his thankless office. His hands were stretched with longing towards those shores of the Black Sea where dwelt his heart.

The Allies were unanimously agreed that Richelieu was indispensable and did their best to rally his spirits. Castlereagh asked Wellington to assure the Duc that he could rely on all great questions of European interest on the fair and liberal views of the British government; they had every confidence in his personal character and principles.

Both through Pozzo di Borgo and his personal correspondence Alexander continued to give all possible moral support to Richelieu. He assured him how happy he would be to see an end to France's unfortunate situation and the restoration of her liberty and political independence. This, the Czar believed, was not the desire of his allies who would be happy to keep France in a state of subjection. The spirit of opposition was most active among the foreign ambassadors. Pozzo's support of Richelieu caused his colleagues to range themselves alongside the Duc's rivals. Most formidable of these was Talleyrand who was damaging the government's prestige by encouraging the most dangerous and intriguing elements in Paris.

Alexander was particularly anxious to reach agreement on a reduction in the size of the Army of Occupation, the great issue between the French government and the Allies. A conciliatory move towards

France would be the first test of the strength of the Quadruple Alliance and the stability of the restoration. The Czar hoped that it would pave the way to a reasonable peace ending the hatred which for too long had divided the nations of Europe.

Pozzo di Borgo was instructed to play his part in the negotiations with *finesse*. Personally he should urge reduction while feigning Alexander's reluctance to concede it. In the event of success all the merit and glory must be ascribed to the Duke of Wellington.

Prolonged and delicate discussion was needed before the Duke finally agreed to take the calculated risk of reducing the army by 30,000 men which would save the French some thirty million francs a year. Characteristically Wellington warned the French government that he would not agree to further reduction in the force before the expiration of the first term of three years laid down in the Conventions annexed to the Peace of Paris. At the same time he reminded Richelieu and Louis XVIII that all Europe had preferred the solution of an army of occupation to a permanent cession of French territory.

The Duke was not primarily influenced in his partial reduction by the desire to save the French money. Bad harvests and the general financial straits of France foreshadowed difficulties in finding subsistence and forage for the armies in the following year. Another factor which weighed with him was the growing agitation against occupation, regarded by the French not as protection against the revolutionary spirit as Wellington claimed, but as a disgraceful condition imposed by the conquerors on the conquered.

Lord Bathurst, Secretary for War, thought that the French had contrived to render the Allies so odious and had been encouraged by impunity to be so audaciously insolent to them that, even should the government still continue to regard occupation as necessary for its own security, its maintenance was doubtful.

Louis XVIII's position was now, however, somewhat happier. Under pressure from Wellington and the Conference of Ambassadors he had dissolved the reactionary *Chambre Introuvable* (so called because its like would never again be seen) and the autumn elections had returned a Chamber more representative of the nation as a whole.

When, on 11 February 1817, the Duc de Richelieu announced the reduction in the Army of Occupation, as envisaged by the Protocol to the Conferences of Paris of 13 October 1815, French spirits rose immediately. The nation looked forward confidently to total evacuation, especially as negotiations had been initiated for a loan to settle her war debts.

Lest the prospect of an end to their humiliation should induce excessive optimism and obstreperousness in the French Lord Liverpool sounded a warning note. Total evacuation would depend on the settlement of all claims on France otherwise, once the troops were all withdrawn, she might fail to meet her obligations. Bathurst took an even gloomier view. Although the occupation might have outlived its usefulness, once the armies departed the whole French fabric would probably crumble to pieces.

Now that the Conference of Ambassadors was less involved in the surveillance of France they were given another task which increased their consequence. They were instructed to mediate on the relations between Spain and Portugal and their respective colonies. Volumes of documents bear witness to the complexity of the problem, which became almost as much a running sore in European politics as war in the Peninsula had been to Napoleon. Happiest aspect of the mediation and a welcome sign of French regeneration was the co-opting of the Duc de Richelieu to the discussions.

Tangled Spanish affairs were still further entwined by British and Austrian suspicion that Alexander was making a secret agreement with Spain. To the discomfiture of the other three members of the Quadruple Alliance the Czar, in default of a new love affair, was now flirting with nations. Metternich, always reluctant to take the lead, refused to make the formal move of protest suggested by Castlereagh. Nothing must be allowed to imperil the general alliance of the Great Powers, therefore open disagreement should be avoided as long as possible to maintain the tranquillity of Europe.

Castlereagh did, however, avail himself of the opportunity for a subtle revenge on Alexander offered by Spanish recalcitrance in toe-ing the British line about the slave trade. Still smarting under his enforced championship of the Holy Alliance he wrote with some irony to Capo d'Istrias,

'It would be unworthy in laying down the maxims of Christianity as the rule of conduct in Europe between state and state, to have assumed a less benevolent principle towards Africa. We may defy moral criticism if our execution shall correspond to the principles we profess.'

One great stumbling block to further progress in securing abolition was the wish of Alexander and other Powers involved that it should go hand in hand with suppression of the Barbary pirates marauding in the Mediterranean. The Czar's suggestion of using repressive measures was recognized as a plausible excuse for sending his warships through the Dardanelles into the Mediterranean, in pursuance of Russia's unvarying policy of securing a warm water port. No British government would countenance such a move.

Castlereagh riposted that he had no doubt but that, if all drew heartily together upon the broad ground of giving repose upon Christian principles to the human race, of whatever colour and in every part of the globe, they would do themselves credit, and render a lasting service to mankind.

The Barbary pirates were for the time being left unchecked and many years elapsed before the brave British hope of suppressing the slave trade became reality.

Whatever policies were dictated by sovereigns and cabinets they had to be implemented by their delegates but friction among them could, and in Paris in these years did, frustrate their entire realization. Under stress of new and old problems agitating the members of the Quadruple Alliance, and after nearly three years of intimate association, signs of wear were apparent in the goodwill of their ambassadors.

Each accused the other of trying to govern France, with Pozzo di Borgo naturally the chief prosecutor. Sir Charles Stuart was convinced that it was Pozzo's influence which secured the sudden removal from the War Ministry of Clarke, Duc de Feltre. Pozzo continued the slanging match by retorting that Stuart's continued presence in Paris was damaging to business; his retention at the Paris embassy was pure retaliation for the Czar's too successful ambassador at Madrid.

That Great Britain, Austria and even Prussia were jealous of Russia's political power Pozzo was convinced. All three, inspired by Metternich's intrigues, were trying to circumvent the Russians. Pozzo believed that the Viennese cabinet governed the London cabinet and influenced that of Berlin. To round off his accusations Pozzo wrote to Nesselrode that the British government was inferior to the circumstances, the times and the country it governed.

When Gentz concurred that on European questions the British government was generally asleep and showed a want of vigour the links in the chain of European opinion were obvious. Both Gentz and

Pozzo were correspondents of Nesselrode but neither of these shrewd political observers grasped the fundamentals of Castlereagh's foreign policy. Unlike Alexander who from a spirit of benevolence was willing to guarantee everything, the British were unwilling to enter into any general guarantees and loath to encourage unnecessary British interference on the Continent. Beyond commitments to the Quadruple Alliance the British would not go, in accordance with Castlereagh's conviction that Great Britain's interposition would always be most authoritative in proportion as it was not compromised by being unduly mixed in the daily concerns of the states of Europe. Nevertheless, Pozzo di Borgo was heard to murmur in conference in a voice designedly audible to Sir Charles Stuart,

'You will see how Lord Castlereagh wants to dictate the work of the Conference.'

Even the mutual admiration society established between Pozzo di Borgo and Wellington was now losing some of its bloom, despite Alexander's reiterated insistence that his ambassador must not act without the Duke's approval.

Obediently Pozzo continued to render justice to the Duke's fine qualities but he now found that they were marred by his defects; he was susceptible to the *nth* degree, capable of receiving mistaken impressions, when he could not bear to be contradicted. His high-mindedness, remoteness from his country's intrigues and profound good sense did not, in the final analysis, prevent his being the instrument of his government.

The final barb was that the British government was embarrassed by the Allied army and its commander. Wellington's reputation was too great to be kept idle and unemployed in London, which was the reason for his being entrusted with the command of the Army of Occupation.

On his side Wellington was tiring of Pozzo's ambivalence; a French minister in the Conference of Ambassadors would be better than Pozzo, who stood in the way of any concerted plan of action upon any subject, however common the interests might be.

'Every word is repeated,' the Duke complained to Castlereagh, 'and the Czar's instructions are acted upon or not, according as it suits the French interests; and they are never communicated, as was at first the practice by all, and is still by the ministers of some, to the Conference.'

Hardest perhaps to stomach was the lofty tone Pozzo borrowed from Alexander. He wrote to Wellington, actuated by his belief that Great Britain was embarrassed more by the superiority of Russian principles than by any other obstacle,

> 'These principles are drawn from two sources equally salutary; that of Christian morality, fortunately in our days become the recognized regulator of general policy, and that of the right of nations which lays down the rules by which this abstract doctrine is effortlessly applied to discussions arising among the states.'

Alexander himself could not have put it better.

CHAPTER V

The European Federation

In February 1818 the appreciably calmer atmosphere in France was abruptly shattered by a shot at the Duke of Wellington as he stepped into his carriage. The assailant missed, but to be the target of however bungling an assassin is an unpleasant experience even for a soldier accustomed to danger.

The Duke's reaction was to lash out in all directions. He suspected that Richelieu doubted the genuineness of the assault, to which some credence was given by the delay and inefficiency of the French police in discovering the culprit. He was further enraged by the slander current that he himself had engineered the attempt in order to retain the command which made him the virtual equal of kings. Lord Bathurst must have felt no surprise to be told in a letter from Wellington that he felt very indifferent respecting the French government, in whose concerns he had interested himself only for the general good and to preserve the peace of the world.

Gentz for one professed to have heard the Duke speak of the French with ill-disguised feelings of hate and scorn. Clearly Wellington saw little to choose between them and the lower classes of England. Their efforts to raise themselves from their humiliation the Duke appeared to regard as a kind of ungrateful revolt against their conquerors.

The French, in fact, were insufficiently grateful for their defeat, for their obligation to supply the vast Army of Occupation foisted on them, for beggaring themselves to pay a swingeing war debt and for maintaining on the throne a reigning house wanted only by a minority.

The cabinet's indignation and suspicions exceeded even Wellington's. This 'diabolical conspiracy' seemed to justify Castlereagh's gloomy fears of the resurgence of the 'Jacobins'; more than ever he was convinced of the danger of leaving France to the uncontrolled administration of her own affairs. Lord Cathcart was instructed to inform Alexander of the serious anxiety felt by the British cabinet about the state of French political parties and the temper of the nation, exacerbated by the occupation and stridently vocal against the Allies.

In Alexander, acutely sensitive to the merest whisper of assassination, Castlereagh found a sympathetic ear. Pozzo di Borgo was wrong to insist that all was well with France; the nature of the French did not change.

'Whatever the success of the institutions on which their government is founded,' said Alexander, 'they will be ready to upset the one by the other, or both together, as soon as circumstances or some pretext gives them the opportunity.'

The recurrent upheavals in France during the 19th century and the endemic instability of her governments during the 20th proved Alexander a prophet. His fellow-oracle was Wellington, who gnomically predicted that the descendants of Louis XV would not reign in France and that the fault would lie with the Comte d'Artois and his adherents. No doubt when Artois, as Charles X, was forced to abdicate in 1830, the Duke congratulated himself on his foresight.

Evidence was at last forthcoming that the outrage against Wellington was not the isolated work of two or three desperate and profligate assassins but part of a wider plot hatched by French exiles in the Low Countries and a party within France. Was there any connection between this attempt and a project uncovered in the United States to effect Bonaparte's escape from St Helena?

Joseph Bonaparte, William Cobbett and Regnault de St Jean d'Angély, all three in exile in America, were involved. Regnault had given an order in Philadelphia for 1100 hats and a comparable amount of equipment to fit out a small rescue force, but he was so obviously insane that Joseph packed him back to Europe. He was now believed to be in Antwerp.

Clearly, whoever was responsible for the attack on Wellington, its inspiration was to be found in the Netherlands. The King must take the blame for constantly disregarding repeated warnings of the danger of harbouring and encouraging proscribed criminals. Wellington remarked caustically that, if the King continued to permit the publication of libels, he would, like the British, have no real friends in Europe.

Discovery of a further plot in the Netherlands to assassinate him in no way surprised the Duke. It was not, he presumed 'because they do not like my face or my manners, or the colour of my coat, but because I am the General of the Allies and the main support of the system of tranquillity and order'.

The spectre of Bonapartist resurgence in Europe did not frighten Marshal Blücher who was cruelly bored. He sent Wellington a message, suggesting that he use his influence to facilitate the escape of their 'common friend', in order once again to try a battle of strength. This frivolous proposal had no sequel.

Wellington, positive that he was the sole prop on which the tranquillity of Europe rested, refused the British cabinet's request that he leave the dangers of Paris for the greater security of Cambrai. His sudden withdrawal from Paris 'would give the most fatal shake to everything that was going forward'. Without him the union of counsels and objects which had prevailed among the ambassadors in Paris would collapse; absence of visible signs of disunion should not be taken as evidence that they were cordially united. Moreover, since the Duke had discovered in himself an aptitude for finance almost as great as his military skill, his departure from Paris would put an end to the negotiations on private claims against France in which he was successfully mediating.

Finally, a cowardly retreat would sacrifice all respect for the only person who, in his own estimation at least, had the power to keep French enmity within bounds. Wellington warned Richelieu that, unless the French fulfilled the conditions imposed on them by the Second Peace of Paris, the Allied troops would remain *in situ*.

By the summer a happier frame of mind prevailed. Both the Duke and the French had rallied their spirits. Where threats and exhortation had failed a rising stock market succeeded. The welcome given to the loans produced greater confidence in the existing order. With great caution Wellington was now ready to concede not only the desirability but the necessity of total evacuation. The final decision on the withdrawal of the army of occupation and the settlement of war debts must, however, rest with the sovereigns. By the terms of Clause V, paragraph 5, of the Second Peace of Paris they were due to meet shortly. On this meeting all attention was now focused.

Early in 1817 Metternich had already written to the Duke that he was looking forward to meeting him somewhere in the following year. He added with typical *wienerisch schwärmerei* that he would always count the moments they would spend together as the happiest of his life. For those moments Metternich considered a meeting of sovereigns superfluous. The same procedure used for the partial reduction of the Army of Occupation would surely suffice, that is an exchange of notes by the Conference of Ambassadors.

Metternich later changed his mind but he was as insistent as Castlereagh that the reunion should be treated not as a congress but as a *special conference*, as the final stage of the negotiations at Vienna and Paris in 1815, a sequel not a beginning. The Prince Regent's government felt strongly that no new matter of sufficient importance had emerged to justify any assembly even remotely resembling the Congress of Vienna with its unwieldy concentration of plenipotentiaries from every state in Europe. Nevertheless, in spite of general determination that the meeting should *not* be considered as a congress, a congress it was called and as a congress it continues to be known.

Once the principle of a sovereigns' meeting was established a decision had to be taken as to its time and place, who would be present and the subjects to be discussed.

The timing was quickly settled. August was the month chosen by Alexander although he later deferred it until the end of September. He added the request that the meeting be as short as possible because domestic affairs required his presence in Russia. The British were only too ready to agree, thankful that a short meeting would postpone his threatened visit to England, at best most inconvenient and at worst susceptible of undesirable intrigues.

Everyone shared Castlereagh's wish that the place of reunion be chosen 'with a view to the course of business being as little as may be broken in upon by any other objects'. This prim caveat was taken to mean that there should be no repetition of the frivolity of Vienna. Deliberation not dalliance, decisions not dancing were to be the rule.

With Vienna thus excluded speculation in the European Press was keen as to the venue to be chosen. Prague had its disadvantages. No one liked Alexander's suggestion of Bâle. From many points of view a North German city was desirable, not least because the Prussian police were more reliable than elsewhere.

Competition among Rhineland cities was great for the honour of entertaining the sovereigns and perhaps still more for the profits their presence would bring. Since the Rhineland, by the territorial distributions made at the Congress of Vienna, now belonged to the King of Prussia, his was the final word. Frederick William opted for Aix-la-Chapelle in preference to Düsseldorf. At Aix he could combine taking the waters with the business of the congress. By April the news was leaked from Vienna that the reunion or interview would be at Aix-la-Chapelle, an admirable choice.

As the ancient capital of Charlemagne and the scene of the coronations of the Holy Roman Emperors Aix-la-Chapelle was a city of great imperial traditions and the site in 1668 and 1748 of two congresses. Almost as much as its history its thermal springs, tested and approved by English doctors, added to its renown. Physically its setting was superb, between the Eifel mountains and the Ardennes, but for the forthcoming meeting its greatest advantage was ease of communications. Standing at an important crossroads between Belgium and France, Aix-la-Chapelle was within near reach of the Duke of Wellington's headquarters at Cambrai, only three days' journey from Paris and four from England.

This comparatively short distance from home was of greatest benefit to Castlereagh, who could not expect to enjoy the same latitude in decision as at Vienna. From Aix-la-Chapelle despatches could be sent to England and answers received in little more than a week. Although both Castlereagh and Richelieu would be furnished with their instructions for the conference it was likely that both would need to refer to London and Paris for further directions.

Ease of communications was immaterial to the Russian, Prussian and Austrian delegations since their 'August Masters' would be present in person at Aix. Alexander would certainly inhibit his Foreign Secretaries, Nesselrode and Capo d'Istrias; without his direct orders they were able to exercise only a 'very limited discretion of stating an opinion'. Metternich was more fortunate. Francis allowed him a great deal of leeway and rarely interfered with his decisions. With monotonous regularity the Emperor marked Metternich's communications 'Read and approved', only occasionally did he make any comment.

The time and site of the meeting settled, the next question to be resolved was who should be summoned to attend. Alexander rushed in with the proposal to invite the whole of Europe to treat all weighty matters at issue, with the tacit intention of acting as arbiter. He could have had little hope of success since his similar essay in involving all parties interested in the negotiations for the settlement of private claims against France had already been quashed by Wellington.

Now Pozzo di Borgo was told that the Duke, who had experienced the delays and complications of Vienna, thought it unreasonable to invite twenty Powers to Aix-la-Chapelle. The result could only be the dragging on of the reunion *sine die*. Pozzo, for once conciliatory, agreed that, while rarely helping the great Courts in their difficulties, the secondary Courts were very active and dexterous in wearing them out with minor problems.

Alexander returned to the charge with a further suggestion, monstrous to Metternich, that a majority vote of the Conference of Ambassadors should decide the point. Democratic ideas had clearly gone to the Czar's head—the Conference was not a parliament; it could act only on the definite instructions of its masters. Gentz ridiculed the mere idea that ambassadors should deal with matters which were the province of cabinets alone. If these were the notions Alexander was packing in his baggage for Aix-la-Chapelle, then beware the future!

Only one way was seen of scotching any belief that the meeting at Aix-la-Chapelle was in any way comparable to the Congress of Vienna. A firm announcement must be made that it originated exclusively in the engagements undertaken by the Four Powers in the Quadruple Alliance signed by them in Paris in November 1815. Hopefully the Four Courts argued that, once the distinctive character of this reunion was made clear, the minor Courts would be under no misapprehensions, either as to the nature of the proceedings or to the relation in which they themselves stood to the conference.

To underline the Allies' insistence that the sovereigns' meeting was limited to the signatories of the Quadruple Alliance invitations to attend were sent to the Four Courts by the Conference of Ambassadors in Paris.

Castlereagh and Metternich thought that this procedure should effectively rule out any invitation to the King of Spain. Although Alexander's flirtation with Spain was languishing, he and Richelieu were both anxious that her King should be invited.

When the Austrian Chancellor and the British Foreign Secretary pointed out the inexpediency of opening the conference at Aix to new matter, 'especially to such an interminable chapter as that which Spanish interests represent', Alexander withdrew his request. Castlereagh gave little credit to the Czar's steadfast adherence to the principle of unity. He merely congratulated himself and Metternich

Robert Stewart, Viscount Castlereagh

Prince Clement von Metternich
in the robes of the Order of the Golden Fleece

that the sentiments of their two cabinets were travelling so closely in the same path.

Different, though still tactful, language was used to Richelieu. He was told that none of the Powers which had made the greatest sacrifices during the war would relish seeing a Power like Spain introduced into their councils.

To make a greater clearance of the decks for action the Conference which had been sitting at Frankfort to settle some of the minor German problems arising from the Congress of Vienna was brought to a close. The expected clash for power in the new Diet of the German Confederation ended in victory for Austria over Prussia, but the dream of a united German state dissolved; the secondary German states preferred their individual to the general interest.

Some outstanding German problems, notably the Baden succession, seemed likely to come under discussion at Aix. The Four Courts protested too much that they were concerned only with the total evacuation of France and the settlement of her war debts. They had no intention of foregoing the opportunity of debating other political questions 'in order to give to their progress that useful impulse which had never failed to result from the immediate superintendence of the sovereigns'.

Agreement had already been reached in principle on total evacuation and loans to pay French war debts were in an advanced stage of negotiation. The most important question to be debated at Aix-la-Chapelle would be the future of France in relation to the Quadruple Alliance.

Richelieu dangled the bait before the Allies of the advantages of co-opting France to the Alliance rather than condemning her to an exclusion as impolitic as it was insulting. His anxiety to secure French admission to the European federation was greater because his hope of a separate entente with Russia was fading fast.

'I could see a more intimate ally in France,' said Alexander, 'but, even if she were guaranteed for ever from any future revolution, I should still refrain from contracting with this nation any closer relations.'

Castlereagh was still prophesying woe. At this moment he was concerned with seeking safeguards against disturbances in France which might imperil the tranquillity of Europe. He feared that, once the Allied armies were withdrawn from France, she would offer no security that she would fulfil her engagements. Castlereagh was still

4

sceptical about the endurance of the present system but Metternich took a brighter view. If France arrived as a great Power at Aix-la-Chapelle, loyally contributing to the general welfare by honouring her commitments, she would offer the most impressive of moral guarantees. Her entry into the Quadruple Alliance would then be difficult to oppose, particularly since French co-operation must materially assist the preservation of peace in Europe.

Gentz was ready enough to concede Castlereagh's fears about the fragility of Allied union, but he held to his opinion that the disastrous alternative would ensure its survival. This European federation, the term he thought most exact for the system, could have a life of fifty years, although ten or fifteen were more probable.

For the benefit of the Hospodars of Wallachia Gentz summed up the European situation as he saw it.

Austria, without enemies and dominating the Confederation of Germany, was in the happiest position.

Gentz was mistaken in saying that the British government had ridden out its crisis and was firmly established; popular movements in Great Britain were by no means contained. He was more accurate in judging that she must continue in the front rank, that she could not tolerate a secondary role. Most encouraging was British determination to support the Quadruple Alliance.

Unlike Castlereagh who feared France above all, only in Prussia did Gentz see cause for alarm. No one would be able to control the factions and intriguers who kept Prussia hovering on the verge of a crisis when Hardenberg, who was old and ailing, died. Since Prussia was in no position to direct her own foreign policy she would submissively follow Austria's lead.

Weakest links in the European chain were France and Russia. Of Russia Gentz' partiality for Alexander led him to take a hopeful view. Neither fear nor necessity but reasoned policy inspired the Czar's adherence to the Quadruple Alliance. French dependence on the European federation was merely temporary. An early dissolution of the alliance would best suit French interests as she would then be able to revert to her traditional policy of choosing her allies where it pleased her. The alliance with Russia everyone believed inevitable would take time to realize—in fact it took another seventy-five years.

Most of all France needed time to cool the fear and hatred she still aroused. She would long continue as an object of suspicion and war with her be the only one popular in Europe, the merest offensive sign on her part would provoke the revival of the coalition of 1815.

Gentz pinned his faith to the alliance of the Four Courts as the nucleus of the wider European league which must ultimately be formed. Could the existing united front but be maintained then the reunion at Aix might well initiate the federal system of Europe. Not normally the most idealistic if possibly one of the shrewdest of contemporary political thinkers, Gentz was enthusiastic about European unity.

He believed that the principle of the balance of power had been superseded by the principle of union. Now at last Europe appeared to be a great political family, whose members guaranteed to themselves and to one another the peaceful enjoyment of their respective rights. If the infant system could be brought to maturity then, despite all the obvious disadvantages, it would be the best possible combination to ensure the prosperity of nations and the maintenance of peace.

Alexander's mind was running along the same lines. Unknown to his allies, Alexander's secretaries of state in St Petersburg were already committing his new vision to paper. Even the Holy Alliance now took second place to the Czar's concept of a world where the vital interests of the continent of Europe would take precedence of the egocentric interests of nations.

Both Alexander and Friedrich von Gentz had grasped the elementary truth that in union lies strength, in disunion weakness, but neither has received his due as a precursor of the ideal of nations united. Their dream had to wait almost exactly a hundred years after the Congress of Aix-la-Chapelle before it assumed the even larger shape of the League of Nations. Those European statesmen who, in 1815, dimly apprehended the advantages of a European bureau only to toss it aside, once again, when a fresh opportunity presented itself, allowed narrow national prejudice to obscure the prospect of a united Europe.

Hints dropped by Pozzo di Borgo that the Czar intended at Aix to put forward some astonishing proposals alarmed the practical politicians. They could only guess at what shape it might take and hope that no new Holy Alliance was involved. Another of Alexander's flights of fancy would embarrass them greatly.

Castlereagh and Metternich took only small comfort from the Czar's assurance, conveyed to them by Pozzo, that at Aix his vote would be in strict conformity with the letter of the existing treaties and his policy as consistent as it had been since 1815, that he was unshakeably attached to the Quadruple Alliance.

So anxious was Alexander not to run counter to his allies that if need be, he was ready to yield up his cherished project. Not to disturb the existing harmony he would even concede to Austria the exclusive glory of directing European policies and admit them to be well directed. This decision was as yet revealed only to his most intimate counsellors.

'I have never intended,' he said, 'to prepare for the future the elements of a federative system in opposition to and contrary to that which in the bosom of the cabinets of Vienna, London and Berlin they suppose already conceived.'

The Czar was not, however, prejudging the effect on his allies of his new proposals. He was still optimistic about bringing the good news from St Petersburg to Aix.

If the jealousy among the Allied ambassadors in Paris was any portent then maintenance of the united front, confidently expected at Aix-la-Chapelle, seemed hazardous. Since dissolution of their Conference was likely to be a minor consequence of the Congress the ambassadors looked at it with a green eye. An invitation from the Czar to Pozzo di Borgo to join him at Aix angered his three colleagues. With deep resentment Sir Charles Stuart argued—and Pozzo believed the poisoned whisper inspired by Austria—that all or none should go to Aix; it would be a great inconvenience if their colleague, more French than Russian, should be singled out.

The *chers collègues*, Pozzo sighed to Nesselrode, were as petty and unjust on this point as many others. Capo d'Istrias had to remind him that it was because they regarded him as the most redoubtable patron of France that they had started the miserable plots to prosscribe him from Aix. Pozzo was instructed to arrive at Aix-la-Chapelle on 7 October; the Russians attached too much importance to his talents and experience to be deprived of them simply because of the 'minor behaviour of great people who regulate the destinies of the world'.

Surprisingly, Richelieu was himself in some doubt as to whether his presence at Aix would be required or not. By July Louis XVIII was agitating for some official notice of the time and principal objects of the forthcoming reunion and for the just and indispensable invitation for the French to participate.

At this delicate moment the French government was gravely embarrassed by the indiscreet publication of a *Note Secrète*, intended by its authors for the eyes of the foreign ambassadors in Paris alone. The source of the Note was the ultra-royalist entourage of the Comte d'Artois who invited the ambassadors to use their influence to force Louis XVIII to change both his liberal policy and his ministry. They further urged that the army of occupation should continue to guarantee the Ultras' safety against the revival of that fearful bogey, the revolutionary spirit.

For once Castlereagh refused to be impressed by the conjuring up of this spectre, normally his familiar. He told the French ambassador in London,

'If this picture is correct, we should immediately have to recall our troops, throw a *cordon sanitaire* around France, and let her devour herself from within. Happily our information is less frightening than yours.'

The Powers had made up their minds to evacuate their troops and they had other measures in mind to preserve France from herself when she was left to her own devices. They refused to be intimidated by the ultra-royalists whose antics had been a constant source of friction since the conclusion of the Second Peace of Paris.

From this impolitic move Artois himself was the only sufferer. On 20 July France duly received her invitation to send her delegation to the conference. Richelieu would naturally be the chief plenipotentiary but Capo d'Istrias hoped that he would be supported by an orator inspiring confidence in Great Britain, Austria and Prussia since the Duc was commonly regarded as a tool of Russia.

At last the time had come to finalize the practical arrangements for the meeting. Routes had to be planned, communications organized for the French and British plenipotentiaries and accommodation found for sovereigns, statesmen, their staffs and secretariats. And, once again, an unofficial tail prepared to make its way to Aix, heedless of strong warnings to keep away.

CHAPTER VI

Eve of a Congress

AIX-LA-CHAPELLE in 1818 was a city of some 40,000 inhabitants and 3000 houses, none of which could be regarded as palaces and few grand enough to house distinguished guests. This was Napoleon's experience when in 1804 the Empress Josephine visited Aix with a suite of fifty persons to take the waters. He was obliged to commandeer the Prefecture as the mansion he bought for her was not sufficiently imposing.

A veil of silence now shrouded Aix's Napoleonic past, the twenty years when it was honoured as one of the Emperor's thirty-six *bonnes villes*, cities enjoying special privileges, and was the centre of the French department of the Ruhr. No one willingly recalled how much of its prosperity Aix-la-Chapelle owed to Napoleon—the restoration of the baths and thermal springs, the flourishing manufactures of pins, needles, cloths and cashmeres, and the neighbouring coal mines.

The Aacheners preferred to point proudly to their more ancient glories—the cathedral with its octagonal chapel and sacred relics, Charlemagne's tomb and throne, and the 14th-century Rathaus, whose magnificent throne room was the scene of the congresses of 1668 and 1748.

Aix-la-Chapelle was also a popular spa, disposing of many more distractions than met with Castlereagh's approval. Under French rule its theatre was visited regularly by two touring theatrical companies and now staged German plays. Concerts and balls were given in the two *salles de fêtes*, the Old and New *Redoutensaalen*. The New Redoute, built in 1782 and magnificently decorated in stucco, had every amenity desirable, a library, a reading-room and, during the season, a gaming room where visitors had ample opportunity to part with their money at *trente-et-quarante*, roulette, *biribi*, or *passe-dix*.

While drinking the waters of the thermal fountain in the Comphausbadstrasse, street of the best houses, curists strolled about a pleasant promenade lined with limes and acacias. The more energetic climbed the Lousberg for a splendid view of the city laid out at their feet and the surrounding wooded hills. For a drive a favoured spot was the Paulinenwald, named for Napoleon's flighty sister, Pauline, who had once honoured Aix-la-Chapelle with a visit and a new love affair.

During the French occupation Aix had its own newspaper, the *Postillon de la Roër*. Now the *Stadt Aachener Zeitung* filled its columns with every available scrap of news about the forthcoming congress. Early in June the paper published an invitation to the inhabitants of Aix to register with the municipal authorities their wish to rent all or part of their houses for the expected influx of visitors. At the same time they were invited to say whether they spoke any foreign languages and, if so, which. Finally the citizens were warned not to charge excessive rentals; the honour of receiving the sovereigns in their city should be compensation enough.

Brooms, brushes, paint pots and paving-stones took possession of Aix-la-Chapelle during the months following this announcement. Houses were redecorated and refurbished, the theatre and the Rathaus renovated, the roads widened and improved, the barracks enlarged and re-equipped and the numbers of horses at the posting-houses increased, all regardless of cost.

The arrival of the King of Prussia's quartermaster to find suitable accommodation for his master was the first external sign of the forthcoming reunion. For Frederick William and his suite of sixty-one persons he took the Offermannischen mansion and the neighbouring houses in the Capuzinergraben and for Hardenberg the Bettendorf house in the Marktplatz, overlooked by the Rathaus.

Hard on the heels of the Prussian commissioner came the Austrian and Russian quartermasters to take first pick of what Frederick William left available—for the Emperor Francis a mansion in the Marschierstrasse and for Metternich the house of Fraülein Brammertz near the thermal baths in the Comphausbadstrasse. Alexander, his aides-de-camp, his Scottish doctor, Sir James Wylie, and his suite of thirty-five persons were found lodgings near Metternich's in the Grossköllnerstrasse. For the duration of their stay the houses in which the sovereigns lived were graced by the name of 'palaces' for their own and the Aacheners' consequence.

As befitted his position, similar to that of Talleyrand in the early stages of the Vienna Congress, Richelieu was housed at some little distance from the other delegations, in the Peterstrasse. His strictly working secretariat of French Foreign Office officials included two historiographers. The Comte de Rayneval, Head of Chancery, drew up a useful résumé of the negotiations while his colleague, the Baron de Boislecomte, compiled a diary of the private lives of the sovereigns at Aix.

Not until all the commissioners had finished their task and departed did the British commissioner arrive at Aix. He managed to secure accommodation for Castlereagh and his party at 218, Kleinborcette-strasse. Those who could not find room in the house were spread out in other dwellings in the same street or in the two hotels, Grand and Grande Bretagne.

Wellington, closer to the spot at Cambrai, and better organized, had already rented the superior house of the Oberbürgermeister Herr von Guaita, in the Jacobstrasse, the street where most of his international staff were housed.

Again, as in Paris in 1815, all the delegates lived within easy walking distance of one another.

Excitement mounted in Aix with the arrival of a great train of Imperial Austrian state carriages with a number of choice horses. Next the guards began to march in, a company each of the Imperial Austrian and Russian grenadiers, followed by two companies of Prussian Landwehr grenadiers, a Rhineland *schützen* battalion and a squadron of hussars with a hundred and forty horses.

Even the spacious barracks in the Grosse Marschierstrasse, on whose wide square hundreds of troops could deploy, were not large enough to house so great a number of men. Those who could not be accommodated in the existing barracks were lodged in temporary barracks in the Tempelherrengraben or billeted on the inhabitants.

Already before the sovereigns' arrival there was so much bustle and extra activity in the city that it was obvious how great congestion would be. Both citizens and strangers were therefore told what roads would be available for their use and their coachmen warned to take extra care with their horses to avoid accidents.

The police had naturally a great deal to do with their security arrangements but, of all those busied with the preliminaries of the Congress, the Duke of Wellington was busiest. In view of the imminent evacuation he had to plan the return of his British contingent, approve the homeward routes to be taken by the foreign regiments under his command, and order the details of the grand review of Allied troops which the sovereigns had commanded should take place in their presence. Finally it fell to the Duke to re-align and augment, but with a firm eye on expense, the existing system of communications with England.

Five messengers were kept permanently on the Continent to carry Foreign Office bags from the British embassies in Paris and the Netherlands to the coast; three were attached to the Paris station and two to Lord Clancarty at Brussels or The Hague. They took their turn by rotation for foreign journeys and were normally stationed abroad for a tour of three months.

Wellington decided that, if Lord Castlereagh fixed on Wednesday as his despatch day to England from Aix-la-Chapelle, three messengers should suffice for his service. One of Lord Clancarty's messengers would be transferred to Aix for the duration of the congress. Lord Castlereagh would himself provide the other two from the pool of messengers shared by the Foreign Office and the Home and War Departments under the control of Lewis Hertslet of the Foreign Office.

The messenger sent from Aix-la-Chapelle on Wednesday would arrive in Brussels on Friday which was the despatch date from the Netherlands to London and vice versa. He would collect Lord Clancarty's bags, together with those sent to Brussels by the Duke by orderly from Cambrai, and leave the same day at 5.00 p.m. On his arrival at Ostend in time for the sailing of the regular packet the messenger would hand over his bags to the British packet agent at the port and await the arrival of the Dover boat. He would then return via Brussels to Aix-la-Chapelle with the bags from London. Except in the event of extraordinary delays at sea these arrangements should be adequate.

For the alternate mails the Duke considered that the Netherlands post office should be adequate. Postal service from the Netherlands to England ran twice weekly; in normal conditions the Tuesday mail was found sufficiently punctual for letters and newspapers.

The regular weekly communication established by the messenger service between Aix-la-Chapelle and England would ensure that at all times the bags remained in the hands of responsible British couriers and packet agents.

Wellington was particularly anxious that the messenger system he devised for Aix-la-Chapelle should be watertight because of his

4*

irritation with Sir Charles Stuart's failure to use it properly. Security was at all times important, less perhaps for the official numbered despatches, whose contents were frequently communicated by an ambassador to the Foreign Minister of the Court to which he was accredited, than for the 'separates', the confidential annexes using more forthright language and opinions.

From embassies abroad there were constant complaints that their letters sent by post were opened and read in transit. This was particularly true of St Petersburg where all letters, even those sent by junior officers of the diplomatic service, were opened 'with no other distinction than in the degree of care in making them up for delivery or transmission after perusal'.

During the summer months Lord Cathcart was frequently able to confide his correspondence to British ships' captains or reputable travellers who were furnished with a special courier's passport. In winter he was forced to rely on the rarer opportunity of a messenger. No regular courier service existed as yet between London and St Petersburg: given the distance and the cost, the return journey by messenger amounted to some £460.

At all times their own couriers and those of other countries were a source of lively interest to Foreign Offices and embassies. Exceptional courier activity between one Court and another might foreshadow some unexpected diplomatic move. When Frederick Lamb, minister at Frankfort, noticed extremely active communication between Prussia and Austria he suggested to Clancarty that it might be worthwhile reporting to Castlereagh that an unusual number of couriers were passing through to Berlin.

Others besides the British and French governments required prompt and efficient communications from Aix-la-Chapelle. Early news, especially about loan negotiations capable of affecting the stock market, was eagerly sought by speculators. Their couriers competed with the official messengers for relays of horses, putting a particular strain on the postmaster at Givet, an important stage on the Paris road.

Finding himself with insufficient couriers to cope with the volume of correspondence passing through his post, he was obliged to ask Richelieu that only those who had his express authority should have the privilege of using *estafettes*. By courier the hundred-and-four-league journey to Paris from Aix-la-Chapelle took sixty-four hours. An *estafette*, who rode, not drove a carriage, offered some advantage in time because he travelled through the night with a flambeau to light him on his way when there was no moon. The difference in time could be important in the buying and selling of stocks.

Organization as massive as for the courier service was necessary for the sovereigns' journeys, especially for Francis of Austria who travelled from Vienna in great state. His own horses had been sent ahead of him but, to avoid congestion on the roads, he intended to do part of his journey on the Rhine from Mainz to Coblenz. Alexander originally planned to join Francis on the boat trip but later decided to make his own way by road to Aix-la-Chapelle. For this occasion he travelled with greater ceremony than in his usual modest calèche. En route he would open the Diet at Warsaw and call at Berlin to return the visit lately paid him by Frederick William. The King of Prussia would precede his august guests to arrive at Aix-la-Chapelle to welcome them on their arrival.

The diplomatists all arranged their routes to get the maximum benefit on the way from preliminary conversations. Metternich's Rhineland estate of Johannisberg was the general half-way house. Gentz travelled towards it from Vienna via Frankfort, whiling away the tedium of long hours in his carriage by an astonishing diversity of reading. He always kept abreast of the newspapers in three languages but on this journey in addition he got through Schlegel on the Provençal language, the secret memoirs of Lucien Bonaparte, the *Quarterly Review*, Bonald on Madame de Staël and Gourgaud's account of the battle of Waterloo. At his nightly halts he still found energy to continue his correspondence with Pilat and the Hospodars, for writing articles and making translations.

Most profitable for Gentz were his encounters with some of his enormous range of acquaintances, especially with the personalities converging from all parts of the Continent on Aix-la-Chapelle. With David Parish, of the Hamburg banking house of Parish, he discussed the French loan negotiations, with the Rothschilds the Frankfort Jews, philanthropy with the 'boring Robert Owen' and with others freedom of the Press. Gentz' conversations with Nesselrode and Capo d'Istrias were naturally concerned with subjects to be raised at Aix, while with the abolitionist, Thomas Clarkson, who intended to present an address about the slave trade to the Czar, its iniquities were the basis of their talks.

Alexander was still the white hope of all who had some humane or religious axe to grind, which led Metternich to make the sour observation that the Czar and his cabinet were increasingly succumbing to moral and political proselytizing.

Metternich had intended to meet Castlereagh in Paris but his father's sudden death obliged the Prince to cancel this arrangement, for which Castlereagh was not on the whole sorry. Much though he would have liked an interchange of views before the congress opened, he was relieved not to be involved in Artois' intrigues. In any event his brother, Lord Stewart, had already assured him that with Metternich he would meet no difficulties.

Castlereagh had already asked that Stewart might be present at Aix. In the absence of the Court from Vienna he would be at a loose end and also bound for Aix was the French ambassador to Austria, the Marquis de Caraman, whose indiscretions were as notorious as his slavish devotion to Metternich. Stewart, said Castlereagh hopefully, would be of considerable use in keeping Metternich steady and apprising his brother of what the Chancellor was about. He would also furnish Liverpool with a private bulletin of all details, anecdotes, etc. Gossip could be an important adjunct to the official negotiations when a careless word might reveal a vital secret.

Not least in importance to a dearly loved brother would be the benefit to Stewart's private concerns since correspondence with Vienna was slow and by post unsafe.

At the beginning of September Castlereagh set out from London, looking, according to report, uncommonly well and anticipating with pleasure seeing his friends again. Avoiding Paris now, he travelled from Calais via Cambrai and Brussels to Spa where he expected to meet Richelieu. All the practical arrangements for the congress were left in the capable hands of his Under Secretary, Joseph Planta, Jr., who took his departure from London a few days later.

Planta had the unique distinction of being born in the British Museum of which his father was librarian. His sister shared with Fanny Burney the tedious duty of attendance on Queen Charlotte whose health was at this moment giving rise to anxiety, chiefly because her death might cause a postponement of the next parliamentary session.

When Planta was still an Eton boy of fifteen George Canning appointed him to a clerkship in the Foreign Office where he soon showed the industry and application of his Swiss origin. His first promotion was to précis writer, no sinecure to anyone obliged to winnow the chaff of meaning from the straw of ministers' verbiage,

Castlereagh's in particular. Few statesmen had the Duke of Wellington's gift of expressing themselves plainly and succinctly.

From précis writer Planta graduated to acting as private secretary
to Castlereagh until in 1817 he was appointed Under Secretary of a
Foreign Office considerably understaffed for the amount of work it
had to do. During these years the average annual number of despatches sent and received was some 6000. These, and all other tasks,
were dealt with by two Under Secretaries, a Chief Clerk with his own
clerk, three Senior Clerks, thirteen Junior Clerks, a Librarian, Sub-
Librarian, the Minister's private secretary, a précis writer, a trans-
lator, a Turkish interpreter, and a collector and transmitter of
papers.

At times Planta felt that, 'burdened as he was with the shafts of
the waggon', it was almost too much for him. Much of his overwork
was undoubtedly due to his excessive good nature; while making him
universally popular it also set him up as an easy target for the im-
portunate. Not surprisingly, Planta ultimately abandoned his career
in the Foreign Office for the leisurely life of a Member of Parliament
for Hastings.

Extra assistance would have been most welcome to Planta in
making his preparations. Forty-two treaties, extracted from the
archives, added considerably to the weight of his baggage since they
were written on gold-edged paper of the thickest texture and bound
in velvet heavily embroidered in gold. Planta had also to choose and
allocate the duties of the clerks accompanying the mission. Their
task would be chiefly copying; for official translations no one
could do better than Gentz, equally fluent in German, French
and English.

Although the Foreign Office could not function without them
clerks were the lowest forms of its life. They spent many weary years
copying despatches, supposedly to give them an insight into the conduct of diplomacy, before gaining promotion. At conferences abroad,
to which they travelled in less comfort than their superiors and
lodged where they could, pressure on them was greatest, because to
meet the deadlines of the courier service they had frequently to work
far into the night.

Several copies of the same despatch were often required in addition to the copy for the Foreign Office records as anything relevant to
their own missions was sent to various ambassadors. Sometimes
despatches were sent under flying seal to be read by an ambassador

en route before being forwarded to their ultimate destination, but this practice could lead to leakage as well as delay in sending the messengers forward.

A further task which fell on the clerks was the decoding of cipher when it was used.

Metternich positively boasted that he could write in two hours what would take a copyist five to six hours to copy, but copyists could not permit themselves handwriting as dauntingly illegible as Metternich's. However weary of dipping their quill pens into their standishes and scattering with sand the finished foolscap page, half left blank for ministerial comments, they were still required to be meticulously legible.

Any failure to form his letters as carefully as he had been taught to do at his dame's school brought caustic reproof down on the unfortunate clerk's head. When Foreign Secretary, Palmerston told one copyist that his lines looked like 'iron railings leaning out of the perpendicular' and another that his letters 'sloped backwards like the raking masts of an American schooner'. Praise for the young gentlemen performing a tedious and exacting task for a minimal salary came rarely. Posterity, however, is glad to make amends and express its gratitude for the greater legibility of their copies than the originals of their masters.

When all arrangements were in train and the horses' heads directed towards Aix-la-Chapelle, Richelieu dropped a bombshell into Louis XVIII's capacious lap. The Duc announced his unalterable resolve to resign after the next session of the Chambers, due to assemble after the Congress ended. In great agitation the King wrote to the Duke of Wellington, asking him to use his influence with the Czar to persuade Richelieu to change his mind. So that every effort was made to weaken the Duc's determination, to his own brief plea Louis added a longer and more explicit letter from the Comte Decazes, his present favourite and Minister of Police.

Until the Czar saw Richelieu at Aix there was little he could do in persuasion, but Wellington expected to meet the Duc at Spa, where the advance British party arrived on 18 September. Lord and Lady Castlereagh, his private secretary, Lord Clanwilliam, and other members of the staff took up their residence at the Hotel de l'Orange where they found Hardenberg taking the waters.

Since the nostrums in vogue were generally unpleasant it was possibly the nauseous taste of those waters, an amalgam of warm iron, sulphur and rotten eggs, which perpetuated belief in their therapeutic qualities. Spa, the oldest watering place on the Continent, deserved its title of 'the café of Europe'; at one time or another every European of note had visited the town. Its thermal springs were praised by English doctors who popularized them with the British and in 1717 Peter the Great spent three weeks at Spa, where he found the waters beneficial. In gratitude for his patronage the Spadois in his honour named their pump room the Pouhon and the square in which it stood *Pierre le Grand*.

A fire in 1807 destroyed much of the old town but left its considerable natural beauties intact. Picturesque walks among the hills of the Ardennes, thickly wooded with beech trees, ran alongside little streams burbling into cascades overhung with honeysuckle and wild raspberries. In the valley itself the 'four o'clock meadow' offered a pleasant stroll after the bath and drinking sessions. The *Promenade de Sept Heures*, shaded by great elms beneath the hill called *Annette et Lubin* after a local legend, was the evening haunt of the *bobelins*, the dialect word for foreign visitors. In addition Spa naturally had its theatre and the inevitable Redoute and Wauxhall for gaming.

Business took precedence of holiday when, a week after Castlereagh's arrival, he was joined by the Duc de Richelieu who took up his quarters in the Grand' Place at the popular English club, founded in 1766 and now with more than five hundred members. Until he met his allies Castlereagh felt bound to speak with reserve so that his conversations with Richelieu were merely exploratory. With greater frankness the Duc made known his intention to press two objects, the evacuation and the admission of Louis XVIII into the general alliance.

As to how he was to gain his second object the Duc apparently had as yet very little idea. 'He obviously perceives,' reported Castlereagh to Liverpool, 'the inconvenience of the King being a contracting party to the existing stipulations, and his mind is afloat, to find some expedient, by which France might be brought more in line with the other Powers.'

The Duke of Wellington confirmed Castlereagh's opinion that in general Richelieu's tone was conciliatory and reasonable, particularly no doubt as his views on Spanish politics appeared to coincide with those of the British government.

Despite the heavy row Richelieu knew he had to hoe at Aix the prospect of early release from the cares of office made him more cheerful. He had also, if only temporarily, escaped the importunities of his 'mad queen'.

Désirée Clary, Queen of Sweden, had for several years been subjecting Richelieu to the most determined assault. Her preference for remaining plain Madame Bernadotte in Paris rather than enjoying royal honours in Stockholm was largely because of her infatuation for Richelieu. Wherever the Duc went, in Paris or on a journey, he was sure of finding Désirée hot on his heels but he was unaware of the fact that she pursued him for the sake of his *beaux yeux*. He believed her to be politically inspired and acting as her husband's police agent.

At Spa Richelieu had a hairbreadth escape. He left for Aix-la-Chapelle a day before Madame Bernadotte caught up with him. Only with great difficulty did her entourage dissuade her from pursuing the Duc to Aix, where her presence would have been particularly unfortunate. Madame Bernadotte's wild passion made her wholly careless of the personal and political impropriety of the inopportune arrival of the Queen of Sweden at the congress where her husband's failure to fulfil Sweden's obligations to Denmark figured on the agenda.

While the city of Aix-la-Chapelle was working itself into a fever of excitement at the now imminent arrival of the sovereigns, the attention of political circles was more coolly bent on the conference itself. Agreement was general that it offered an interest quite distinct from the meetings of 1814 and 1815; no one made any extravagant claim for the results. At least it promised to be less fatiguing.

Edward Cooke, a former Under Secretary at the Foreign Office, looked for no more than the total withdrawal of Allied troops from France and her admission to the alliance. He believed all would have succeeded for the best if another sovereigns' meeting was fixed within a reasonable period; whilst such reunions continued peace would be secure.

The first official to arrive at Aix was the Prussian Foreign Minister Count von Bernstorff, who took up residence at the Golden Lion. He was quickly followed by Castlereagh, Metternich and Richelieu. Next came Hardenberg, fortified by his cure at Spa to tackle the problems of the conference. The Russian ministers would arrive with the Czar.

Little notice was taken by the Aacheners of the arrival of Alexander Baring of the banking house of Hope and Baring although as negotiator of the French loan, he was the most important of the private visitors. Baring had promised Wellington to be present in person and he came with Castlereagh's approval of the loan project, 'an outstanding service to the whole of Europe and the deed of a good British citizen'.

The long-awaited arrival on 27 September, a lovely autumn day, of their sovereign lord, King Frederick William III of Prussia, made the congress a reality for the Aacheners. The King was accompanied by his son, Prince Karl, and a host of princelings, body servants and adjutants, among them names which strike a contemporary chord, Flügel-Adjutant von Brauchitsch, and Colonel von Falkenhayn.

Frederick William was so delighted with his tumultuous reception, especially with the troops who paraded before him in the Capuziner-graben, facing the old thermal spring of the Elisenbrünn, that on the spot he promoted their colonel, von Clausewitz, major-general. The arrival on the same day of the 'great Marshal, the royal Great British ambassador', the Duke of Wellington, was more quietly welcomed.

Greatest jubilation was reserved for the arrival, heralded by a telegraphic signal, of the Emperor Francis on the following day. Lord Clancarty's shrewd prediction that Francis' course through his former territories would be a triumph was wholly justified—so was his suspicion that Metternich had planned the Emperor's route with the ulterior motive that enthusiasm for one great German sovereign might detract from acclaim of the other. The Rhinelanders were, in fact, finding it hard to settle down to their arbitrary transfer to Prussian rule.

Since there was no Queen of Prussia to do the honours at Aix Francis' fourth Empress remained in Vienna. His third wife had, as he had expected, failed to stand up to the strain but fortunately he was not obliged to seek a fifth consort; the Empress Caroline Augusta succeeded in outliving him.

Frederick William received Francis in great state outside the walls of Aix-la-Chapelle. As the sovereigns, both in uniform, entered the city through the Kölnthor, escorted by a squadron of hussars, the entire population seemed to be in the streets. The church bells rang in unison, the bands played martial airs and a salute of 101 guns was fired as the procession made its way to Francis' 'palace' on the Marschierstrasse.

Ten flunkeys, fifteen coachmen, nine postillions, cooks galore—

the Emperor's fondness for toffee was well known—a saddler, a harness maker, even a Court official to do the dusting, and innumerable gentlemen in attendance, made up Francis' household. Nothing and nobody was lacking to underline his Imperial consequence in Charlemagne's Imperial coronation city.

Last of the sovereigns and his suite to arrive was Alexander. His arrival was delayed until the evening because he halted outside Aix to change his travelling clothes for the uniform of his favourite regiment. He was welcomed by Frederick William with the same state as Francis before being driven to his 'palace' through roads beflagged and lit by torches. Here all the diplomatists, generals and the city's civil and military authorities were assembled to welcome the Czar of Russia while a large crowd huzzaed outside in the Kölnstrasse.

This day, momentous in the history of Aix-la-Chapelle, ended on a note of comedy. Immediately after the committee of welcome had departed Alexander set off to pay a courtesy visit to Francis. As the Austrian Emperor had the same idea both sovereigns missed each other on the way, but the ceremonial visits were paid in form next day.

All was now ready for the deliberations of the Congress of Aix-la-Chapelle to begin.

CHAPTER VII

The Congress of Aix-la-Chapelle

'You seem to be very gay and comfortable at Aix-la-Chapelle, drinking probably the old toast of "Happy to meet, sorry to part, happy to meet again" ', wrote Lord Melville from the Admiralty to Castlereagh.

Lord Melville had guessed correctly. The reunion at Aix had the character of a family gathering rather than that of a congress. Since everyone had long ago taken the others' measure no personal surprises were in store. The plenipotentiaries would act not as a managing committee, as at Vienna, but as a corporate body free from external pressures. Not all perhaps would be happy to meet, nor all sorry to part, but to begin with at least everyone's spirits reflected the golden glow of the superb autumn weather.

Happy to meet? The Duc de Richelieu was particularly happy. Although much arduous work and many difficulties faced him at Aix it marked the first stage on his road back to the Crimea. As soon as the congress came to an end he would slough off the burden of office. He for one would feel little sorrow at parting from colleagues simultaneously his masters, happy even to meet none of them again except his 'idol, Alexander', in whose orbit he longed to end his days.

Prince von Metternich, whose vanity convinced him that *he* would be the linchpin of the congress, was happy to meet his friends and looked forward to triumphing over his enemies, chiefly Capo d'Istrias and Pozzo di Borgo. To his wife Metternich wrote that he had never seen such a pretty little congress; he was sure it would give him no trouble.

Happy to meet? Freiherr von Gentz was complacently aware that no congress could function efficiently without him. At Aix he would undoubtedly once again emphasize his indispensability and increase both his prestige and his bank balance.

Happy to meet? Viscount Castlereagh, 'agreeably surprised to find how much solid good grows out of the reunions which sound so terrible at a distance', fell into the error he deplored in the Czar, excess of enthusiasm.

With most uncharacteristic excitement he wrote to Lord Bathurst, acting Foreign Secretary in his own absence, of the advantage of periodical direct contacts between cabinets,

'It really appears to me to be a new discovery in the European government, at once extinguishing the cobwebs with which diplomacy obscures the horizon, bringing the whole system into its true light, and giving to the counsel of the great Powers the efficiency and almost the simplicity of a single State'.

Unconsciously Castlereagh was drawing perilously close to the plan for a European federation which Alexander was about to spring on his allies.

No one could doubt the Czar's happiness in meeting his fellow sovereigns and their ministers. He was as confident as Metternich of being the dominant personality in the congress, to which he was entitled, not by virtue of his rank, but by his unwavering adherence to the Quadruple Alliance. Most of all he was gratified by his certitude that the proposals he intended to submit to the congress would enhance the value of that alliance.

Both Frederick William and Francis were in a happy frame of mind. Francis was basking in the respect and affection lavished on him by his former subjects of the Rhineland. Frederick William was proud that to him fell the honour of acting as host in the city of Charlemagne which was now his own; for once his would be the pre-eminent position.

Audiences of the Austrian and Prussian sovereigns strengthened Castlereagh's belief in his new discovery. Both received him with great cordiality and both assured him of their great satisfaction with the Czar's pronouncements on his way to Aix-la-Chapelle. Frederick William in particular promised Castlereagh that he would find His Imperial Majesty in the best possible disposition. Although the King of Prussia's views nearly always coincided with those of the Czar of Russia any further evidence of their agreement gave him renewed pleasure.

Happy to meet? No one's happiness rivalled that of the Herr

Hofrat Karl Franz Meyer, the city's official chronicler of the 'Congress of the Monarchs'. Jaundiced opponents of the Holy Alliance dismissed kings 'lashing with their lordly tails' as 'bores paramount, royal zeros', but to this arch-sycophant they were indisputably earth-gods. His pen never wearied of shaping the styles and titles of the All-Highest—Imperial Majesty, Royal Majesty, Imperial Highness, Serene Highness—as he unctuously recorded the trivia of their daily routine.

Only when his superlatives were momentarily exhausted did the Herr Hofrat condescend a glance from the empyrean at the labours of the plenipotentiaries whose presence at Aix-la-Chapelle was merely incidental to that of the regents of the earth.

Those labours began immediately all the delegates were assembled without waiting for the first official meeting. As an earnest of their good faith Metternich, on behalf of the Four Powers, informed the Duc de Richelieu at once, rather than wait for the end of the congress, of their agreement to terminate the occupation of France; all foreign troops would be marched off her soil by 30 November.

Richelieu, appropriately grateful, urged immediate publication of news so welcome to France and certain to have a favourable influence on the government in the current electoral compaign, but Castlereagh demurred. Reverting to his habitual caution, he objected to undue haste. Gentz must first draft the necessary protocol. Although the document was not signed until 9 October it was backdated to 30 September. Publication to satisfy French impatience was then agreed, but with the caveat that evacuation was still subject to the conclusion of satisfactory financial arrangements.

Congratulations on this early success and excellent augury for future discussions flowed into Aix. Planta, reporting to Bathurst the good progress made, paid a special tribute to Gentz; he was doing all the hard work of reduction [*sic*] in the negotiations. As the secretariat of the Prussian Foreign Office was not available, Gentz was, in fact, obliged to do everything himself, but was never too occupied to lose sight of the main chance. Adroitly, hopeful of further largesse from the British, he allowed Planta to learn of his profound admiration of Lord Castlereagh's views.

Lord Clancarty added his congratulations on the prospect of an early and satisfactory termination to the conference. Richelieu's friend, the Marquis de Vérac, cheered him with news of the universal happiness felt in Paris, for which even Richelieu's enemies gave him credit. When Alexander paid his expected visit to Paris, added de Vérac, he would be most warmly welcomed but, if Frederick William accompanied him, his reception would be much colder; the incident of the Pont d'Iéna was not forgotten.

Castlereagh was given an early opportunity of testing the King of Prussia's optimism and Lord Cathcart's report of the change in Alexander. The day after his arrival the Czar gave a series of audiences to Castlereagh, Metternich and Wellington, and later to Stewart. To each man Alexander spoke in approximately the same terms.

His sole object, he said, in coming to Aix-la-Chapelle was to strengthen the cords binding him to his allies and to consult with them how their union could best serve the general advantage. He indignantly refuted the base calumny, spread by intriguers in Paris and elsewhere, that he sought a closer connection with France and Spain—a veiled reproach for the secret agreements he believed existed between Great Britain and Austria.

Metternich suavely concurred with the Czar that, if the Allies remained faithful to their unity, then the present conference would lead to the greater glory of the sovereigns, a glory inseparable from the happiness of their peoples. The Chancellor's own view was that the congress had assembled to 'new-mould and new-model existing arrangements—to pen all those doors for discontent, speculations and diplomatic intrigues which it was so much in the interest of the Quadruple Alliance to keep for ever closed'.

Alexander's patent sincerity convinced Castlereagh that he might be aiming at sway but not at changing his allegiance. His continuing horror of the revolutionary spirit explained his present severity to France. The Czar dwelt on his mistrust of the French nation, on his persuasion that Europe's only safeguards from possible dangers arising in France lay in unity and vigilance. She must be reminded that any fresh outbreak would meet the same resistance which had previously reduced her to reason. Richelieu's ideas, continued Alexander, did not correspond to the true situation of his country. To hope for French entry into a Quintuple Alliance was imprudent at the very least if not stupid.

The Czar ridiculed the idea that he maintained his army with any hostile intent; his sole concern was to preserve peace.

'With whom should I go to war?' he demanded of his listeners. 'I have as much territory as I can desire and more than I can well manage. Suspicion would be justified were my army that of the Russian empire to be used for Russian ends, but I regard my army as the army of Europe and as such alone shall it be employed. I will not admit that it can be employed otherwise than with Europe to repress any attempt that may be made to shake the system of which my empire forms only a part.'

If the army were called upon, it would act to show disturbers of peace that in Allied unity lay the pledge to maintain the existing order.

At the end of his audience of Castlereagh Alexander again affirmed the principles upon which he was determined to found his conduct and from which *religious duty*, coupled with a sense of character, would never suffer him to deviate. In parting, he declared,

'I now renew those assurances to you and, if you ever find me knowingly violate them, I submit myself to every reproach that such a failure can bring me.'

The Czar had laid his cards on the table. He now departed on a short visit to Spa, leaving the ministers to ponder on the way he intended to play them. Even Metternich's cynicism was not proof against the Czar's obvious honesty of purpose. Not only were the Chancellor's suspicions somewhat allayed but he even went so far as to confide in Castlereagh his belief that the Allies' only guarantee against the danger of Russian power was Alexander's personal character.

So close was the association between the two ministers that Metternich gave Castlereagh a copy of his own memorandum on his audience with the Czar to be forwarded to the cabinet in London. From both their audiences two important points had emerged; the Czar's cordiality, sincerity and firm intention to pursue a peace policy and his abandonment of his former idea of an intimate relationship with France in favour of the more fascinating prospect of a Europe united. His enthusiasm was not shared by his allies.

Castlereagh, with this fear in mind, deprecated in his report to the cabinet a 'degree of exaltation of mind' capable of leading to some proposition as absurd as the Holy Alliance. Eager though Castlereagh was to applaud the merit of European diplomatic gatherings, neither he nor Metternich was ready to go farther with the Czar.

For any minister, particularly the Foreign Secretary of a constitutional government, it was awkward to be obliged to deal directly with a sovereign on matters normally the province of his staff. While all the plenipotentiaries and ministers paid lip service to their own and their colleagues' 'August Masters', it is highly doubtful that they shared the Herr Hofrat's belief that they were earth-gods.

With Charles Stewart Alexander could be more man than monarch, could use a far less formal tone than in his harangue to Castlereagh. The Stewart brothers were totally different in temperament. Where Castlereagh's formality repelled, Charles's warmth and impetuosity attracted. Where Robert Stewart was cold and cautious, Charles was expansive. His dashing career as a soldier until appointed minister to Vienna and his undoubted charm had earned him the sincere friendship of two characters as dissimilar as the Prince Regent and the Duke of Wellington.

Stewart's military career, especially the campaign in which he fought bravely alongside the Russian Guards, recommended him to Alexander. Charles was better-looking than his brother and his manner far easier. Like Alexander himself, Stewart was a man of the world who appreciated its pleasures and was not slow to indulge in them. From the Czar, who in his time had loved greatly, he found ready sympathy for the difficulties he, a widower of forty, was experiencing in his wooing of Lady Frances Vane, one of the greatest beauties and heiresses in England.

Although many of his contemporaries found Stewart a somewhat absurd swashbuckler and underrated his abilities, his judgments of men, formed in the camp and on the field, were frequently more astute than his brother's. Most people failed to understand Castlereagh's devoted attachment to his junior by nine years. They did not know of the shy and lonely little boy, whose mother died when he was a baby, who discovered a welcome playmate and an object to cherish in the son of his father's second marriage.

Even in his 'separates' Castlereagh was moderate in his language. Stewart had no inhibitions about cutting an autocrat down to size. The Czar's cordial and affectionate embrace did not deter Stewart from satirizing his convictions, although he would not agree with the opinion expressed by Metternich in Vienna that Alexander was the falsest man in the world. (His opinion changed somewhat when he met Alexander again at Aix.) The Czar, said Stewart, must be sincere or 'hypocrisy certainly assumed a more abominable garb than she was ever yet clothed in'.

Nevertheless, Stewart could not resist ridiculing Alexander's 'religious rhapsody' nor the 'seeming delight and animation of countenance expressive of *self*-satisfaction' with which the Czar dwelt ecstatically on the reunion of sovereigns which he described as 'affording positive proof to Europe of the unity, justice, moderation and morality upon which all their system and conduct had been founded'.

In common with the majority of his colleagues Stewart felt a slightly uneasy contempt for an idealism they did not share, which embarrassed them and which they patently distrusted. Undoubtedly Alexander's theatrical language and gestures contributed to their discomfiture. On this occasion he declared, 'looking up to heaven and putting his hand on his heart, that he was actuated by a religious and conscientious feeling which would render it impossible for him to be unequitable and unjust.'

When Stewart boldly pointed out the dread and suspicion inspired by the immense Russian army, so gigantically ready to march beyond the rest, he was waved aside. The Czar would never deviate from his chosen path; he would act upon the great rules of right which guided his career.

'I desire,' he said, 'to establish and hand down to posterity for the welfare of mankind an edifice which will leave it out of the power of any one nation again to revolutionize the world.'

Happy for Alexander that he did not know it was the Russian nation, almost a hundred years after the Congress of Aix-la-Chapelle, which sought to revolutionize the world, beginning with the great Russian empire itself. Unhappy for that world that in 1818 Alexander's vision aroused only amused irritation among men who refused to grasp its tremendous possibilities.

Diplomatically Stewart assured Alexander that it was impossible to hear him deliver such noble sentiments without applause. The Czar responded by embracing him twice and making kind enquiries as to how Stewart liked his residence in Vienna.

Stewart's tribute to Francis' 'kind condescension' set Alexander off on another tack, 'a great eulogium upon the Emperor of Austria's rare endowments and personal quality'; he would never have been able to achieve the work now so far completed had not the Austrian empire been governed by a sovereign of the enlightened and liberal principles which characterized Francis.

Did Stewart suppress a smile? While Alexander was clearly beginning to see in Francis a father figure, Stewart had the cynical satisfaction of knowing that the Emperor entertained no paternal feelings towards the Czar. Before Francis left Vienna he caustically imparted to Stewart his hope that at Aix Alexander would be made to see reason. The Emperor was careful to add that it was impossible that he could ever be too sensible of all he owed to Great Britain and his great personal attachment to Castlereagh.

While Francis might have echoed Alexander's final words to Stewart, 'Let us continue in the path we are treading—nothing can then interfere with our tranquillity, nothing can disturb the peace of the world', he would strenuously have rebutted Alexander's claim to lead the way. The Emperor jealously plumed himself on being the pivot on which the whole European world turned and his own moral conduct as responsible for the present repose of Europe.

Francis was by no means the cypher he appeared to be but he did not keep a Metternich to bark himself even though his Chancellor all too often showed himself a dilettante. According to Stewart, Metternich desired to do a great deal and yet put off actual decisions or did nothing until the last moment. With more firmness and greater moral courage he might have succeeded in asserting his own authority over the intriguers to whose whispers Francis lent only too ready an ear.

At Aix the Austrian Emperor had no intention of rivalling Alexander's industry nor imitating his practice of playing a personal part in negotiations. Francis' presence at Aix was ornamental rather than useful. His aloofness from the congress deliberations relieved the plenipotentiaries of any interference on his part and he delighted the Aacheners by acting the perfect tourist. In the words of Herr Hofrat Meyer, he left behind him 'an impression of graciousness, condescension and piety which the city would never forget'.

Francis' first visit was naturally to pray at the High Altar of the Cathedral, do reverence to the relics and inspect the tomb of Charlemagne. Thereafter no church, no factory, no coal mine, no thermal spring was neglected by him in his indefatigable tour of the city and its environs. No opportunity was lost for sunning himself in popularity as he informed himself of how things were done and with great affability expressed his royal satisfaction.

Whatever Francis' dislike of social gatherings he could not wholly escape his obligations. His was the first formal dinner to all the leading lights of the congress, including the two most glittering, Alexander and Frederick William. The diplomatists were also present in full force with the exception of Richelieu since, as yet, he had not been officially invited to take part in the discussions.

The city of Aix-la-Chapelle promptly followed suit by giving a ball in honour of the sovereigns for a thousand guests in the new Redoutensaal. As the day chosen was Francis' name day it was unfortunate that colds kept him and Metternich away but happily the presence of the two other 'enthroned Heroes' gave Herr Hofrat Meyer ample material over which to rhapsodize.

When the Peace of Aix-la-Chapelle ended the Seven Years War in 1748 five separate entrances were made in the Throne Room of the Rathaus to avoid any dispute about precedence. Now in 1818 the Czar of all the Russias and the King of Prussia entered the ballroom familiarly arm in arm, greeted by a triple *Lebhoch*.

Out of compliment to Alexander the ball opened with a polonaise. He led out the Princess of Thurn and Taxis, acting as hostess for her brother-in-law, Frederick William. The King danced with her 'Princess daughter', his niece. (Strange that the Herr Hofrat whose favourite reading was indisputably the *Almanach de Gotha* never discovered her first name.) Lady Castlereagh was partnered by the Duke of Kent, his brief visit to Aix some slight compensation for the absence of the Prince Regent. Castlereagh manœuvred awkwardly with the Duchess of Kent, already pregnant with the child born on 24 May in the following year, to be christened Alexandrina for her godfather, the Czar, and Victoria for her mother. Behind them tripped all the princely personages and distinguished foreigners whose numbers caused Aix to burst at its seams.

A quadrille followed the polonaise and the monarchs changed partners for yet another polonaise. After a pause for the All-Highest to take some refreshment dancing was resumed; when they departed early with their suites the glow of their presence continued to bathe the Aacheners who kept up their entertainment until midnight.

Courtesy demanded some reciprocal hospitality from the Foreign Ministers, however reluctant they were to allow any interruption to business. Metternich and Wellington, the two most socially minded, both gave musical parties graced by the singing of Angelica Catalani, as inevitable a figure of a congress as Gentz. Her enchanting voice and incomparable trills, brilliant as the diamond stomacher bestowed on her by the Czar, thrilled everyone but Gentz, who thought her vulgar and her husband, Balabrègues, revolting. Frederick William was especially ravished by her rendering of the English air, *God Save Great George our King*, which became the congress song.

Even the genuinely musical like Wellington, Metternich and

Frederick William, found a surfeit of music at Aix. A large number
of singers and artists had crowded to the city, anticipating the
sovereigns' customary largesse of diamond rings and golden snuff-
boxes. Among them were such famous virtuosi as Napoleon's
favourite tenor, Garat, but also infant prodigies like the boy of four
and a half who played the double bass, to Metternich the last straw.

So continuous were the arias, the sonatas and intermezzi of
military bands that their notes for Herr Meyer at least drowned any
echoes from the conversations of the plenipotentiaries although his
ear was always tuned to the slightest word dropped by a monarch.

Aix-la-Chapelle did its best to ape the pomp and panache of
Vienna with curiously assorted distractions. Balls, concerts, art
exhibitions and a panorama of Waterloo were more generally acceptable than the displays of fisticuffs given at five francs a ticket in the
old Redoutensaal by three English pugilists imported for the
occasion. To make the flesh of the credulous creep the Parisian sybil,
Mademoiselle Lenormand, prophesied woe while concealing
smuggled goods for sale beneath her muffled draperies. Her services
were mainly sought by the unsophisticated Aacheners. The delegates were fully capable of making their own gloomy prognostica-
tions.

No self-respecting gathering was complete without at least one
balloon ascent. Aix did better by inviting two rival female balloonists
to defend the honour of Germany and France. Frau Reichard, the
German, inspired no doubt by the presence of Frederick William on
the launching site, not only made her fifteenth perfect ascent, throwing flowers at the King as she rose through the air, but succeeded in
sailing some thirteen hours' distance from Aix before making a safe
landing.

Herr Meyer wept crocodile tears at the misfortunes of Mademoiselle Garnerin, the French balloonist. 'The Garnerin' made
several attempts to get her balloon to rise but France failed where
Germany succeeded; once again Jena was avenged. Mademoiselle
Garnerin could not get off the ground.

Some of the balloonists' difficulties were now being experienced
by the congress. The preliminary meeting with Richelieu had been
followed by the official opening at Hardenberg's lodging on the
Marktplatz and thereafter the delegates met either here or at
Metternich's in the Comphausbadstrasse.

No procedure as formal as at Vienna was necessary or desirable.

This congress would not merit Rousseau's satire on an assembly which deliberates whether the table should be round or square, the room have more or fewer doors or whether this or that plenipotentiary had his face or his back turned away. Informality was the keynote and the discussions always serious.

Each delegation produced a memoir or memorandum which was worked over in private conversations before being brought to the attention of the conference. These documents and any further proposals introduced by the plenipotentiaries were annexed to the protocols drawn up by Gentz and signed, though not necessarily read, by them at the following meeting.

The word 'protocol' in this context is somewhat misleading; it was used both in the sense of a *procès-verbal*, a report of minutes of decisions taken but also of an agreement between governments of less importance than a convention or treaty. At Aix-la-Chapelle forty-seven protocols in all were drawn up by Gentz who was also responsible for their printing and proof-reading.

The question of evacuation could be speedily dealt with because agreement had been reached in advance. With Baring's aid Richelieu anticipated no difficulty in obtaining the desired reduction in that amount of the French war indemnity as yet unpaid. Equally easy to deal with was the section of Louis XVIII's instructions that the French delegates were free to make their own decisions on all minor matters provided they were guided by French interests. Easiest of all for Richelieu was to neglect no opportunity of convincing the congress that the King of France cherished one ambition only—to heal France's wounds.

The most crucial and delicate part of Louis' instructions dealt with the Quadruple Alliance. Richelieu was to exert the utmost pressure both to secure its annulment and its replacement by a Quintuple Alliance to include France. Should the Allies admit France to their alliance but still insist on preserving their Four Power compact, then Richelieu must declare French preference for withdrawal into a system of total isolation.

This vital issue for France had to wait on Allied settlement of a problem of equal weight—the expediency of a prolonged surveillance of France and what, if any, military measures ought at this stage to be taken as a precaution against the renaissance in some other shape of 'the revolutionary spirit which had convulsed Europe'.

However alarming the prospect of a resuscitation of French

military power through a revolutionary outbreak, views on how to prevent it differed widely. No one wished to depart either from the spirit or the letter of the clause in the Quadruple Alliance which defined the conditions under which it would again become operative, i.e. armed federation should France in revolution again become a Power threatening to overthrow the European system.

In anticipation of the congress Castlereagh had prepared several memoranda, arguing the pros and cons of the decisions he hoped would be made at Aix-la-Chapelle; the military surveillance of France was one of his cardinal points. In order to speed a satisfactory conclusion to a concentrated debate which had been proceeding for several weeks and to leave the congress free to approach the question of French admission to the Quadruple Alliance, Castlereagh, in agreement with Wellington, decided to submit the substance of his final memorandum to his colleagues. He had already found that, in general, British and Austrian views on the question were similar.

Castlereagh spent long hours with Gentz in re-defining the *casus foederis*, the grounds upon which hostilities against France would be justifiable should the worst fears of the Powers be realized. As now worded, the clause submitted to the approval of the congress read that 'intervention in France would become operative only if the catastrophe compromised the tranquillity of her neighbouring states and the general security of Europe'. The difference in wording was a subtle revelation of a change in the British point of view.

Francis' solution of throttling the revolutionary spirit at source did not detain the delegates long; it was wholly impracticable. The Emperor considered that, like himself, Louis XVIII could suppress 'the Jacobinical impressions rapidly encouraging on all sides' by steady adherence to all the forms and usages of his ancestor. This was no example for the King of France to follow; it would have led him only to the same disaster as his brother, Louis XVI.

Alexander had arrived at Aix with a ready-made system of security, for once not visionary but practical. He proposed the setting up of a military commission, ready to act should the need arise; every sovereign would know his duty and his obligations while Allied forces would be disposed at strategic points.

The Czar's proposition was loudly acclaimed by the Prussian generals present at Aix, but not by Castlereagh and Wellington. Their objections were manifold. Despite Alexander's assertion that his army was the army of Europe neither Austria nor Great Britain viewed with any enthusiasm Russian troops being stationed in the heart of the continent. No suitable centre for a standing Allied force existed. Even if its purpose was his own defence the King of the Netherlands would undoubtedly resist the occupation of his territory by an Allied army. France would equally regard such a force as an excuse for augmenting her own army, with the inevitable sequel of the revival of the military spirit, wholly inadmissible to the Allies.

Wellington tactfully pointed out to Alexander the unfortunate effect not in France alone but in every country in Europe of rumours that a new plan of campaign had been drawn up in advance of any aggression. He used the common-sense argument that a measure so alarming would focus attention on the poor opinion held by the highest military and political authorities of France's stability. However strenuous the attempts to keep the work of this military committee secret, inevitable leakages would arouse the cruellest anxiety as well as furnishing the malcontents in France with an excellent pretext to cry out against the perfidy of the Allied cabinets. They would say that the evacuation was a hollow sham, cloaking continued hostility to France.

An alternative to the creation of a special force was to strengthen the existing bulwarks by including other states in the Quadruple Alliance. This suggestion found no favour with the British; any amendment to the treaty would require parliamentary sanction for which the cabinet was not prepared to ask.

Alexander finally showed himself amenable to opposition arguments and his military committee died stillborn. As a conciliatory measure a document was, however, drawn up, outlining some preliminary dispositions to be made should the Allies ever again find themselves obliged to resort to arms.

The Powers at last agreed on the impossibility of keeping France under a longer surveillance; it would do more harm than good. Should the necessity arise then no doubt common danger would give birth to a more general alliance. All other dangerous and difficult projects were rejected in favour of the maintenance of the Quadruple Alliance of 1815 which, like its parent, the Treaty of Chaumont, was to remain in force until 1825. Its terms should be adequate to meet any contingency.

In order not to shock French susceptibilities, the protocol enshrining this decision, which in this case was given all the force of a convention, should remain secret, together with the document annexed to it concerning tentative military plans. However, so that the King of France should be under no illusions as to his position, the protocol was communicated to the Duc de Richelieu for confidential transmission to Paris.

Castlereagh in particular was relieved that a settlement had been reached. Although discussion had been essentially harmonious it might well have been critical in its consequences. The cabinet was certain that Parliament would neither endorse a new treaty nor finance an army whose existence could not be justified by policy.

Parliament was the shadowy presence hovering over the British delegation at Aix-la-Chapelle. Bathurst and Liverpool repeatedly reminded Castlereagh of the unpleasant reaction to be expected from Parliament in the event of any new treaty or further commitments on the Continent. He must impress on the Powers that:

> 'The general and European discussion of these questions will be in the British Parliament, new, untried, of a doubtful character, and certainly not accustomed to look at foreign questions as Parliaments were some years ago, when under the pressure of immediate recollection of great foreign danger.'

Again and again the same warning reached Castlereagh in the couriers' bags; the Russians in particular must be made to feel that 'we have a Parliament and a public to which we are responsible, and that we cannot permit ourselves to be drawn into views of policy which are wholly incompatible with the spirit of our government'.

Everything done at Aix-la-Chapelle must be 'within the limit of the principles which could be maintained in Parliament', of which the cabinet quite plainly went in the greatest fear.

Devoted though Alexander was to constitutionalism—for nations other than his own—possibly this nearer insight into the workings of a parliament gave him a distaste for parliamentary institutions when he contrasted his own liberty of action with the limitations which hedged Castlereagh. With kindly contempt he assured the Foreign Secretary of his readiness to lend himself to any plan which might relieve the Prince Regent's ministers from parliamentary difficulty; amongst parties for so long accustomed to act in confidence, everything requisite might be done by protocol or declaration, without re-opening existing engagements to debate.

The Czar had already told Stewart sympathetically that he was

a, Wohnung Sr. Majestät des Königs   g, Wohnung des Herzogs von Wellington
b, ——————Kaisers von Russland   h, ——————————von Richelieu
c, —————Kaisers von Oesterreich   i, der Dom
d, —— des Fürsten von Hardenburg   k, das Rathhaus
e, ———————————— von Metternich   l, Cassernen
f, ————— Gesandten von Alopäus   m, Landw. Zeughaus

Aix-la-Chapelle in 1818, showing the residences of the
sovereigns and some of the delegates to the Congress

View of the Bathous at Aix-la-Chapelle

aware that Castlereagh had difficulties to contend with greater than his own, but he misjudged the situation when he added,

'When he can go back to his Parliament and detail what he has heard from the lips of the sovereigns here assembled, and bring their present conduct as confirmed proof of their former declarations and actions, the people of Great Britain are too enlightened not to be convinced.'

Only a complete lack of comprehension of the British character and the nature of British democratic institutions led Alexander thus to delude himself. The peoples of the British Isles cared nothing for any declaration by a foreign sovereign; they were a sovereign people.

Autocracy imposed no restraints on Alexander's political actions nor did he permit any circumscription of his private behaviour. In common with everyone else at Aix he came and went like an ordinary citizen, no considerations of etiquette or security precautions interfering with his enjoyment of its amenities and the persistent fine weather.

As an occasional change from poring over papers and endless conversations with his own and the other ministers, Alexander made brief excursions to Spa, either alone or accompanied by Frederick William. Naturally the Spadois were anxious to fête the successor of Peter the Great who had honoured their town, but unfortunately the talent available was not equal to the occasion. All that they could manage when Alexander went to the theatre, accompanied by his sister and brother-in-law, the Princess and Prince of Orange, were some vile laudatory verses. Only the tune of *Et, gai, gai, gai, mon officier* was, however, unexceptionable and struck the military note so dear to the Czar.

More to Alexander's taste were the reviews of troops which Frederick William organized for his friends' enjoyment but which the plenipotentiaries felt no obligation to attend. Only on the occasions when the troops paraded did the sovereigns don the be-starred uniforms they usually avoided. They then, out of compliment to one another, wore the dress of the foreign regiments of which, by an innovation in international courtesy, they had been nominated as colonels-in-chief. Nobody in this respect was more punctilious than the Czar who in one day changed his uniform four times, from Prussian to Russian, then to Austrian and once again to Prussian.

Most spectacular of all the reviews which were held at Aix was that on 18 October, anniversary both of the signature of the Peace

5

of Aix-la-Chapelle and of the Battle of Leipzig, which terminated Napoleon's domination of Europe. How many quill pens must the Herr Hofrat have discarded to describe lovingly the smallest detail of this most marvellous of anniversaries, of the day which restored to the Fatherland its natural pride, peace and power.

The three sovereigns, all wearing Prussian uniform, accompanied by Field-Marshal the Duke of Wellington, the Czar's brothers, the Grand Dukes Constantine and Michael, the Prussian Prince Karl, the Prince of Orange and the generals of their suites, rode out of the city, followed by the foreign delegations riding in open carriages. This was one occasion they could not escape attending.

A salvo of guns greeted the sovereigns' arrival at the Ketschenburg where, in a hollow square, infantry, cavalry and foot and mounted artillery were drawn up before an altar on which a silver crucifix glittered in the flickering light of supporting candles.

When the first cannon shot was heard in the city below the Duc de Richelieu with the entire French delegation left Aix. However little a Bonapartist, however much engaged in repairing the damage done by Napoleon to Europe, no Frenchman could take part in celebrating a great French defeat, any more than the diehard French aristocracy will remain in Paris on 14 July to commemorate the fall of the Bastille.

The Herr Hofrat reached the pinnacle of his eloquence to record how the three sovereigns who had survived the battle of Leipzig to join hands in the Holy Alliance of Princes, dropped to their knees before the altar raised to the Holy Spirit, to hear a religious service, intoned to an obbligato of cannon.

All Aix-la-Chapelle crowded the streets to gape at the monarchs, the troops and the fine carriages as they made their way down from the Ketschenburg after the service. The *haute volée* rode first to breakfast with Alexander before proceeding to the Rathaus where covers were laid in the throne room for Frederick William's hundred guests. The less important people were entertained by Hardenberg in a new building on the Lousberg. Illumination of their city ended the glorious day never to be forgotten by the citizens of Aix-la-Chapelle.

To mark the occasion Frederick William distributed a hundred ducats to the city's poor and, as a permanent reminder that Aix had housed the 'Congress of the Monarchs', the streets in which they lodged were re-named in honour of Francis and Alexander the

Franzstrasse and the Alexanderstrasse. Frederick William did not forget himself—the Foggengraben on which his own 'palace' abutted was henceforward to be known as Friedrich-Wilhelmsplatz.

Neither Alexander nor Frederick William was ever sated with reviews. They now moved off to Valenciennes for the even grander review of the Allied armies, organized for them by the Duke of Wellington. In spite of the additional work entailed by his dual role as second British plenipotentiary and Commander in Chief of the Allied Armies, the Duke remained as ever imperturbable. No detail was neglected. Now he was occupied in arranging the overnight accommodation at Namur and Valenciennes for the sovereigns and their suites, now for the large numbers of horses required to be ready for them at each staging post. Dinner must be at four o'clock exactly; there must be a play on the first evening and a ball on the third. Alexander would review the Russian army by itself before the sham fight, the Duke's 'harlequin farce', staged with the combined forces.

Wellington had no doubts about pleasing the sovereigns but this did not deter him from keeping his staff on their toes by reminding them that the Czar and the King of Prussia were 'the first critics of reviews in Europe'. In accordance with the Duke's expectations all went off extremely well with, for him personally, a gratifying sequel. 'As a mark of their favour and confidence' Alexander and Frederick William appointed the Duke of Wellington Field Marshal in their armies, an example shortly thereafter copied by Francis of Austria.

From the review the Czar and the King drove on to Paris, Alexander reluctantly, Frederick William eagerly, to pay a courtesy visit to Louis XVIII. Alexander escaped after only twenty-four hours in the city but Frederick William lingered for a few days to go to the opera.

How much less lively was Aix-la-Chapelle during the sovereigns' absence, mourned Herr Meyer. Francis, who generally hunted alone, did not accompany his brother monarchs to the review but, as he had now exhausted every possible excursion, he was rarely seen in public. The Aacheners had no royal personage on whom to feast their eyes. In desperation the Herr Hofrat was compelled to recollect that a congress was in progress.

CHAPTER VIII

Peace and Security

HERR Hofrat Karl Franz Meyer found Aix less lively during the sovereigns' absence. Metternich did not find Aix lively at all; the high sophisticate was bored. No ladies caught his eye, wandering without an object on which to fix since his break with the Duchesse de Sagan, during the Congress of Vienna. The sum total of women at Aix in the orbit of the Congress was the Princess of Thurn and Taxis, Countess Nesselrode, Lady Castlereagh, a few Russians and three or four Englishwomen between fifty and sixty—the age in London, sneered Metternich, of youth.

Metternich's established routine was far from exciting. In the morning he conferred with his colleagues; he then went for a walk, dined, played his game of whist with the bankers—people who wouldn't mind losing a good few millions which he was not at all averse to winning—and then went to bed.

For visitors bent either on business or pleasure the plenipotentiaries kept open house in the evenings. Anyone wanting to talk seriously to Lord Castlereagh made the Kleinborcettestrasse his first port of call but, according to Metternich, the charm had gone from Lady Castlereagh's salon. The visitor quickly gravitated to Metternich's or to Nesselrode's, whichever suited his political complexion.

At the beginning of November Metternich told his wife that all the foreigners, unable any longer to stand the dullness, had left Aix. Decidedly the Prince was disenchanted. He complained that there were no shops worth the name nor was anybody buying anything but what was absolutely necessary. Apparently Metternich failed to notice the fabulous oriental emporium near his house on the Comphausbadstrasse set up specially for the Congress by merchants from Constantinople. He also ignored the great influx of merchants trying to tempt visitors with silverware, porcelain and diamonds worth a million gulden.

One visitor certain to be tempted was Gentz. As soon as his pockets were sufficiently well lined he was always ready for a shopping spree. How many of the nine million francs from secret service funds expended by Richelieu at Aix-la-Chapelle went into Gentz' pockets? If from Rothschild he 'won' 800 ducats in English securities was it likely that David Parish or Alexander Baring neglected so useful an intermediary? Giving *douceurs* to Gentz was, however, a practice too universal to arouse comment.

When Clancarty reported a rumour that Pozzo di Borgo received three million French livres from the contractors of the French loan and that Metternich had accepted from Hope and Baring a million florins on the Austrian loan this was held to be a foul calumny. No one was ready to credit that from the bankers Metternich would take anything more than his winnings at play.

In return for his 'gifts' Gentz kept his part of the bargain. Like a bee he buzzed from one delegation to another, carrying the pollen of confidences. His routine was similar to Metternich's but considerably more charged with work. After attending the morning conference he had a business lunch with Metternich, then a stroll in the afternoon sunshine, as often as possible to the gardens of the famous botanist, Asselborn, at Burtscheidt on the outskirts of Aix. One of Gentz' most amiable characteristics was his love of flowers and plants which were a certain purchase for his garden in the suburbs of Vienna.

Gentz was a clear believer in the philosophy of *solvitur ambulando*. His companion on his walks was generally someone with whom he could converse usefully on congress matters, a Russian, a Prussian or one of the bankers.

Gentz' evening began with an obligatory visit to Castlereagh with whom his talks were always relevant to the day's deliberations. He then escaped to the more relaxed and congenial atmosphere of Nesselrode's, for whom he professed great attachment. When he assured the Russian minister that he was one of those men on whom one congratulated oneself to be with in fair and foul weather in all probability Gentz had his eye on the Russian gratifications which Nesselrode dispensed.

The sessions with Nesselrode, Capo d'Istrias and Pozzo di Borgo frequently lasted until midnight before Gentz returned to his lodging to draft protocols, wrestle with Castlereagh's memoranda to translate into French and write his lengthy letters to the Hospodars of Wallachia and directives to Pilat. For visits to brothels there was no spare moment but possibly the unexpected arrival at Aix of Gentz' protégé, Karl, dispensed with the need for further 'libertinage'.

In days so crowded time was lacking for little more than a brief record in his diary of comings and goings. On 8 October Gentz noted that, when he dined with Lord Castlereagh, among the guests were Count and Countess Lieven, the Russian ambassador to the Court of St. James's and his wife. At Countess Nesselrode's on the 20th he again met the Lievens and yet again on the 22nd at Metternich's. On the 25th, a glorious warm Sunday, the Lievens went on an excursion to Spa and Metternich was of the party.

To Gentz these dates were of no special significance but to Metternich they were all-important. Dorothea Lieven's arrival made his emotional desert blossom like the rose; the vacuum in which his heart had been beating was now filled with a new and exciting interest.

Pretty women were a necessity to Metternich, but they had to come from a milieu which enabled them to feed him, in the intervals of lovemaking, with political secrets. In this way he had used to his professional advantage the Caroline Bonapartes, the Laure d'Abranèts, the Princess Bagrations and the Duchesses de Sagan. Now, where and when least expected, a ripe plum dropped into his lap from a most valuable tree.

In 1818 Metternich was forty-five, the dangerous age of the *démon de midi*, Dorothea Lieven thirty-three. In beauty Madame de Lieven could not compare with his previous inamoratas but her intelligence was keener, she belonged wholly to the world of diplomacy and her main interest and activity in life was political intrigue. Her greatest quality was her capacity to listen and retail what she heard, most frequently with a point of malice, titillating to a jaded palate.

Since each fulfilled the other's need it was almost inevitable that Dorothea and Metternich fell into each other's arms, but was this really the *coup de foudre* or was the apparent passion of their love affair less genuine than the lovers' satisfaction at having a foot in each other's camp? During the eight years of their liaison their meetings were few but the connection was kept alive by a correspondence which served as an unofficial channel of information between the Austrian and Russian courts rather than one of love.

Metternich naturally concealed from his wife that the origin of his boredom was the Lievens' departure from Aix, and that his eagerness for an end to the congress was to join Dorothea in Brussels. Release for Metternich, however, was not yet. Much work remained to be done.

Before the sovereigns left for the review at Valenciennes they gave notice to their ministers that they wished all business to be concluded by 15 November, showing no disposition to push the discussions beyond the point chalked out by the circular convening the meeting. Gentz was sanguine that this date would be met, although neither the question of the admission of France to the Alliance nor the most 'vexatious' Russian memoir had yet been fully thrashed out.

The Russian memoir fulfilled all the British, Austrian and Russian fears. Murmurs of its content heard before the congress had swelled into a diapason.

'When the Duke of Wellington and myself,' Castlereagh wrote to Bathurst, 'came to consider this paper together, although abounding in the principles of union and peace, we felt some dismay in observing the abstractions and sweeping generalities in which it was conceived.'

Castlereagh, however, had no cause for the further complaint that Capo d'Istrias, who had drafted the memoir, had a literary style both verbose and unintelligible. With sublime obtuseness Castlereagh failed to see the beam in his own eye; in an age when prolixity was the rule even his style was regarded as slovenly nor was Capo d'Istrias alone guilty of 'shrouding his most common thoughts in a voluminous drapery of words'.

In this instance Castlereagh and Wellington were justified in complaining of the difficulty in reaching the core of this involved document, buried beneath long digressions on the principles of Christian morality, concord and fraternity.

The present European system *might* have been the work of Providence but Castlereagh had thought it to be largely his own. He certainly had greater faith in its practical terms for combating the revolutionary spirit rather than rely on moral influence alone to quell the doctrine that might is right.

Most irritating to Castlereagh was the Czar's renewed suggestion of inviting all the Powers which had signed the Final Act of the

Congress of Vienna and the Treaties of Paris to join in a general association of the European family. Alexander wanted to see all the Powers of Europe 'bound together in a common League, guaranteeing to each other the existing order of things, in thrones as well as in territories, all being bound to march, if required, against the first Power that offended, either by her ambition or by her revolutionary transgressions'.

Neither of the two pragmatists, Castlereagh and Wellington, had any more intention of admitting this proposition of Alexander's than of subscribing to the Holy Alliance. What had now to be avoided was becoming entangled in the endless discussion certain if they answered the memoir in writing. By dealing in person with Capo d'Istrias Castlereagh congratulated himself that he had to a considerable degree succeeded in getting him to 'descend from his abstractions'.

To open the question of admitting all the European Powers to a league before the status of France with regard to the Quadruple Alliance had been determined was putting the cart before the horse. The British cabinet was itself in a high state of confusion. While holding to the opinion that great inconvenience would be caused by inviting France to accede to the Alliance at the same time it believed that to exclude her from any further deliberations of the Four Powers would be most disadvantageous.

Castlereagh's own preference was a diplomatic concert with France, supported at its back in case of need by the Quadruple Alliance. Were France left in isolation, almost inevitably she would be driven to intrigue and cabal against the Alliance with consequences everyone was anxious to avoid.

Obviously to invite Louis XVIII to become a party to an association avowedly constituted to keep him under surveillance would put him into an intolerable position vis-à-vis his subjects; that surveillance of France in the future had, moreover, already been dismissed as impolitic and impracticable. A way had to be found to surmount this difficulty, to reconcile the conflicting views of the British cabinet and to meet the changed attitudes of the other Powers. The value of direct contacts between cabinets was again underlined since, except by personal intercourse, no basis of understanding could have been reached so fully and in so short a space of time.

On his arrival at Aix Alexander, in common with Francis and Frederick William, objected to a quintuple alliance to include France as suggesting a confidence in her they did not feel. To accept France as an equal partner might, they feared, jettison their treasured security which Europe had a moral claim on them not to relinquish lightly.

In the course of his many conversations with Castlereagh Alexander had now come round to the view that, if the object of the reunion was to strengthen the general tranquillity, then French participation was not only desirable but essential. He suspected that rivalry and jealousy on the part of Austria and Great Britain had for so long held them back from reaching this conclusion.

Before the Czar's return from Paris to Aix on 30 October the congress ran into some anxious days as it groped for a formula both to meet the sovereigns' views and one possible to maintain in Parliament. Gentz reported a fierce tussle with Capo d'Istrias about the editing of some important documents in which victory finally fell to him. This argument was followed by an unpleasant scene with Castlereagh and one still more unpleasant with Stewart. Most likely money was the cause but possibly also the fact that Castlereagh had considerably neutralized a protocol drafted by Gentz. This first serious disagreement he had met with at Aix distressed Gentz considerably but he was able to console himself with his own 'blameless conduct and the imbecility of the British ministers'.

Even when agreement had been reached in principle that France should be admitted to the Alliance difficulties did not cease. Drafting of the necessary documents ran into trouble. Castlereagh's first draft was inadmissible to the Russians because by making French entry into the Alliance purely formal, it would leave her still in a state of isolation.

A Russian draft more favourable to France was objected to by Austria, Great Britain and Prussia. Discussion became animated and even at times acrimonious before concessions were made by all the Powers.

Castlereagh gently reproved the cabinet which seemed to be trying to direct the congress from London or Walmer Castle where Lord Liverpool was in residence as Lord Warden of the Cinque Ports.

'In such a body as we have to deal with, we cannot hope to give the documents precisely our own complexion and there are reasons why a phraseology *must be tolerated*, which would be better avoided. We
5*

must take care in substance not to break new ground, and if this is secured, I should hope, in matter of taste, the cabinet will be disposed to make some allowance and not be too severe in their criticisms.'

Liverpool might argue that no practical question was now at issue as formerly, that it was more a discussion as to words than things, but Castlereagh was looking into the future when failure to find the right words might provoke deeds. In his estimation Four Power security must be maintained. France should join the Alliance, not as one to four, but as one of five, with her fair share of influence, so long as she did not infringe upon the spirit of the Concert. While she behaved well the Powers were at five but, should she not do so, the existing Treaties imposed on the Powers the *obligation* of being again as four to one.

Admittedly co-opting France to the Quadruple Alliance was a calculated risk but, in Castlereagh's eyes at least, preferable to throwing her at some future time into the arms of Russia. Daily contact with Alexander and his ministers had not abated his fear of Russia. On the contrary, his prime consideration in going to every reasonable length to restore France to an honourable place in Europe was to lessen the chances of that Franco-Russian alliance which he believed to be the only one which might prove really formidable.

The British system, and those of the countries which had common frontiers with France, must always in some measure be regulated upon the French. Bad relations with France would not only leave Britain dependent on Russia but might lead France to form a rival association to the Quadruple Alliance. The danger might then arise, possibly in another reign, that Russia would seize upon this association, if she decided to separate herself from the Quadruple Alliance, to dictate to the rest of the world, either by joining or dominating the new system which would be a serious source of danger to the balance of Europe.

With these considerations in mind agreement was finally reached that France should become a member of the Grand Alliance to take part in all negotiations having as their object the common good of Europe. Richelieu was wise enough not to press for this decision to take the form of a treaty, which would have to be referred by Castlereagh to the cabinet and by the cabinet to Parliament.

On 4 November the plenipotentiaries of the Four Powers

addressed a Note to Richelieu whereby he was invited 'to convey the wish of their August Sovereigns to the knowledge of the King his master that henceforward His Most Christian Majesty should unite his councils and his efforts to those which they will not cease to devote to so salutary a work' as preserving to their peoples the benefits which peace had assured to them.

Nevertheless, on the same day, the Four Courts signed a secret and separate protocol to determine under what circumstances and when to renew the Quadruple Alliance.

The Note of 4 November, sent forward to Paris, was received by Louis XVIII with 'real satisfaction'. His approbation was made known to the Powers by Richelieu in a Note and on 9 November the Duc was admitted as a full partner to the deliberations of the Four Powers.

Only three years after France's total defeat by Europe in arms she was in a way to paying off her colossal war indemnity, her soil was relieved of the odious presence of an occupying army and she had regained her important place in the European community. All this she in great part owed to the unwearying and selfless persistence of the Duc de Richelieu. How ironic that this man, who had foresworn his country rather than see it wrecked by the forces of revolution, should, by his reluctant return, have been the means of leading France triumphantly out of the morass into which that revolution had finally plunged her.

Praise for this eminently satisfactory conclusion to a problem agitating the councils of Europe was due also to Castlereagh as author of Article VI of the Quadruple Alliance which had made possible this congress where such vital decisions had been reached. Like all diplomatists, however, he found that what seems best to the man on the spot is seen in a different light at his home base. Many times during his stay at Aix Castlereagh must have wished himself in the comparative independence of Vienna where exhortations from the cabinet arrived far less frequently.

Castlereagh's faith in the value of diplomatic meetings was still lively. He was more than ever convinced that, 'together with past habits, common glory, displays and re-pledges, they were among the best securities Europe now had for a durable peace'. The cabinet disagreed. Castlereagh was obliged to back down from his agreement with the Czar at their first meeting at Aix when Alexander spoke confidently of their next reunion, three years hence.

Never had Castlereagh felt in so much charity with the Czar as when Alexander predicted that 'increased experience, both of their own work and of each other, would make them, if possible, still more satisfied with the result of their labours and with the ties uniting them'.

With this part of Alexander's belief no diplomatist would have disagreed. Their intimacy, extending now over a long period, had taught them to plumb the depths and shallows of one another's sincerity and political intelligence; dissimulation was now difficult and anything but frank and open discussion virtually impossible.

Still musing on the future, Alexander had declared that, although he could ill be spared from the interior of his dominions, and that he might not then enjoy the good health he now happily did, he had it so much at heart to meet his Allies, that no inconvenience should prevent his so doing, whenever the meeting might be fixed. Rather than fail them, added the Czar, he would come in a litter.

Castlereagh, normally so wary of Alexander's enthusiasms, dropped his guard. He could not fail to be gratified that the Czar had so wholeheartedly adopted the principle of Article VI of the Quadruple Alliance. Not to have been chagrined by the cabinet's reaction would have been less than human.

Throughout the month of October despatches hurtled back and forth between Aix-la-Chapelle and the Foreign Office in London with Castlereagh urging the benefits to be gained by further reunions and Liverpool and Bathurst counselling caution and reluctance to agree.

Only a lukewarm reception was accorded to Castlereagh's contention that the review of existing engagements and their application to the sequel of evacuation 'could not have been taken by the ordinary course of diplomatic intercourse, not only without delay but without the hazard of the most serious misconception, and complication of views'.

Bathurst countered with the cabinet's great doubts as to the advisability of publishing to Europe the intention of the Four Powers to hold continued meetings at stipulated periods. Castlereagh's retort that difficulties had been obviated and any prejudicial divergence of opinion avoided by the presence of the cabinets side by side failed to impress the British cabinet.

Bathurst did not object to the system so much as to the expediency of declaring it in a circular letter, which seldom did any good. He raised the worn old spectre—such letters were generally productive of much inconvenient discussion in Parliament.

The prominent necessity for reunions would cease, said Liverpool, whenever the French government proved itself capable of maintaining tranquillity abroad and peace at home. The Prime Minister might argue that it was often as unwise to look too far into the future as to put narrow and contracted limits to the cabinet's views but, in fact, the cabinet looked at France and France only. They seemed unable to envisage any other possible source of trouble in Europe. They would go so far as to permit, if it was thought advisable for keeping France in some order, a period to be fixed at which the sovereigns would again assemble. A succession of meetings could not form part of a permanent system; the advantages might well be nullified by possible great embarrassments and inevitably create jealousy among the other European Powers.

Should the Powers meet again in two or three years' time they would then be at liberty to decide, in the light of the state of France and Europe at that time, whether a further meeting was necessary or advisable. The cabinet did not wish to abrogate Article VI of the Quadruple Alliance; simply they felt it was impolitic to reinforce it by any new declaration of a general nature. While willing and ready to fulfil British obligations to the Alliance the government was reluctant for further commitments on the Continent.

The cabinet feared that the other European Powers would be alarmed if they were excluded from future meetings of the Four Courts. In answer Castlereagh protested that their resentment could be anticipated by an Allied denial of any intention to 'interfere in the politicks of other states in any manner not strictly warranted by the Law of Nations'. His words fell on deaf ears.

Not surprisingly the most unsympathetic ear in the cabinet belonged to George Canning, already defining his future attitudes and 'plucking the grey hairs out of a question, and then again the black'. In a cabinet largely composed of aristocrats Canning, as a mere Irish squireen, was at a disadvantage. Perhaps consciousness of his inferior background led him to self-assertiveness and self-seeking. Not only were his faults those of the parvenu but his temperament was his own worst enemy. For his happiness his temper was too uncertain and his wit too satirical. In 1809 he and Castlereagh had fought a duel and, although they were reconciled thereafter, the incident could not be forgotten.

Canning was not the man to neglect the opportunity of opposing Castlereagh when he might legitimately do so; Great Britain's role was not 'to dictate and domineer over the whole world' nor yet to hold the balance of Europe but 'to creep into our shells and draw in our horns'. He, therefore, considered that 'the system of periodical meetings of the Four Great Powers, with a view to the general concerns of Europe, new and of very questionable policy; it would necessarily involve the British deeply in all the politics of the Continent, whereas true British policy has always been not to interfere except in great emergencies and then with a commanding force'.

Canning allowed himself to be carried away by his own rhetoric, 'reasoning a tissue of glaring sophistry in language a cento of florid commonplace' as Hazlitt put it.

'All other states,' declaimed Canning in cabinet, 'must protest against such an attempt to place them under subjection; the meeting might become a scene of cabal and intrigue; the peoples of Great Britain might be taught to look with great jealousy for their liberties if their Court were engaged in meetings with great despotic monarchs, deliberating upon what degree of revolutionary spirit might endanger the public security and therefore require the interference of the Allies.'

As rhodomontade Canning's speech was first class; what was lacking was Castlereagh's greater lucidity of intelligence. Neither Canning nor the cabinet was willing, or perhaps able, to admit that the devils he painted on the wall might possibly be exorcised by the adoption of the Czar's proposal to 'bind all the Powers of Europe together in a common league'. They could not foresee that the Alliance might evolve into something quite different nor that the revolutionary spirit might not always endanger the public security. An unpopular government, clinging to life, had neither time nor inclination for idealism, even practical idealism.

Bathurst did assure Castlereagh that Canning's views had met with no agreement from himself or the other members of the cabinet. He tried to placate the Foreign Secretary by telling him that it was very natural that, having experienced the advantages of the meeting at Aix-la-Chapelle, he should wish to see a continuance of such reunions. Bathurst did not, however, withdraw his caution against fixing a date for any meeting beyond the next, even were the cabinet assured that subsequent meetings would be as cordial as the present one. Settling and announcing the date for the next meeting was even very desirable, but nothing more was necessary. Canning himself did not object to an understanding with the Powers that they would continue to meet.

Castlereagh was now in no doubt that, however happy he personally would be to meet his colleagues again, such a meeting did not have the cabinet's approval. Indeed, Bathurst's pleasure seemed to lie in repeating the obvious truth that all political systems have their day. He even seemed happy that only three years were necessary to emasculate that Article VI which, at the time it was drawn, seemed so solid a guarantee for the tranquillity of Europe.

Obediently, albeit reluctantly, Castlereagh on 29 October wrote in a private and confidential letter to Bathurst,

'Your Lordship will observe that there is no reference (in the various protocols attached) to any specified periods of meeting, nor is there any intention, as far as I am informed, of *now* naming any particular time for reassembling.

'In proportion as the subject has been canvassed, the general tendency of opinion has been in the same direction as that of the cabinet, viz. to say and to do as little as possible to provoke feeling or comment, and to point the eventual reunions to the maintenance of the late peace, and European settlement, as resting on the particular treaties, rather than to the more general political interest of Europe, extra these transactions.'

Alexander might be disappointed but the cabinet could prepare to meet the new House of Commons in January 1819 if not with a conscience wholly clear, at least with one skeleton less in its cupboard.

Now that the tetrarchy had to all intents and purposes become the pentarchy the major work of the congress had been successfully done. Most of the cobwebs which had obscured the horizon had been blown away and the atmosphere was considerably clearer.

Although Alexander had still one or two more cards up his sleeve to play, in general for the sovereigns there was less to do; individually they had visited every possible factory and coalmine in the vicinity of Aix, tasted the waters of all the thermal springs, held as many reviews as there were troops to be inspected, gazed at the panorama of Waterloo and listened on various occasions to Catalani.

The arrival of the Duc d'Angoulême on a flying visit to thank the sovereigns in the name of his uncle, Louis XVIII, for their exertions on behalf of France at least provided the occasion for a royal luncheon party and some employment for the idle Court pastry-cooks.

Courtesy demanded that Alexander and Frederick William attend the weekly tea dances given by the Princess of Thurn and Taxis, although Alexander danced now from duty not inclination; he was in his element in the atmosphere of the congress, revelling in his long and intimate discussions with the delegates, whom he still hoped to convert to his own credo of a European federation.

All three sovereigns found some occupation for their leisure hours in fulfilling an obligation to the absent Prince Regent. The Prince had commissioned from Sir Thomas Lawrence a series of portraits of the Allied sovereigns and their chief ministers to commemorate their joint victory, portraits which now hang in the Waterloo Chamber at Windsor Castle.

Some of these portraits had been begun and some finished in London in 1814, notably those of Metternich, Castlereagh, Marshal Blücher and the Ataman of Cossacks, Platoff. These Lawrence had brought with him to exhibit at Aix but for many weeks he was frustrated of any further painting and obliged to kick his heels in idleness. The studio, ingeniously prefabricated for him in England to be shipped for erection in the garden of Lord Castlereagh's house, failed to arrive in time to be of use.

The city fathers of Aix-la-Chapelle came to the rescue. They set aside part of the large gallery with a good north light at the Rathaus as a studio for Lawrence, the best, said the painter, he had ever had. Graciously the authorities let it be known that they counted this not as a special privilege but as an opportunity of doing honour to themselves since the monarchs of Europe would visit their city hall to sit for portraits commissioned by the Prince Regent of England.

The Emperor of Austria was the first monarch thus to honour the city of Aix-la-Chapelle. He came to the Rathaus to be painted while Alexander and Frederick William were at Valenciennes and Paris. In the seven sittings Francis gave him Lawrence found Francis' long, thin face, grave to the point of melancholy, difficult to fix on the canvas. In Lawrence's opinion only when the Emperor spoke did benevolence light up his countenance with the most agreeable expression, making it 'the perfect image of a good mind'.

Since Francis was accompanied always by the same aide-de-camp, conversation must have been limited in scope. Fortunately the sittings were enlivened by the fine Prussian military band playing in

the Marktplatz. Lawrence shared Frederick William's fondness for
the English air, *God Save Great George our King*, rendered with
many charming variations.

Only six sittings were necessary to complete Frederick William's
portrait. Painting his wooden stance and expression must have been
like painting a lay figure but Lawrence was confident that he had
portrayed his good features and the reserve of manner he noticed in
the King. At any rate Frederick William was sufficiently satisfied to
commission for himself a copy of his own portrait together with
copies of those of the two Emperors and of the Prince Regent.

To a man of business like Alexander seven sittings for a portrait
involved a sacrifice of valuable time. Unlike Francis and Frederick
William, however, Alexander used the sittings for profitable talks
with Stewart, Richelieu or others of the delegates.

The Czar was a subject of interest to the Aacheners greater even
than Francis. They admired the Emperor's splendid state, particularly his magnificent carriages and they flocked to the Marktplatz
to watch him come and go and greet him with enthusiastic cheers.
To see Alexander the approaches to the studio were more thickly
crowded with 'respectable people and foreigners', eager for a close-
up sight of the Czar, wearing the uniform he had worn at the battle
of Leipzig in which he chose to be painted.

A crisis developed at one moment when Lawrence, dissatisfied
with Alexander's stance, had him on the canvas with four legs. His
entourage was scandalized and even the Czar himself showed some
displeasure until 'the vessel was righted', an indication perhaps that
affability and condescension on Alexander's part in his intercourse
with ordinary mortals was only a veneer.

The finished portrait shows the Czar in characteristic pose, leaning
rather on one leg and with his hands clasped in front. It depicts a
man of resolution and the expression of the mouth is stern but the
eyes 'look to far distant horizons of a world of charity and brotherly
love'—or so Lawrence decided.

Metternich, not entirely influenced by his own highly successful
portrait, considered Lawrence's works as *chef-d'oeuvres*, praise
echoed by all who saw them. That no official group portrait like the
one done by Isabey at the Congress of Vienna was painted is a
matter for regret. Individually the characters of the men painted by
Lawrence leap from the canvas. Collectively they would have shed a
great deal of light on the corporate personality of the congress.

For Lawrence this excursion to Aix-la-Chapelle was a highly profitable one since, as well as the sovereigns, he painted Hardenberg, Nesselrode and Richelieu, whose leonine head made him an admirable subject. In addition to his fee of five hundred guineas for a full-length Lawrence was given a thousand pounds by the Prince Regent for his expenses and loss of time in travelling, plus further fees for his copies.

When Lawrence moved on to Vienna to complete the Prince Regent's plan, in his baggage he took diamond rings, the gifts of Alexander, Frederick William and the Empress Dowager of Russia. The Czar's mother, who came to Aix-la-Chapelle on her way to Brussels to see her daughter, the Princess of Orange, positively screamed with pleasure at the excellent likeness of her son.

More than the monetary rewards Lawrence was delighted, as he wrote to his niece, that his exertions had been repaid by complete success.

> 'The family, attendants and the subjects of each sovereign unanimously declare that the portraits I have taken are the most faithful and satisfactory resemblances of them that have ever been painted, and the general voice of all unites in common approbation—a word, I assure you, much below the impression I use to describe it.'

Only one fly had entered the sweet ointment. Lawrence had seen his rival but much inferior painter, George Dawe, 'creeping round the Czar's lodging'. His sole contribution to memorializing the congress was an allegorical portrait of the three monarchs mounted on a triumphal chariot.

Lawrence need fear no comparison with Dawe. Rarely can there have been such reciprocal satisfaction between an artist and his sitters, all, with the exception of Francis, handsome, some extremely handsome men. Although Alexander's hair was receding, he was stouter and the eager expression of his youth had gone from his face, the indefinable aura of charm still surrounded him. Stewart had great dash and, in his portrait by Lawrence, if somewhat effeminate, appears better-looking than his brother, although the painter considered Castlereagh as the most handsome of his sitters. Castlereagh's loose-limbed figure does not, however, show to the same advantage in ordinary dress as the sovereigns and Metternich in uniform.

If the painter admired his sitters he himself was admired even more than his portraits. Was Lawrence's early biographer wholly innocent of *sous-entendu*—since the painter's tendencies were well known to his contemporaries—when he wrote:

'The Emperors acknowledged that his manners and deportment formed a fine specimen of the English gentleman, and they were not insensible to the symmetry of his form, and to his fine expression of countenance.'

Gentz, who did not conceal his sexual ambivalence, might have added his voice to those of the sovereigns but, even among the least epicene of men like Metternich, Alexander and Francis, the latent attraction of handsome men for one another existed, perhaps unrealized. Subconsciously this attraction may well have had some influence on their friendships and therefore on their political alignments. The possibility exists and cannot be wholly dismissed.

CHAPTER IX

End of a Congress

THE Four Powers, while insisting that their discussions at Aix-la-Chapelle would be limited in scope, had still reserved the right to consider such matters of general interest as might appropriately be brought to the sovereigns' attention. Although these matters were of minor importance the list was formidable—the affair of the Spanish colonies, the dispute between Sweden and Denmark, the succession to the Grand Duchy of Baden, the dukedom of Bouillon, the state of Monaco, the Barbary pirates and the inevitable slave trade.

The sovereigns' presence likewise acted as a magnet to draw many individuals to Aix, hopeful of airing their favoured projects—if they could get a hearing. Foremost among them was the Bonaparte family.

According to Hugh Elliot, writing from Madras to Lord Bathurst, the shades of oblivion were manifestly deepening round Buonaparte. In India this may have been true but at Aix-la-Chapelle the ministers had ample evidence that he was not, as Lord Liverpool had once so confidently predicted, forgotten. Elliot's only criticism was that an atrocious culprit, who was over fortunate to have escaped condign punishment, was too liberally treated. This opinion the Bonapartes fiercely disputed; they were desperate to secure for the Emperor at least some alleviation of his mental and physical sufferings.

As soon as he returned to Europe from St Helena the Comte de Las Cases, Napoleon's faithful adherent and scribe, had bombarded the monarchs and the British cabinet with letters, eloquently descriptive of all that Napoleon was enduring. In the Congress of Aix-la-Chapelle Las Cases saw an opportunity to seek a full-dress re-assessment of the conditions under which the Emperor was held captive.

Las Cases simply refused to believe that Napoleon's wife, his father-in-law, and those monarchs to whom he had so recently been friend and good brother, would not be moved by his recital, but his greatest faith was in Alexander. He tried every conceivable channel to reach the Czar's heart, hoping from him something 'noble, great, humane and philanthropic'. Las Cases begged La Harpe to use his influence to persuade Alexander to deal magnanimously with an old friendship or, should his former affection have lamentably changed to enmity, yet to show himself capable of rising above it. When the Czar learnt that Napoleon himself had not forgotten the ties which once united them, surely some memory of the raft on the Niemen would stir in Alexander? Could he remain impervious when told that the Emperor still said,

'My war with the Czar was merely a political war; it bore no relation to individual feelings, and I cannot think he nourishes any personal animosity.'

Letters from the Emperor's mother, sisters and brothers to the sovereigns and the British plenipotentiaries supported Las Cases' own frenzied efforts. Most pathetic was the letter written by Napoleon's mother. In her anxiety that no maladroit move should prejudice her son's cause she consulted Las Cases for advice as to whether her appeal would be more favourably received if she signed herself 'Letitia' or 'Madame Mère'. For all the effect her pleading produced she might have signed herself Mammamouchi.

Castlereagh reported with satisfaction that in no instance had the letters from the Buonaparte family received any direct reply. They had been tabled before the conference and thereafter ignored.

Las Cases suspected that the sovereigns let fear over-ride any generous feelings they might have harboured towards Napoleon; he especially accused the British of fabricating an escape plot to justify reinforcing their security measures on St Helena. Not even such a partisan as Las Cases could, however, deny that, ever since the Emperor landed on the island, one escape project had followed another.

In the United States the British minister continued to keep an eye on Joseph Buonaparte's activities, his reports were forwarded to Aix-la-Chapelle for Castlereagh's information. Joseph was quoted as saying that the present state of affairs in France could not last long. Incredibly—except that Joseph's political acumen was on a par with his courage—he looked forward to the moment when Austria might be setting up his nephew, the young Napoleon, as Emperor of the

French. Admittedly the ex-King of Rome, now the Duc de Reich-stadt, held in silken chains in Vienna, was a focus for French dis-content and a potential means of disturbing the tranquillity of Europe. For this, if for no other reason, Francis felt that the care of the boy was better in his hands than in anyone else's but he was also a most engaging and much-loved grandson. Austria was quite as much aware as Joseph could be of Reichstadt's value as a pawn to be used for her own advantage, but if she had ever wanted thus to use him the time for it had long since gone by.

Joseph, nevertheless, blandly professed himself ready to lend Austria and England whatever aid was in his power to forward what he considered must be their joint policy, the restoration of the Empire. Such an offer from a proscribed exile to two great European Powers had in it something both pathetic and ridiculous, had the statesmen had bowels or a sense of humour, but where the Bona-partes were involved, they had neither.

Only fourteen years before, Napoleon, in the early flush of his Imperial dignity, had spent ten days at Aix-la-Chapelle. Like the monarchs of 1818 he received an enthusiastic welcome from its citizens, visited factories, attended fêtes and in the cathedral heard a Te Deum in his honour as the sacred relics were brought out for his inspection. (Josephine was offered a holy bone which she gracefully declined.) Napoleon, too, had gazed at Charlemagne's throne and tomb as if seeking inspiration for his own infant empire. That empire now lay in ruins and the Emperor himself was a prisoner of his enemies who were debating his future in this self-same city.

For the consideration of the congress the Russians had prepared a memoir relating to the detention of Napoleon Buonaparte on the island of St Helena. Was it merely unfortunate coincidence that this paper was read to the conference immediately after Protocol 31 which discussed the depredations of the Barbary pirates? The plenipoten-tiaries might have been forgiven for confusing the two documents, so strong was the language used by the Russians about the fallen Emperor. Since the memoir was drafted by Pozzo di Borgo Castle-reagh was not surprised—when it was *Corse contre Corse* he expected a little cayenne.

Buonaparte, proclaimed the Russians, had no right to expect the consideration due by the civilised nations to public power. Before the battle of Waterloo he was a powerful rebel, after the defeat a vagabond, whose schemes had been disrupted by Providence. The

word 'vagabond' especially shocked Castlereagh—it was at no time
an Imperial expression, still less so after the peace of Tilsit. His
memory was unfortunately long. Who else now remembered Tilsit?
It was the name of a place, nothing more. Where now was Alexander's
chivalry to a fallen enemy, where now his affection for an erstwhile
friend, where now his declaration, 'I never loved anything as I loved
that man'?

Why did the Czar permit Pozzo di Borgo to frame such an indict-
ment? Was this another of his celebrated *volte-faces*? Certainly
Russian obduracy towards Napoleon did not accord with the words
of Christian charity and fraternity so frequently on Alexander's
lips.

The Russian ministers stood firmly on the measures taken and to
be taken 'for the strictest maintenance and execution of the Convention of 2 August 1815' whereby the Four Powers had declared
Napoleon their prisoner. When the final Protocol was drawn up by
the congress, incorporating the resolutions taken by the plenipotentiaries, Pozzo di Borgo was seen to have won the final victory in
his long battle with Napoleon Bonaparte.

'By his own act,' read Protocol 42 of the Congress of Aix-la-
Chapelle, 'Napoleon Buonaparte is deprived of any rights other than
those humanity demands in his favour.'

Humanity's demands yielded to Pozzo di Borgo's rancour. No
reproof was administered to Sir Hudson Lowe for the indignities he
heaped on his prisoner, no alleviation was permitted of that prisoner's
sufferings. Castlereagh indeed considered it inadvisable to object to
a clause in Protocol 42, which required the British to procure access
for the Allied commissioners on St Helena to verify Buonaparte's
personal presence, a principle fully sanctioned by the 1815 Convention. Thus, one of the most galling circumscriptions of such minimal
liberty as Napoleon enjoyed was maintained. Surely now he would
be forgotten?

The harshness of the Allies' final decision with regard to the
Emperor was undoubtedly influenced by the Russian allegation that
yet another escape plot had been engineered by members of the
Emperor's suite, timed to coincide with the evacuation of French
territory by Allied troops and the unrest which the Bonapartists
hoped would ensue.

Infinitely more alarming to the Russians was the discovery of a
plot much nearer home and involving the sacred person of His

Imperial Majesty the Czar of Russia. He was to be kidnapped on his way from Aix-la-Chapelle to Brussels where, before returning to Russia, he intended to visit his sister, the Princess of the Netherlands.

For three years the Allies had been remonstrating with King William of the Netherlands for permitting his kingdom, particularly the Belgic provinces, to become a hotbed of Bonapartist intrigue. Their efforts had at last met with some success. For more than a year, Lord Clancarty was now able to report, there had been no lack of vigour on the part of the Netherlands authorities in endeavouring to control the intrigues of the French emigrants. The unmasking of yet another 'diabolical plot' again undermined confidence in the sincerity of King William.

With little evidence to show that Alexander intended to support them, the Bonapartists since 1814 had clung to the hope that he could secure the Emperor's restoration, or at least his liberation. When the Czar left Paris in 1815, in addition to the letter from the 'Captain of the Regicides', his desk was found littered with anonymous letters, all bent on the same object of obtaining his co-operation in championing the cause of the King of Rome. Alexander's visit to Brussels offered a unique opportunity to force his hand.

The Czar was to be kidnapped and made to sign a proclamation in favour of Napoleon and his son. When this was published the conspirators believed that a Bonapartist rising in the Netherlands would follow, in its turn fomenting revolution in France.

The proclamation was short and to the point but, in drawing it up in the name of the fatherland and Alexander, the plotters betrayed their ignorance of the nature of the congress of Aix-la-Chapelle.

'By virtue of Our Congress of Aix-la-Chapelle' read the first article, 'we decree that the evacuation of the Army of Occupation shall be carried out during the last days of this month and the troops shall return home.'

As propaganda this article was valueless since the decision to evacuate the army had been made public on 9 October.

The second was the operative article:

'By the above-mentioned assembly of sovereigns We proclaim by the deliberations of Our Congress that, in the name of France, Napoleon should be brought back to France under the responsibility of the British government, and that Prince Charles François Napoleon should be proclaimed Emperor of the French and Marie Louise Empress and Regent.

'Done at Our Congress of Aix-la-Chapelle on the date of Our assembly of 1818. Signed: Alexander.'

Only the date and the authentic signature were lacking.

So amateurish was the plot that, within five days of the discovery of its existence, the ringleaders were arrested. Baron Nagell, the Netherlands Foreign Minister, to whom it fell to deal with the affair, believed the root cause to be the flood of print pleading the cause of the prisoner of St Helena. The widest circulation had been given to a spurious pamphlet, selling like hot cakes at three and four francs apiece, in which the Archduchess Marie Louise was made to protest at her husband's captivity.

Only the mass was credulous enough to believe anything so stupid. The higher cadres of French exiles knew only too well that Marie Louise preferred adultery with Count Neipperg at Parma to immortality with Napoleon on St Helena.

That the conspirators had a link with Paris was reasonably certain, probably with a Bonapartist organization known, from its recognition sign of a black pin, as the *Chevaliers de l'Epingle Noir*. After an abortive conspiracy in 1816 some of the *Chevaliers* had been brought to a trial which dragged on for months only to end in the damp squib of an acquittal.

None of the distinguished exiles in the Netherlands was involved in the plot. Cambacérès, formerly Arch-Chancellor of the Empire, was known to have refused to have any truck with it. Old soldiers of the Grande Armée of minor rank were responsible for the idea of kidnapping Alexander. Baron Nagell primly conceded that it was legitimate for the French exiles to hope for the evacuation of France. What was not permissible was for them to nourish guilty expectations of a change of régime rather than accept things as they were in the interests of the tranquillity of Europe.

Why blame these men for attempting to bring about a Bonapartist restoration when all the tranquillity of Europe offered them was a penurious exile? 'All great devotion is heroic,' Napoleon himself had said, and what more heroic than the fidelity of these humble people to an ideal for which they were ready to risk their lives as they had so often in the past risked them in battle for their Emperor?

In reporting the plot to the Duke of Wellington Nagell was tactful enough to couple it in iniquity with the attempt in February on the person of His Highness the Prince of Waterloo (as Wellington was invariably known in the Netherlands). To the great regret of some uneasy spirits, fed on exaggerated memories and dreaming of changes each one more outlandish than the last, that attempt had failed. Nagell allowed it to be implicitly understood that he shared the universal relief that Wellington had not succumbed to an assassin.

The Duke, still smarting under the cavalier treatment meted out to the assassination attempt on himself, did not take the plot seriously, but, as Commander in Chief of the Allied Armies until 30 November, the date of its disbanding, he was responsible for the sovereigns' security. As the Czar was involved the Duke felt obliged to lay the documents before him. They were a farrago of comedy, credulity and ineptitude.

The conspirators appeared to be well informed about the members of the Czar's entourage, the number of carriages which they would use and the one in which he himself would travel, but they were vague about the most important fact, the date of his journey from Aix. They calculated that he would arrive in Brussels on 10 or 11 November but this was pure guesswork and, in the event, wrong.

Their plan was simple: Alexander's carriage was to be held up, the traces cut and he himself taken to the nearest town, there to sign the proclamation. He would then be invited to send a message to the Emperor of Austria, asking him to announce his own adherence to the proclamation. If Alexander refused to sign—and apparently no one knew how he was to be persuaded so to do—he would be killed. What advantage the dead Czar would be to the cause or what the consequences of his murder to the plotters they had not stopped to consider.

To reinforce their own numbers they decided to co-opt some smugglers, many of them former members of the Red Lancers of the Old Guard. Each was to receive a louis to rush out, pistols in hand, from the wood where they would be hidden alongside the road taken by Alexander from Aix-la-Chapelle to Brussels. The money to pay the smugglers would be provided by someone vaguely described as a lame man wearing a shiny hat.

One Laborde, a former aide-de-camp to General Vandamme, would recruit the smugglers in Hainaut and lead them in small parties by side roads to the appointed spot. The authorities had, in fact, observed some ferment in excess of what was normal on the frontiers where smuggling was always rife. More foreigners had been seen to cross the frontier, many of them former soldiers of the Grande Armée.

Rendezvous of the chief conspirators was an inn—naturally of ill repute—the *Tête d'Or* in the Rue Haute in Brussels, suspect already as a port of call of Bonapartists.

These details and many more were disclosed to the police by a former French officer named Pouillot de la Croix, whose identity had been revealed by another Frenchman named Buchoz. When Pouillot was apprehended and questioned by the police his ideas grew increasingly grandiose. By the time he had finished telling his story the numbers involved in the plot had risen from some thirty men with forty smugglers in support to a thousand or even 1600 men.

What puzzled the Public Prosecutor most was the identity of the lame man, whose limp may have been a disguise, who had frequented the *Tête d'Or* with Pouillot. Was he the man with the shiny hat and possible chief of the conspirators or was that another man who manufactured combs? What might have been a tragedy turned into farce when it was discovered that the man with the limp merely had bandy legs and was, in addition, a police informer.

Thanks to the vigilance of the Netherlands police the arrest of the conspirators had nipped the plot in the bud. Nevertheless Wellington was in a quandary. However absurd the plot, his duty was to protect the Czar and to protect him in face of Alexander's known dislike of any protection. Finally, feeling that a certain degree of ridicule attached to precautions, the Duke advised their not being adopted.

'With miscreants such as those with whom we have the misfortune to deal,' he said, 'it is better to incur some risk rather than appear to be afraid of them.'

He advised that, in case of need, the King of the Netherlands should merely station cavalry and gendarmerie on the high road from Liège to Brussels as the Czar would most positively refuse any escort.

Similar discreet arrangements should be made for the Czar's safety during his stay in Brussels, where his habit of walking about alone would be more imprudent than in a smaller city like Aix-la-Chapelle.

Castlereagh wrote the last amen to the affair, when he said that he must render justice to the Czar and his *faiseurs*; they had been most handsomely anxious to court an irreparable breach with the Jacobins of all countries,

'The plot at Brussels is sufficient to prove that they begin to discover that His Imperial Majesty is not disposed to enlist in their service.'

One person only was involved in the protocol concerning the detention of Napoleon and also in the plot to kidnap Alexander. Now, in its closing stages, the congress turned its attention to a people, to the liberation of the Jews. That they were persuaded to do so was due to the unremitting efforts of the Reverend Lewis Way and to Alexander.

'Every sage, wit and saint jostled shoulders with every crank and freak in Christendom,' said Way himself, 'and each at Aix-la-Chapelle had some project to further, some object to obtain.'

In whatever class Way put himself he was undoubtedly the most energetic of all who came to Aix to plead the cause they had at heart, but few were so fortunate as to have gained the ear of Alexander. This Way had been successful in doing earlier in the year when he journeyed in the hope of seeing the Czar to St Petersburg and later to the Crimea.

Lewis Way by an extraordinary series of chances had inherited from an eponymous stranger a vast fortune, the bulk of which he devoted to his chosen life's work, the conversion of the Jews. By profession a barrister, he had taken Holy Orders the better to fulfil his task. Way was no mystic like the Baronne de Krüdener but a man of real piety and religious feeling which naturally attracted Alexander when Way was brought to his notice.

Both in St Petersburg and the Crimea Way was privileged to have long conversations with the Czar on religion, occasions when Alexander would reach for his much worn Bible to read aloud some favourite passages. Especially dear to the Czar was the 91st psalm, whose verses brought him inspiration and comfort—'He that dwelleth in the secret place of the Most High shall abide under the shadow of the Almighty.'

Although Alexander did not share Way's optimism about the possibility of converting the Jews to Christianity he respected his zeal and was sufficiently impressed by his sincerity to assure him of his own aid. He professed himself as prepared to make special provision for converts in his dominions.

The congress at Aix-la-Chapelle offered Way the opportunity of a wider forum for his projects. Here he renewed acquaintance with the Czar, whom he found 'dearer than ever' and eager to do everything in his power to assist him. Together they spent much time working on the manifesto which Nesselrode had instructed Way to prepare. Alexander himself read and fully approved all Way's documents and arranged for them to be brought to the attention of the congress. Small wonder that, when Way saw Lawrence's portrait of the Czar, he exclaimed enthusiastically,

'It ought to do for a head of St Michael, so full is it of spirit and benevolence.'

Way's all too well-known enthusiasm caused his uncle, Edward Cooke, to write apologetically to Castlereagh,

'I do not suppose you can have given much attention to the wild schemes of my nephew, Mr Way. The Czar, who knows how to mix piety and self-interest, and is as political as he is chimerical, has been flattering his vanity, and will, I fear, continue to do so.'

Cooke was doing less than justice either to the Czar or to his nephew. Only cynics could throw cold water on the Czar's religious sincerity. What political advantage it could be to him to help emancipate a scorned and downtrodden people whose advocates were few is a mystery perhaps Edward Cooke could solve. He had little concern with the fact that Alexander might be looking to gain a seat in heaven.

Way's schemes were by no means as wild as his uncle alleged. For the time being he had discarded all thoughts of conversion and now sought only to repair the damaged clause in the Final Act of the Congress of Vienna whose alteration had frustrated the gradual extension of civil rights to the Jews of Germany.

Two memoirs, 'dedicated and presented to Their Imperial and Royal Majesties assembled at the Congress of Aix-la-Chapelle', incorporated Way's arguments. To lend greater weight to his own views he co-opted the help of several writers on the Jewish question, among them the veteran champion of the Jews, the Protestant pastor Dohm, who had come to Aix to support Way. Dohm had written that:

'The oppression experienced by the Jews in nearly every country since the extinction of their own state, is in contradiction to humanity, to the Christian religion and above all to the principles of wise policy.

'The moral and political depravity of which the Jews are accused does not arise from errors peculiar to this nation, but to the state of oppression, servitude and scorn in which the Jews were placed for so many centuries.'

Alexander kept his promise nobly to Way, who was allowed to expound his theories, of which the keynote was tolerance, to the assembled sovereigns together with their ministers.

'The final re-establishment of the Jews in their native country is a fact based on the infallible authority of the word of God,' declared Way in an eloquent speech. 'It is clear, therefore, that any measures opposed to this gracious dispensation would frustrate the intention of Providence and prove futile. Consequently, the present considerations relate to their intermediate state and the treatment which must be meted out to them during the period of their exile.'

Way insisted that he was concerned only with the moral and social status of the Jews, that he intended to advocate neither blotting out their nationality nor depriving them of the full and free exercise of their religion—a generous concession for a dedicated proselytiser.

On the contrary, the Jews should enjoy civil and social rights in equality with Christians. Governments should instruct their priests to show the greatest charity towards the children of Israel by example as well as precept. They should also encourage arts and crafts, especially agriculture since, when the Jews returned to the land of Israel, they would again become an agrarian nation. Furthermore, Jewish children should be permitted to share education with Christians in the same schools and universities.

To implement a plan essential for the well-being of the Jews a central committee should be established at Frankfort, Berlin, Warsaw or some other place, made up of Christians and enlightened Jews.

The presence of Nathan Mayer Rothschild at Aix-la-Chapelle ensured that all the financial support necessary for Way's proposals would be forthcoming. Rothschild's conversations with Gentz were not concerned only with financial arrangements for France and loans to Austria and Prussia; Gentz had been set to work to write a memorandum for the Frankfort Jews.

Rothschild had his own method of dealing with the non-fulfilment of the clause in the Final Act of Vienna concerning his co-religionists.

He declared publicly that his house would 'refuse to accept bills drawn in any German city where the Jews were denied their treaty rights'.

Whatever part Rothschild was playing through Gentz, official recognition of Way's project came from Alexander. Protocol 44 of the Congress of Aix-la-Chapelle, signed by Metternich, Castlereagh, Wellington, Hardenberg, Bernstorff, Nesselrode and Capo d'Istrias, read as follows:

'Without entering wholly into all the views of the author of this document, the Conference renders justice to its general tendency and to the praiseworthy aim of its proposals. The Plenipotentiaries of Austria and Russia have declared themselves ready in both monarchies to give all the information necessary on this question which might serve to solve a problem of equal concern to the statesman and friend of humanity'.

This resolution was engraved on a diced oblong snuff box of Russian gold and presented to Lewis Way on 25 November.

Way could not but be gratified by his reception at Aix, but he may have hoped for too much from the congress. Only the Austrians and the Russians promised any action and then only of the vaguest. They, apart from Prussia, had the largest Jewish populations on the Continent. Great Britain could give no undertaking; she was still in her equivocal position with regard to the Catholics. The Jews must wait for their own on Catholic emancipation in 1829. Even then it was not until 1858 when, after many setbacks, Lionel de Rothschild was finally enabled to take his seat as a Member of Parliament, that the Jews came to enjoy full civil rights in Great Britain.

Not all Way's time at Aix was spent with the Czar or with memoranda. His fortune and his social connections assured him of entry into the highest diplomatic circles. Although he gave up a concert by Catalani for a long talk with Capo d'Istrias, he was present at another soirée which was attended by all the monarchs. Way met them again at the Duke of Wellington's where, he said, 'dear Alexander shook me by the paw like an old friend' and on another evening he dined with Lord Castlereagh.

Castlereagh did not belong to the select band of Old Etonians with whom Lewis Way 'drank the health of old Eton in champagne' one evening, but enough of them—Planta, Clanwilliam, to say nothing of Wellington—were present at Aix to make it a nostalgic reunion.

From Aix Way carried with him consciousness of a job well done and memories of old associations happily renewed.

The British did not need to show the same reserve with regard to the slave trade as to the emancipation of the Jews. Once again the odious traffic was brought to the attention of the Powers, linked with the activities of the Barbary pirates who endangered shipping in the Mediterranean.

Thomas Clarkson met with less success in his mission than Lewis Way. All the pressure exerted by Great Britain and her dedicated abolitionists failed to secure that unanimous condemnation of the slave trade on which their heart was set. With the connivance of Powers possessed of less sense of social responsibility and less humanity the slave trade flourished unchecked. Castlereagh's proposal of a reciprocal right of search was rejected; no Power was ready to admit British supremacy over every ship afloat.

In the face of this refusal Alexander could hardly expect a welcome to his suggestion of establishing an international squadron in the Mediterranean to control the Barbary pirates. His renewed attempt to get Russian warships into the Mediterranean and the fulfilment of the old Russian dream of a warm water port was too transparent.

By the second week in November it had become rare to see any of the statesmen abroad in Aix-la-Chapelle; they were working at full pressure and already it was clear that they would not be able to meet the deadline set by the sovereigns. Their chief preoccupation was now to debate the final form to be taken by the closing declaration without which no self-respecting assembly could disperse.

Minor matters were finished off; a subsidiary commission consisting of some of the foreign ambassadors at Aix and British and French Foreign Office officials, among them Planta and de Rayneval, completed their examination of individual claims. Wellington concluded his arrangements for evacuating the Allied troops and satisfactorily settled which officers of the Army of Occupation should receive the Orders the Czar had graciously announced his intention of bestowing on them.

When his command came to an end the Duke would not be allowed to remain idle; he had a choice of two employments, to go to Spain as suggested by Russia and France to mediate in the question of the Spanish colonies, or to enter the cabinet as Master General of the Ordnance. Wellington chose the second alternative,

Arthur Wellesley, Duke of Wellington

Armand-Emmanuel du Plessis, Duc de Richelieu,
Prime Minister of France

made more attractive by Liverpool's assurance that he need not follow the party line but was completely at liberty to adopt the conduct he deemed most proper and advisable.

In declining to go to Spain the Duke was not influenced only by his desire to return home after so long an absence. He judged his success in Madrid, where he knew no member of the government, to be less likely than in Paris where he had dealt with people known to him and to whom he was known. Wellington was underlining the truth already endorsed by Castlereagh that,

'By treating personally we speed affairs
More in an hour than they in blundering months'.

An end was in sight for the Conference of Ambassadors in Paris as well as for the Congress at Aix-la-Chapelle. They had one final fling of authority when they wrote to Wellington, complaining that they had not been furnished with the information necessary to sanction the evacuation of certain fortresses. Then the curtain was rung down on their activity. Protocol 47 announced the Four Powers' decision that, as the Second Treaty of Paris might be considered fully and finally executed and, therefore, the chief objects of the ministerial conference in Paris accomplished, the conference would now cease and the protocol thereof be closed.

Metternich was increasingly impatient to be gone, but at his colleagues' request, he postponed for a few days his departure for Brussels. There he was to have important discussions with the King of the Netherlands about a possible military arrangement for the occupation of the frontier fortresses, should the *casus foederis* ever become operative, and also about the Confederation of Germany. The Prince moaned that his four days in Brussels would be hedged with infernal etiquette; he failed to add that all formality would be absent from his reunion with Dorothea Lieven which was the most important but unavowed object of his visit.

The arrival at Aix of his dearly loved daughter, Marie Esterhazy, and her husband enlivened these dog days for Metternich. Together on 12 November they attended Catalani's final concert at the New Redoute, given in aid of the poor of Aix-la-Chapelle, which netted them 10,000 francs. Innocent Herr Meyer, unaware that Catalani was unenviably famous for her extortionate fees and rapacity for money, was ecstatic about her noble and generous heart and how her

6

sublime voice rose heavenwards toward the throne of the Almighty while the earth-gods listened below.

Only now, when the congress was drawing to a close, did the Herr Hofrat begin to take any real interest in its deliberations and the great decisions being made at Aix-la-Chapelle. He did not, of course, neglect the sovereigns who were infected with the general *abschied-stimmung* and hastily remedying any omissions of duty or pleasure. For Frederick William it was a visit to a cashmere factory which he had unaccountably overlooked, for Alexander a long ride incognito into the countryside and, for both, a final review at the Adalbertstor and distribution by Alexander to his Prussian Guard regiment of diamond rings.

For the plenipotentiaries and for Gentz these were the busiest days of their whole two-month stay at Aix. Gentz was drafting innumerable documents but now with the help of de Rayneval and Mounier of the French Foreign Office. Since 9 November, when Richelieu became an equal partner with the others, the Duc was spending his evenings with the Russians, trying to repair the breach in Franco-Russian relations. These sessions with Nesselrode, Capo d'Istrias and Pozzo di Borgo were the only indulgence Gentz now permitted himself although he did snatch a few minutes to visit the Rathaus to see the portraits about which there was such universal enthusiasm. He was gratified that Lawrence expressed a wish to paint his portrait; in Gentz the painter obviously recognized one partially at least of his own kind. Time was lacking at Aix for Gentz to sit for Lawrence and the portrait had to wait on Lawrence's visit to Vienna.

A certain atmosphere of flurry now prevailed over the congress; Gentz worked far into the night to have ready for signature on 15 November the numerous documents which would conclude the Congress of Aix-la-Chapelle. The daily conferences were meeting difficulties particularly tiresome at this stage—the question of the succession to the duchy of Baden proved unexpectedly intractable. News of a financial crisis in Paris once again threw doubts on French stability. Nevertheless all was done in time for the evening session of the congress on 15 November. Not surprisingly it took three hours for all the delegates to sign all the documents; so many annexes were attached to the Protocol of the day.

Annexes A and B were the Notes addressed to and by the Duc de Richelieu concerning the final completion of the General Peace and the invitation to and acceptance by France to take part in the deliberations of the Allied Powers. Annex C was the Final Declaration of the congress, to be communicated to all the Courts of Europe, which, despite strenuous efforts, Castlereagh had not succeeded in avoiding. This annex merely recapitulated briefly the subjects dealt with in greater detail in the Protocol, under three heads—the Treaties signed since 1814 and the convention of 9 October; the Union of the Five Powers and Future Meetings of Sovereigns or their Representatives.

The phraseology of the preamble and the first two Articles of the Protocol clearly showed Alexander's influence. 'Under the auspices of divine Providence' and 'linked by the bonds of Christian unity' the Five Courts were firmly resolved never to depart from the principle of intimate Union whose object was the maintenance of general peace, founded on religious respect for the engagements contained in the Treaties.

Castlereagh's hand was equally visible in the cautious wording of the last article relating to future meetings of the sovereigns or their representatives:

'Should the Powers judge it necessary to establish particular meetings, there to treat in common of their own interests, in so far as they have reference to the object of their present deliberations, the time and place of these meetings shall, on each occasion, be previously fixed by means of diplomatic communications.'

The second paragraph of this article was especially designed to soothe the fears of the secondary States that the Five Powers would arbitrarily interfere in their affairs. It read:

'In the case of these meetings having for their object affairs specially connected with the interests of the other States of Europe, they shall only take place in pursuance of a formal invitation of such of those States as the said affairs may concern, and under the express reservation of their right of direct participation therein, either directly or by their Plenipotentiaries.'

No Power could object to the echo of the Holy Alliance, the clause in which the sovereigns of the Five Courts bound themselves to consecrate 'all their efforts to protect the arts of peace, to increase the internal prosperity of their States, and to awaken those sentiments of religion and morality, whose influence has been too much enfeebled by the misfortunes of the times'.

What would alarm the secondary Courts was any pretension on the part of the Five Courts of the right to discuss their affairs without specific authorization. The Final Declaration was, therefore, at pains to disclaim any such intention in terms stronger than those used in the Protocol. In this document the sovereigns pledged themselves never to depart, either among themselves or in their relations with other states, from the strictest observation of the principles of the Right of Nations, which alone could effectually guarantee the independence of each government and the stability of the general association.

Not annexed to the Final Declaration was the Protocol reserved to the Powers who had signed the Treaty of the Quadruple Alliance on 20 November 1815. While anxious to disclaim hostility to France or to inspire alarm in other states the Protocol nevertheless specifically laid down that the first four articles of the Quadruple Alliance were applicable only in the case of war against France.

Although Richelieu had not succeeded in frustrating a renewal of the Quadruple Alliance France had given her adherence to the Quintuple Alliance. However temporarily, she needed the association which was the only link between her and the other Four Courts. They had the additional tie of the Treaty of Chaumont, the only one Great Britain recognized as entailing definite obligations on her part. France must in her own interest lend her wholehearted support 'to the maintenance of Peace and the guarantee of those transactions on which the Peace is founded and consolidated'.

By a happy accident of timing the evening of 15 November had been chosen by the merchants of Aix-la-Chapelle for a ball in the New Redoutensaal. Satisfaction that their task was virtually over and the prospect of an early departure made the congress personalities particularly gay and relaxed. For once the sovereigns lingered at the ball where Marie Esterhazy repeatedly danced polonaises with Alexander and even with Francis. Her father was amused to see her amazement that he was on such good terms with the Czar. Previously she had only seen them glaring at each other.

Their accord reflected the perfect harmony Metternich believed now existed among the cabinets. This view was somewhat over-optimistic. For Austria everything had certainly worked out for the best; at the moment she wanted nothing from her allies.

Britain's situation was on the whole less satisfactory. She had given her agreement to the main objectives of the congress but at the same time she had clearly shown her reluctance for further commitment in Europe. Castlereagh continued to see the chief threat to peace arising from France but he pinned his faith to the Quadruple Alliance as a powerful deterrent. He hoped that Britain's vigilance would produce a more conciliatory attitude from Russia because he believed that 'there was nothing of which the Czar was so much in awe as the character of Great Britain in Europe'. He flattered himself that Alexander had never yet caught the British at work to any little purpose but, to keep him always in order, Britain must stand upon broad principles which the Czar dare not publicly impede.

No compromise with Alexander was possible on the idea of a European federation which was now his principal concern in foreign affairs. To humour him the British were ready, however, to tolerate the vocabulary which was *sacramental* to the Russians. They would suffer the constant use of words like *legitimate* and *constitutional* so long as they remained words and were not translated into deeds.

France was the chief beneficiary of the congress but, if she ceased to be a threat to Europe, no one would regret the concessions made to her. All in all, as Metternich had decided, the Congress of Aix-la-Chapelle had indeed been a pretty little congress but, never-theless, no one present would really be sorry to part from the rest.

Once again the delegates had travelled far from home, put up with all the boredom, fatigue and inconvenience of long hours spent in a carriage, of sleeping in strange beds, eating unfamiliar food, lodging in other people's houses, always even in their most relaxed conversations being on their guard. Argument about words and phrases, about principles and protocols were all part of doing the job but little account was taken of the personal frictions inevitable in the circumstances, and the irritations which develop as a result of fatigue. And with it all the responsibility, for Castlereagh in particu-lar, to the King, Parliament and people of Great Britain, neither to do nor to say anything prejudicial to their interests.

The praise showered on Castlereagh and Wellington was well merited, a new experience for the Foreign Secretary but not for the Duke; he knew praise to be his due. Lord Bathurst told only half the story when he congratulated Castlereagh on 'the favourable termination of a negotiation of so much delicacy which presented so many difficulties in the way of a satisfactory conclusion'.

The Prince Regent was always able to find the felicitous phrase. Bathurst was charged to convey his entire approbation of Castlereagh's frank and ingenuous conduct in the course of the complicated negotiations in which he had been engaged. His temper and discretion, his spirit of accommodation where principles were not implicated, and his firmness where she might be committed, had enabled Great Britain to maintain at the congress with weight and consideration what the valour of her arms and her unexampled exertions had acquired, and the anxious wish she had uniformly shown to preserve the peace and liberty of Europe which for the common interest she should continue to enjoy.

Castlereagh's epitaph was far from being so adulatory.

From Madrid Sir Henry Wellesley, the British ambassador, voiced his own sincere congratulations on the satisfactory termination to the Congress of Aix-la-Chapelle. The arrangements taken had relieved him from all anxiety as to the alliance which might have been in contemplation in Madrid—in other words the possibility of a Russo-Spanish entente.

Sir Henry's letter again underlined the hazards that must be encountered so that the despatches should get through. Crossing the Pyrenees in winter was no easy matter. 'The messenger charged with your Lordship's despatches arrived in so bad a state of health and has since been so ill, that he was only able to set out to-day, and I fear that he will be a long time on the road.'

Wellington came in for a special meed of praise for his handling of the financial negotiations. He had impressed the French government with such a sense of his justice, impartiality and exertions that he had the gratification of receiving assurances from His Most Christian Majesty that, but for his intervention, the intricate negotiation could not have been satisfactorily concluded.

Praise for Gentz took a more material form—from France 800 ducats and a snuff box, 800 ducats but no snuff box from Russia, instead the coveted Order of St Anne, and from Prussia 800 ducats and the Order of the Red Eagle. England's 'gift' was £700 sterling. Most galling to Gentz was that Francis continued to overlook his merits. He was impelled to write to Metternich complaining about the Emperor's hostility which Metternich answered in a long interview. Possibly Francis did not care much for Gentz' morals. Nevertheless, although Francis' failure to recognize his worth rankled, the two months crowded with work and by no means trouble-free had undoubtedly been the most interesting, agreeable and glorious of his life.

Before the earth-gods left Aix they acted the part of the Olympians, showering Aix like Danaë with gold—for Wellington his field marshals' batons in the Russian, Prussian and Austrian armies, for Oberbürgermeister Guiata a third class of the Prussian Order of the Red Eagle, for the restaurateur of the Redoutensaal a gold box—no one was forgotten.

Of the sad moment when the princes of the earth departed Herr Hofrat Meyer could scarcely bear to write. With them they took the city's liveliest thanks for their graciousness and the honour paid to the ancient royal city of Aix-la-Chapelle.

First of the sovereigns to leave was Alexander, undeterred by the kidnapping plot from going to Brussels. Then Francis turned eastwards for Vienna, leaving affectionate memories behind him at Aix, while with Frederick William to Berlin went the Aacheners' fond hopes of an early return.

Now at last Metternich was free to join Dorothea in Brussels. Then Castlereagh and Richelieu took the Belgian capital as the first stage on their journey to Paris. Richelieu's object in going to Brussels was very different from Metternich's; he wished to see the Czar again and receive his blessing before 'plunging into that frightful abyss of passion, vice and corruption', Paris—but not for long. Neither Alexander nor Wellington had been able to dissuade him from resigning at the end of the congress.

The merchants packed up their wares, the owners again took possession of their houses. Aix-la-Chapelle returned to its normal quiet and Herr Hofrat Meyer picked up his pen to relive in his chronicle of *Aachen der Monarchen* those unforgettable months forever in the city's grateful memory.

In so golden an aura of royalty was the Herr Hofrat bathed that he even found a kind word for the distinguished statesmen who had worked with inexhaustible energy for the good of the entire European continent.

Then there was nothing more to say but to assure the sovereigns that the city's deepest gratitude would accompany them to the grave. In the name of the citizens of Aix-la-Chapelle the Herr Hofrat fulfilled his sacred duty of calling down on the monarchs Heaven's greatest protection and wishing them long and happy years in which to reign. To their continuing favour he recommended the ancient imperial city in which they had re-affirmed their Holy Alliance.

The glorious autumn weather had held out to the end.

CHAPTER X

The Turbulence of Europe

ALMOST before the copyists had finished transcribing the final declaration of the Congress of Aix-la-Chapelle its professed ideals of permanent peace, stability and the repose of the world were seen to be threatened. The years immediately following the congress were of turbulence not tranquillity.

No *casus belli et foederis*, no diplomatic dispute loured over the nations; the turbulence was all internal in origin. Popular unrest and a wave of political assassination swept across Europe like the ten plagues over Egypt, nor could the infection be isolated.

'The world,' commented Metternich, 'was in perfect health in 1789 compared with what it is to-day.'

Almost universal restlessness arose from the clamour for political liberty and social reform, but the aspirations legitimate in developing nations were degraded by the means employed to realize them. Murky activities of secret societies, subversive presses and riotous gatherings rendered serious disservice to their cause.

The statesmen responsible for preserving the tranquillity of Europe had some excuse in confusing desire for reform with rampant revolution. In their bitter experience 'Jacobinism' led to revolution and revolution to war. While they remained convinced of the accuracy of this equation their reactions were dictated less by a punitive spirit than by caution, excessive perhaps but in their eyes justified by what they themselves had seen in twenty-five years of war.

Under the assault first of the revolutionary and then the Imperial armies of France nearly every sovereign in Europe had felt his throne totter. Their survival may have been due less to their own exertions than to Napoleon's mistakes, but what more natural than that they should make strenuous efforts to preserve that which at times they had been in imminent danger of losing altogether?

6*

War had not yet so far receded that Austria could forget that the French had twice dictated peace from Vienna itself. Jena and Napoleon's Berlin decrees festered deep in the heart of Prussia. The ravages of war in Russia were not obliterated by Alexander's expressed willingness to forgive them. France was the worst sufferer of all, but in Europe there was no country which did not mourn a lost generation and its unborn sons.

Great Britain's experience of war alone differed from that of the Continental nations. The line of martello towers strung along her southern coasts was never put into service to repel an invader. Patriotic volunteers and fencibles had drilled in handsome scarlet jackets frogged with gold lace, yeomanry had marched bellowing,

'We be the King's men, hale and hearty,
Marching to meet one Buonaparty.'

None of them met the enemy on his own soil.

England, her frontier the sea guarded by her impregnable wooden walls, was psychologically divided from these countries of Europe whose frontiers, made by man not nature, had been so constantly overrun. A nation immune from invasion since 1066 could never understand the trauma of hostile occupation, could not in her blood and bones feel what the Continent understood as war. Fear of further damage to her economy was possibly less responsible for British apprehension of further conflict in Europe than that her perpetual safety could not be guaranteed.

After Waterloo, to the statesmen war in the body politic was what fever is in the human body; the germs might never perhaps be wholly eliminated but at least fresh outbreaks of fever could be anticipated, and their duration and gravity moderated, by sedatives chosen with discernment and applied with art.

Since the prevention of war was the imperative duty of the watch-dogs of Europe they were obliged to seize any means to hand of scotching 'Jacobinical' disturbance in the egg. If repression was the price of keeping war at bay then repression was defensible.

Every ear in Europe was strained to France for rumblings of the revolutionary spirit, but the tocsin sounded first in Germany. In August 1819 August von Kotzebue, dramatist, publicist, Russian agent and reactionary, was stabbed to death at Mannheim in Baden by a fanatical student, Carl Sand.

Metternich refused to believe that the murder was an isolated act done in a state of exaltation; he saw it as the initial attack on the existing system by some secret society poised for further outrages. Hardenberg feared that, were this contagion allowed to spread unchecked, civilized states would be precipitated into an abyss of calamity. Both German Chancellors agreed that jealous defence of the sovereigns' authority was the only safeguard against disorder; any concession to the spirit of the times must be avoided lest appetite grow by what it fed on.

Metternich's reaction to Kotzebue's murder was the summoning of the States of Germany to meet at Carlsbad to concert measures of restraint on the press and universities where the liberal virus was most active and the cry all for representative institutions on the French and British models. Constitutions founded on the ancient customs of Germany had been contemplated when the German Confederation was created by the Congress of Vienna, but not the kind which England and France had won by bloody revolutions—embodying popular elections, dual Chambers, ministerial responsibility and daily reports of debates. Similar institutions in Germany would totally undermine the sovereigns' authority, lead to revolutionary outbreaks and finally to the disruption of the Confederation itself with incalculable consequences to the European system.

By a series of repressive decrees Metternich succeeded in straitjacketing the most turbulent elements of 'Jacobinism', acts generally approved by the nervous states of Germany. Hanover and Württemberg defied Metternich by granting simulacra of representative constitutions to their peoples but in Prussia the constitution gestating for years never reached its term.

Alexander was naturally furious at the murder of his agent while all his ministers and state counsellors saw it as a threat to themselves but what, asked Varnhagen von Ense, could the Czar with all his power do? Against whom could he turn? Varnhagen was himself so distressed by the news that he was unable to eat his dinner. His wife, the famous Rahel, was overcome by an attack of nerves.

The severest critic of the Carlsbad resolutions, probably because he had no share in them, sneered Gentz, was Capo d'Istrias. 'He is especially piqued that no one asked his advice in a matter in which he is quite incapable of giving it.'

The Czar's reaction was less hysterical than Rahel's to Kotzebue's murder and more prudent than Capo d'Istrias' to the Carlsbad decrees. A tranquil Germany was essential to that European system which he continued to hold as sacred and indestructible. He must be the sincere friend of any measures taken to ensure the repose of Europe.

Castlereagh saw 'with lively satisfaction' that, even with no consultation between Russia and England, Alexander's opinions on German affairs coincided with his own views and principles. Both Courts recognized the importance of not giving even the appearance of intervention in German affairs, although the British cabinet manifested some sympathy with the Carlsbad decrees and showed the same friendly interest when the talks were transferred to Vienna.

Alexander, suspicious of the rapprochement between Austria and Prussia, did not favour Metternich's avowed object of strengthening the federative system in Germany which might ultimately constitute a threat to Russia. Nevertheless in Vienna it was being suggested that the Quadruple Alliance was merely a great skeleton from which a Triple Alliance would emerge between the three central Powers. That Alliance did later take shape as the *Dreikaiserbund* when Bismarck not Metternich was the arbiter of Europe and when, as foreseen by Talleyrand at Vienna, Prussia had thrust her way into European predominance at the expense of Austria.

Prussia was now in no position to protest against Metternich's unavowed object of magnifying Austrian influence, to make her in fact as well as name 'the House of Lords of Europe'. Hardenberg was too old and too infirm to challenge Metternich's pretension. He was finding sufficient difficulty in absorbing into Prussia the new territories acquired at Vienna, different in habits, pursuits and religion. As Lord Clancarty observed,

'It is never an easy thing or the work of a moment to reconcile a people to a new government placed over them by others. We all know how much the better part of a century it took to reconcile Scotland to her union with England.'

Although Prussia's weakness obliged her in foreign policy to follow Austria's lead she found a subtle riposte to Austrian claims to supremacy. By gradually binding the smaller economically unviable German states to herself in a *Zollverein*, or customs union, she substituted economic for diplomatic advantage. By the time Austria awoke to the fact that economics rather than politics had become the dominant force in international affairs, it was too late; Prussia had stolen a march on her.

Metternich now argued that Austria, by virtue of her central position in Europe, was a vital *point d'appui*; any weakening of this stronghold might well cause the collapse of the ancient structure of Europe. His first object was to keep Austria secure from the symptoms of contagious fever now obvious in Europe.

'I need all my faculties to keep Austria on an even keel,' he wrote. 'Any false step, even any misguided view of the Austrian cabinet could have fatal consequences.'

At this moment the British were too occupied at home to spare much time for manœuvres abroad. The public no longer had any interest in foreign affairs; they were concerned only with liberty, social and political progress, and reform. The cabinet, so far from riding out its storms, as Gentz had confidently predicted, in 1819 met crises even graver than those of 1817. The fault lay, in Pozzo di Borgo's contemptuous estimation, in the weakness and irritability of the ministers governing a nation of turbulent proletarians and an opposition of factious aristocrats.

The cabinet's most perilous moment came in August 1819. Whoever coined the word, 'Peterloo', understood the value of a slogan. The suppression by the military of a reformers' meeting at St Peter's Fields in Manchester assumed in the eyes of government and people a significance almost as great as the fall of the Bastille in 1789.

Retaliatory measures were even more severe than those taken in 1817. Metternich was justified in preening himself that the 'Six Acts' passed to suppress disorder after the 'massacre' of Peterloo were modelled on the Carlsbad decrees. Castlereagh hoped that these would be equally successful. He wrote to the Prince:

'Your Highness will observe that, although we have made an immense progress against radicalism, the monster still lives, and shows himself in new shapes; but we do not despair of crushing him by time and perseverance. . . . Wherever the mischief in its labyrinth breaks forth, it presents little real danger, whilst it furnishes the means of making those salutary examples which are so difficult whilst treason works in secrecy, and does not disclose itself in overt acts.'

What was overt and clamorous was protest, particularly from the

poets who, as 'the unacknowledged legislators of the world', took it
upon themselves to pour out their vitriolic verse on the government.
In Leghorn the torrent of Shelley's indignation boiled in his veins as
he anxiously waited to hear how the country would express its sense
of this 'bloody, murderous oppression of its destroyers'.

Castlereagh was always the chief target. Since Liverpool as Prime
Minister and Sidmouth as Home Secretary bore a greater share of
responsibility for repression at home one can only suppose that the
poets found it easier to find a rhyme to Castlereagh than the obvious
one to Liverpool and the difficulty of finding one for Sidmouth.

Castlereagh's satisfaction in suppressing radicalism—Jacobinism
writ differently—was short-lived. As the year 1820 vaulted from
one upheaval to another it was seen to have no frontiers. The question was again urgent as to how far the internal convulsion of any
one country might affect the general tranquillity of Europe.

When revolution in Spain coincided with the new year of 1820
alarm seemed justified. A military junta forced the effete King
Ferdinand to accept the liberal constitution drawn up in 1812 with
terms of universal suffrage, a single legislature and truncation of his
own powers. The most sinister feature of the revolution and most
pregnant with future dangers was its military, not 'Jacobinical'
origin.

Alexander reacted predictably. Wholly committed to the value of
united action, he sprang into the arena to demand that the Quadruple
Alliance fulfil its sacred duty of arresting the torrent devastating
Spain. He urged the examination of the Spanish question either by
the ambassadors of the Four Courts in Paris, together with the
French, or preferably by another sovereigns' reunion.

Either proposal hovered too dangerously close to Alexander's idea
of European government to appeal to Metternich. He came out with
a formal but vague declaration that 'the sovereigns of Europe, unanimously and inviolably resolved to keep the peace at all costs,
would march together without deviation to repel everything which
might disrupt or compromise the existing state of affairs'.

Castlereagh had no intention of marching in a literal sense. He
cited the Duke of Wellington's unflattering opinion of the Spaniards,
based on his unhappy experience during the Peninsular War. The
Duke considered it madness even to contemplate military intervention in a country as impervious to attack and as unconquerable as
Russia. Such intervention would not be welcomed; even he had

found the Spanish resentful of foreign advice and arrogantly averse to their allies.

Any opinion on military matters expressed by the Duke of Wellington carried great weight in Europe. Great Britain must also be attended to where constitutions were involved. Although the British carried some share of moral responsibility for the Spanish constitution framed while they were fighting in the Peninsula, the cabinet was sceptical of the wisdom of imposing by force on a politically immature nation a constitution regarded as too radical for the politically mature British.

In Castlereagh's cool analysis any intervention in Spanish affairs was a chimera. A ministerial conference, still more a sovereigns' meeting, would only intensify public alarm. He scoffed at the idea that Spain, too isolated and weak to cause serious anxiety in other states, was capable of disturbing the tranquillity of Europe.

Once again Castlereagh drew the now familiar rabbit out of his hat. Intervention in Spain was for Russia a purely logistic problem, but the British government had to render account of its actions to Parliament. Whatever reformers might choose to say, that Parliament still had an all-powerful voice when clearly pronounced. In its turn Parliament was responsible to a nation wanting to know the whys and wherefores of foreign policy as well as holding the cause of the Spanish king in horror.

While stressing Britain's attachment to the Quadruple Alliance Castlereagh emphasized that the interest of her allies lay in avoiding angry parliamentary discussions on Continental politics. Since in this instance Britain could not act together with her allies the just and sensible line for them to adopt as the only means of safety for Europe was one of strict neutrality.

After reams of paper had been covered with Notes and admonitions the Powers came round to Gentz' belief that, unless something unforeseen occurred, the Spanish revolution would neither endanger the rest of Europe nor create a greater stir than if it had erupted in the heart of Africa. Spain was left to work out her own destiny unmolested by interference from the Quadruple Alliance.

While Castlereagh was congratulating himself on the great moral change so quickly wrought in England he was obliged to eat his words. Troubles gathered thick and fast round the heads of the government. A conspiracy of extreme radicals to assassinate and mutilate the whole cabinet was discovered at the eleventh hour.

Since political pressure in England rarely takes the form of assassination the Cato Street conspiracy aroused greater indignation than in a country where political murder is endemic.

The cabinet recovered from this evidence of the phoenix properties of 'Jacobinism' only to become involved in a crisis less lethal but almost as unpleasant. On his accession in January 1820 George IV determined to divorce his wife, Caroline of Brunswick, who for too long had plagued him with her extravagant and squalid antics. In demanding a divorce this lecher and *bon vivant* alleged that his imagination was haunted and his rest disturbed by the prospect that the Queen's name should be included in the Litany and that she should receive the benefit of the people's prayers.

The King truculently rejected the cabinet's advice to compromise, threatened dismissal and, to crown the government's humiliation, asked the Austrian ambassador, Prince Esterhazy, to invite Metternich to England to tell his ministers what to do. In face of the King's immovable will the cabinet was impotent. The ministers could only piously entrust their fate to Providence, hoping that on this, as on so many previous occasions, it would vouchsafe them its protection.

Caroline's trial was set on foot. Canning resigned from the cabinet in protest but his colleagues sheltered behind her skirts and lived to fight another day. Lord Liverpool might have echoed the words of the Abbé Sieyès who, when asked what he did during the French revolution, answered simply, 'I survived.' Survival appeared to be Liverpool's chief aim and object, in which he succeeded so well that he remained as Prime Minister until 1827. The nation, shocked into greater calm by the Cato Street conspiracy, was diverted from pursuing the will-o'-the-wisp of political reform to the more immediate and titillating expectation of seeing the Queen of England arraigned for adultery.

To Castlereagh the Queen's trial was particularly vexatious because the visit planned by Metternich before George IV made his irascible remark to Esterhazy he now, with great delicacy, postponed until it should be over. His expressions of solidarity were, however, balm to the wounded souls of the cabinet. A few days of personal intercourse with Metternich Castlereagh felt would have been of great benefit to a proper understanding between England and Austria—certainly the difficulties which arose between them later in the year might have been avoided.

Loss of valuable discussions with the Prince on plans to keep the world at peace was not Castlereagh's only disappointment; he would not now be able to observe for himself the intriguing change in Metternich. Stewart reported, confirming what Gentz had already remarked, that Metternich was a very different man from what he had been at Aix-la-Chapelle or Vienna:

'His labour is incessant now. He has laid aside all trivial passions, neither play, women nor conviviality engross him. The two former he has quite abandoned, and he seldom goes into society. His whole time and mind is devoted to his *cabinet de travail*, which he scarcely ever leaves. His work of late has been gigantic, and yet he avails himself of no occasion to shorten business or get rid of a question. He always hangs on to a contested point as to an old friend whom he cannot shake off.'

To this transformed Metternich Castlereagh would have been happy to unburden himself *on the spot* of the many peculiarities attending the management of foreign affairs in Britain—above all why greater circumspection was demanded of a British Foreign Secretary than of his colleagues abroad, especially with regard to France, so long a rival and enemy of Great Britain.

According to Gentz, resistance to France was the one absorbing care, the beginning and end of British statesmanship, but French unpredictability did not agitate the British alone. Suspicion and terror in all the Courts of Europe continued to exaggerate every move made by a Frenchman. All eyes were bent on France because the rest of Europe felt that all their misfortunes were her fault. The responsibility for the present and future tranquillity of Europe rested fairly and squarely on France.

Yet, while Europe stood tremulously on the *qui vive*, hourly anticipating an outbreak of the revolutionary spirit in France, the French refused to gratify her. No nation more than the French was sensitive to the connection between internal upheaval and foreign war. No country therefore had a greater interest in preserving peace. Whoever tried to disturb the repose of France was certain of incurring the hostility of the nation at large.

Those who nourished the criminal hope of troubling both French and European tranquillity found no delight in the erstwhile nursery of revolution. The general malaise affected the French only slightly; disturbances at the Ecole de Droit in Paris were recognized for what they were, mere youthful high spirits in the student body.

France's financial state, once the balance of her war indemnity had been settled, was equal or superior to that of any other country in Europe, not excluding Great Britain, burdened with a huge public debt and overwhelming taxes. Since the withdrawal of the Army of Occupation the French administration had shown itself inoffensive and irreproachable in its relations with other Powers.

Strongest proof of essential French stability was her smooth weathering of the governmental crisis after the Congress of Aix-la-Chapelle. The Duc de Richelieu, disdaining the laurels he had won at Aix and ignoring the royal family's expressed fear that his resignation presaged their ruin, left office on 28 December 1818 as he had pledged himself to do. Once again his word was seen to be as good as a treaty.

Richelieu had declared himself ready to surrender all the decorations lavished on him and all the snuff boxes with which he had been deluged to return to Russia, but his delicacy was too great to accept the Czar's cordial invitation to do so; the Duc felt he would seem to be deserting France. Instead, to Pozzo di Borgo's indignation, he left Paris, which he held in such horror that he hoped never to come back, to roam 'like a vagabond' about Italy and the French provinces. Out of Paris he was gratified to find that business took precedence of politics, making money of greater moment than the making and unmaking of governments. Revolution was unthinkable in the provinces; it could happen only in Paris.

Richelieu's resignation was bewailed by no one more than Pozzo di Borgo. With France in the hollow of his hand and the acclaim of all Europe in his ears the Duc had thrown it all away! Bitterly Pozzo hoped that, for the Duc's own peace of mind, he would never know what harm he had done to the world—and especially to Pozzo himself whose influence was now substantially diminished.

Alexander's disapproval of Richelieu's resignation was as deep as, if less vehement than, Pozzo's. Both Great Britain and Austria shared the Czar's opinion even though they remained mute about the change in government. Everyone was agog to know who the new Prime Minister would be. According to Alexander Baring, in Paris to finalize details of his loan to France, the change of government had been five long acts of drama and the principal entertainment of the Parisians.

As effective head of the new government Louis XVIII chose his favourite, the Comte Decazes. The question then agitating Europe was whether he would be equal to the position into which he had dexterously forced himself, or whether his talents were good only for intrigue and legerdemain. Alexander had little confidence in Decazes while Francis, whose hostility to France was unabated, expressed doubts as to whether France was as sound as she appeared to be. No one, however, saw any cause for intervention in French internal affairs even when with dramatic suddenness the spotlights which had been switched on Spain and Great Britain swivelled back again to France.

On 13 February 1820 the Duc de Berri, the white hope of the Bourbons, was assassinated on his way to the Opéra. Although prodigally fruitful of illegitimate children, de Berri had so far produced only one legitimate daughter. The Duchesse de Berri was, however, pregnant. When later in the year she gave birth to a posthumous son, the Duke of Wellington's prediction that the family of Louis XV would not continue to reign in France seemed unlikely to be realized. The Duke was, of course, right. The young Duc de Bordeaux never reigned.

Louvel, the Duc's assassin, had acted purely on his own initiative but he was known to have Bonapartist sympathies. From 1815 onwards sporadic Bonapartist plots had broken out all over France, individually insignificant but collectively a source of anxiety. Was Louvel's deed the herald of a major Bonapartist uprising was Europe's anxious question.

In St Petersburg Alexander adjured the French ambassador, 'Watch out for yourselves, watch out carefully, because it is in Paris, in your own centre, that the real heart of these terrible and frequent revolutionary outbursts is to be found.'

So deplorable an event as de Berri's assassination might have been expected from a nation as gangrened as France! The Czar, with no evidence to support his belief, was convinced that Louvel had criminal connections with Carl Sand. According to Alexander, France had reached such a degree of corruption and immorality that the most impious and sacrilegious maxims could be spread abroad not only with impunity and effrontery, but with certitude of success. The immediate effect of the murder was to arouse fears that new and very great misfortunes were preparing for France.

Pozzo's despatches painted the government's situation in the most gloomy colours. He shared Francis' scepticism about French tranquillity: France was in the hands of people imbued with the interests and spirit of her old army and of anarchists, but Metternich would not concede that the dangers of Bonapartism were greater in France than in Austria. Napoleon's health was known to be declining. When he died then the Duc de Reichstadt would be at the fulcrum of a whirlpool.

De Berri's assassination meant more than a grievous loss to the French royal family. The Ultras triumphed, all hope of any reconciliation between them and the liberals died and, in the ensuing reaction, the rising tide of Bonapartism ebbed. Against his will and with bitter tears Louis XVIII was forced to dismiss Decazes, on whom as Minister of Police fell the major share of blame for de Berri's murder.

Choice of a new Prime Minister wavered briefly between Talleyrand and Richelieu who, despite all his protestations, had returned to Paris. Once again Talleyrand, anathema to Louis XVIII, was passed over and Richelieu accepted office as his painful patriotic duty, but now in a different spirit. With no less longing for the shores of the Black Sea he reconciled himself to the waters of Babylon. He showed so much energy, courage and resolution in the conduct of affairs as to be almost unrecognizable as the nervous and irritable man he had been during his first term as Prime Minister.

With Richelieu back as head of the government almost regretfully the Powers could see no occasion for intervention in France. Should the monarchy be upset to be succeeded by a revolutionary régime France should not be surprised to see a new coalition forming against her but, until agitation in France threatened the peace of Europe, she must be left alone.

The expected thaw in Russo-French relations failed to take place; Alexander's sensitivity to the accusation of the French press that he seated and unseated French ministers at will kept the temperature near freezing point. The Czar was equally angry at the allegation that both countries' aims and policies were running in such close harness as to make it possible that they would withdraw into an isolation overturning the general European system.

Much that was attributed to Alexander personally was well known in inner diplomatic circles to be the work of the 'intriguing ministers of the North', especially Capo d'Istrias and Pozzo di Borgo. To Gentz it was a mystery why the Czar of Russia, 'incontestably one of the greatest men of his times and one of the greatest sovereigns of modern history', permitted his ministers abroad to speak with different voices while at home his ministers showed such independence, a singular phenomenon in an absolute monarchy, particularly under a sovereign of such personal superiority as Alexander.

Omnipotence is not necessarily omniscience. In council his ministers were obliged to take the Czar's directive but in their correspondence they allowed themselves greater liberty. Chief culprit was Pozzo di Borgo. No amount of remonstrance could make him subdue his French loyalties to his duty to Russia. Repeatedly he now had to be reminded that, as Minister of Russia, he must act with great restraint towards Richelieu since in the public mind their personal intimacy and official policy could not be separated. Pozzo was not suddenly to reverse his distant relations with Decazes' government because Richelieu was now Prime Minister; he might see the Duc frequently, their conversations could be frank but all must be in secret.

The warnings were timely because rancour between persons was again distrust of policies. Since the dissolution of their Conference the ambassadors in Paris had little to do in common except discuss the eternal problem of the Spanish colonies until Pozzo di Borgo resumed his witch-hunt of Sir Charles Stuart. He now had the support of Baron Vincent who bayed the louder because Metternich was anti-Stuart and pressing for his recall.

With time the tale of Sir Charles's iniquities had grown longer; he had embraced Decazes' ministry wholeheartedly because it promised the end of Russian influence in France; now he was talking Richelieu down; the Duc himself was amazed by his conduct. Wellington had openly blamed Stuart for his injudicious behaviour about the Spanish revolution. Castlereagh, while disapproving of Stuart, kept him in Paris so that everyone should be on the *qui vive*, to the great detriment of affairs and his colleagues' discomfiture.

In vain did his cabinet instruct Pozzo to give his relations with Stuart at least the appearance of confidence and intimacy. An unfortunately timed shrugging of Sir Charles's shoulders triggered off Pozzo's most determined attack and diplomatic activity almost as great as that employed to maintain the tranquillity of Europe.

Castlereagh, at Lieven's request, inspired by Nesselrode, urged by Pozzo di Borgo, wearily instituted an investigation into Stuart's conduct in an effort to keep the peace among the turbulent ambassadors in Paris. Pozzo rejoiced that, if Stuart was recalled, his colleagues would be able to 'speak, to confer, to understand one another and communicate their most intimate thoughts without interference; their intercourse would be all good with nothing odious attached to it'.

Pozzo's joy was premature. After an official investigation almost as delicate as the one concerning Queen Caroline the storm blew itself out; Sir Charles was reprieved to remain in Paris glaring at Pozzo di Borgo until 1830.

Harmony among the Allied representatives in Paris was now more than ever imperative because a permanent ministerial conference was again on the *tapis*; nothing however as radical as the European bureau mooted in 1815 was suggested. Metternich disliked the idea of a standing conference although he conceded its usefulness as a confidential point of contact for discussion of interests linked to the Quadruple Alliance, but not if its seat was Paris.

His counter-proposal of an association of the ministers of the Four Courts accredited to Vienna was too transparent a manœuvre to ensure Austrian influence to be seriously considered.

By raising the still small voice of common sense Capo d'Istrias finally quashed the project and once again the nucleus of a centre for European negotiation was rejected. What action, asked Capo, would these ministers take if their respective cabinets were not agreed on what *they* wanted to do and say?

The unanimity of views among the Powers, once assumed, could no longer be relied on—yet one more sign that, with everyone but Alexander, the Quadruple Alliance was going very much out of fashion. Already in treating the Spanish question the uniform direction from which the Alliance drew its force was seen to be relaxed.

Pozzo di Borgo, relentlessly hammering out his personal theme of *perfide Albion*, held Britain responsible for weakening the Quadruple Alliance. Everyone was the victim of the English malaise, due to the egoism and disagreements of the cabinet. More elevated and frank conduct would serve Britain better than all the palpable finesse and duplicity which had for so long characterized her. Britain, while ostensibly still closely associated with Europe, was daily increasing her isolation; only when a *casus belli et foederis* threatened her own existence would she make common cause with her allies. In the meantime all must give way to English interests and convenience, however transitory—thereafter the world could arrange itself as it pleased.

Notwithstanding his prejudices Pozzo was an acute political observer. His language might have been more temperate, his bias less obvious; his conclusions were none the less just. Great Britain felt that she now had little of common interest with the Continent. Only with Austria did she feel much sympathy, mainly because of the friendship between Castlereagh and Metternich rather than from any real community of purpose.

This intimacy between the two statesmen was precisely what aroused the suspicions of the Russian ministers under the influence of Pozzo's sneers at the pusillanimity of the British cabinet. Just how far, they asked, did the confidence existing between Castlereagh and Metternich agree with the principles of the general alliance of one for all and all for one? Would Great Britain and Austria disclose to Russia everything in the way in which Russia openly communicated to them her slightest démarche?

Both Alexander and Castlereagh answered these questions in the late spring of 1820 in circulars to their ambassadors abroad. Once again Alexander exhorted the Russians to use their influence with the Courts to which they were accredited to preserve the general alliance, the letter of the treaties and the inviolability of the engagements undertaken.

The general system, said the Czar, was the logical outcome of rights and obligations consecrated by the treaties and acts of Vienna, Paris and Aix-la-Chapelle; no deviation from these premises was permissible.

'The doctrine of Aix-la-Chapelle as a rule of conduct applies without distinction to all your official relations with the French government, with your colleagues, the ministers of the Allied Powers, and the affairs which are confided to you in common,'

so Nesselrode wrote at the Czar's dictation to Pozzo di Borgo.

Alexander himself took up the cudgels in defence of the European system. Solidarity and respect for the engagements into which all the Powers of Europe had entered required them to act against any state seeking to destroy the integrity of the rights on which the peace of the world reposed.

The Czar strenuously refuted the idea that the alliance was a pious abstraction, nor did it veil any colossal ambition. It ruled out the preponderance of any one nation and cast ambition into the void. The Quadruple Alliance was not designed to endow the cabinets of Great Britain, Austria, Prussia and Russia with dictatorship of both hemispheres, still less was it a league of sovereigns representing absolute power directed against nations aspiring to the benefits of legal government. On the contrary, all acts and treaties were founded on the right of nations to lawful and regular administration.

Alexander reiterated his intention of extending the benefits of a representative system to the whole of the Russian empire. He was still saying that 'liberal principles alone can form the basis of a nation's happiness'.

Sir Charles Bagot, Lord Cathcart's successor as ambassador to St Petersburg, refused to credit Alexander's sincerity. In the teeth of the Czar's strenuous insistence on his devotion to the Quadruple Alliance Bagot was convinced that Russia wished to shake off its inconvenience by extending and generalizing it as much as possible. Lamb in Munich echoed Bagot; Russia's object was to embroil everything.

Castlereagh still held tenaciously to his conviction that only embarrassment could result from generalizing the true and correct principles of the Quadruple Alliance. Bagot was instructed to decline, but in a manner least likely to give umbrage to the Czar's personal feelings, his renewed overtures for transforming the Treaty of the Holy Alliance into a treaty of general guarantee among all the European Powers. Castlereagh apparently forgot that all the European Powers, with the exception of Great Britain, had already declared their adherence to the Holy Alliance and that the Treaty of Chaumont had laid down that the guarantees of mutual security given by the Four Powers to one another might at some future date be extended to the rest of Europe. About Alexander's wishes to extend the Quadruple Alliance there was nothing new; he had already put the suggestion forward at Aix-la-Chapelle.

In an age when personalities dominated policies the great misfortune for Europe was the inability of Castlereagh and Alexander to get alongside each other. Castlereagh was unable to see the genuine idealism beneath the autocratic surface which hid a basic insecurity while the Czar was wholly out of sympathy with Castlereagh's cold pragmatism. Castlereagh mistakenly believed that there was nothing of which Alexander stood so much in awe as the character of Great Britain in Europe and that he dared not publicly impede the British firm stance upon broad principles. Had he approached the Czar with greater suavity and less stiff a back compromise might have been reached between two viewpoints diametrically opposed. In the event Metternich prevailed where Castlereagh did not attempt to succeed.

Now, by his own instructions to British ambassadors abroad, Castlereagh adopted the lofty tone which was so disliked by the Continental Powers. He invited the principal cabinets to attend to the means of security within their reach 'to the improvement of which, especially against the danger of military revolt their immediate efforts should be directed instead of occupying themselves with distant considerations of policy, over which they could, in point of fact, exercise no effectual control whatsoever'.

While pouring icy water on Alexander's dreams Castlereagh did admit that many of his 'wilder notions' were conceived under the influence of Capo d'Istrias, whom he disliked as a tiresome logician and the *coryphée* of liberalism. Capo's reciprocal dislike had been somewhat modified in the course of a visit to England in 1819 but he himself continued to be unpopular everywhere. With Metternich he was in a state of almost open hostility while Francis, speaking to Stewart about him, used language most unbecoming—'scoundrel' and 'good-for-nothing' were the gentlest of the Emperor's expressions. Hardenberg still nursed a grudge against Capo for the trouble his sophisms had given him at Aix-la-Chapelle; the Prussian Chancellor especially deplored Capo's mistaken ideas and opinions which were leading Alexander to act in opposition to his own very good principles.

Gentz successfully tempered praise with malice. Capo d'Istrias was highly intelligent, possessed of almost every virtue but, without wishing anyone harm, was at outs with the whole world. The chief disadvantage for those who had to deal with the Greek was his belief that nothing of moment could happen in Europe without his cooperation. Capo's greatest error of judgment was thinking that, in some chimerical way, liberalism and conservatism could be reconciled and the maintenance of order made compatible with the ascendancy of liberal ideas.

Belief in liberal ideas was put to a sharp test when in July 1820, revolution broke out in Naples, followed in August by revolution in Portugal. The rallying cry was again for a constitution, that same Spanish constitution of 1812 'blindly adopted with all its imperfections in the wild desire of effectuating some theoretical reform in the constitution of the country', sneered Castlereagh.

As in the case of Spain it was the military nature of the revolt which aroused the greatest alarm. If armies were unreliable who would maintain order? What terrible dangers threatened to engulf all governments if a handful of soldiers and their officers, incited by a band of conspirators, could with impunity overthrow public authorities and do as they pleased with throne and state?

Metternich remarked that the ease with which revolutions and constitutions were upsetting nations was increasing to such an extent that soon it would need only a drummer walking up and down to proclaim a constitution in every country in Europe.

This bitter witticism hid Metternich's real fear that revolt in Naples, spawned by revolt in Spain, might spread to the German states. Gentz had never seen him so struck with anything as by this revolution. Although the Carlsbad decrees had apparently been effective in suppressing revolutionary disorder in Germany who knew when the lust for a constitution might burn again?

Nevertheless, at this moment Metternich was looking southward to Italy rather than northward to Germany. Already on the eve of the Spanish revolution Nesselrode had observed that Austria was feeling the weight and price of her Italian crown. How much greater must now be her alarm with revolution rampant next door to her Italian possessions. Everyone agreed that the Neapolitan revolt was an event terrible for Europe in general and highly dangerous for Austria in particular.

Sir William à Court, the British Minister in Naples, warned the cabinet that, although the word 'constitution', which gave the King of Naples an attack of nerves, acted like a charm on the Neapolitans, they were no fitter than the Spaniards to be entrusted with political power. The military aspect of the revolt, Sir William believed, merely cloaked the triumph of 'Jacobinism', the war of poverty against property.

The Powers had for so long been convinced that France was the only secret hotbed of revolution in Europe that they would scarcely credit that conflagration should break out elsewhere. Yet they were aware of the Italian origin of the *Carbonari*, the secret society whose slow fires smouldered all over Europe and were spreading gradually but surely into the Romagna and northwards in Italy.

Byron in Italy fervently embraced the cause of a brave nation 'defending itself against the self-called Holy Alliance, which but combines the vice of hypocrisy with despotism'. Gladly he waved the red, blue and black flag of the *Carbonari*, red for fire, blue for smoke and black for coal. For their eternal hatred against all monarchies, and for the independence of Italy for which they were ready to give their lives, the *Carbonari* found another ally in Shelley. He heaped the vials of his wrath on

> 'Princes, the dregs of their dull race, who flow
> Through public scorn, mud from a muddy spring,
> Rulers who neither see nor feel nor know'

and longed for the free to 'stamp the impious name of "King" into the dust'.

To kings and princes Shelley was somewhat unjust. They all saw and felt and knew what the Neapolitan revolution meant to them. Argument about its origins paled in importance before the means to be taken to suppress this political saturnalia. Clearly agreement was going to be harder to reach than in the case of the Spanish revolution. The new crisis revealed how wide was now divergence among the Powers.

CHAPTER XI

Congress or no Congress

'THALASSA! Thalassa!' cried the Greeks as they came in sight of the Black Sea which saved them from the pursuing armies of Persia.

'A Congress! A Congress!' was Alexander's cry whenever a crisis arose in Europe. Since Aix-la-Chapelle the Czar nourished an almost superstitious faith in the value of a congress as a nostrum for all ills, coupled with the certitude of the magical properties inherent in assembled sovereignty.

Whether the ministers of the absolute monarchies shared the Czar's feelings about their mystique is questionable; they lived at too close quarters to it. Those of constitutional monarchs certainly did not. Even Castlereagh no longer had the same confidence in the efficacy of congresses while his colleagues had no desire for the extra work involved which fell not on Alexander but on themselves.

As for the peoples of Europe, they picked their way through the maze of alliances—Holy, Quadruple and Quintuple—with little understanding of the aims and functions of each, but the Holy Alliance was always an object of suspicion. L. P. E. Bignon, a severe contemporary critic, raged that the autocracy of Napoleon had been exchanged for the oligarchy of the Holy Alliance.

For once the architect of the Holy Alliance and his ministers, Nesselrode and Pozzo di Borgo, spoke with the same voice; they were convinced that only a congress on the lines of Aix-la-Chapelle would give to any resolution about the Neapolitan revolution the full weight and authority of the Powers. The Naples affair was far too grave to be discussed by anyone less than the sovereigns in person. Alone the wisdom and will of the united cabinets, guardians of Europe's social order, could halt a process threatening to all.

Among the Powers there was disagreement only about how this was to be done. What measures could be taken to safeguard their own security without interfering in the right of another nation to alter its own form of government as it pleased? Would moral force suffice or must it be armed intervention?

Austria had a special relationship with Naples. In 1815 King Ferdinand had specifically agreed not to change his country's régime without previous notice to the Court of Vienna, which had a strict obligation to oversee the tranquillity of Italy. Nevertheless Metternich was anxious that the Neapolitan affair should not be regarded as an exclusively Austrian problem but one involving Europe as a whole. He had no intention of marching without his allies' formal approval.

In the earliest stages of international consultation Castlereagh hesitated to commit Great Britain to take or refrain from action in order not to 'embarrass Austria' until Metternich had made up his mind what course to take. Castlereagh believed that the Prince was essentially weakening his position by seeking to drag the Quintuple Alliance into a matter essentially Austrian. His high regard for Metternich was in this instance tempered by regret at his preference for a complicated negotiation rather than a bold and rapid stroke.

With no greater indulgence towards the revolutionary spirit Castlereagh insisted that, since Great Britain was not herself directly menaced, she had no defensible grounds for that intervention in Naples for which the Continental Powers had a reasonable case.

Castlereagh's views about Naples and Spain were identical; in states of the second and third order revolution was less dangerous than if it occurred in the states of any of the Great Powers. Military action involved greater risks to national independence and freedom than the triumph of a revolt which sought to establish them.

Until the British attitude was clarified Metternich had been temporizing. Stewart was now instructed to inform him of what Castlereagh had already told Esterhazy in London. The British government might lament so disastrous an innovation as that in Naples, but it could not take any part forcibly to counteract or controvert it.

Revolution in Naples had exposed Europe's division into two systems, rapidly becoming irreconcilable. One was dedicated to the maintenance of absolute monarchies and repression of the spirit of the age, the other to representative constitutional government. Pozzo di Borgo took a comprehensively gloomy view when he said,

'We live in a time when perverse doctrines and insatiable ambitions try to legitimize any kind of revolt under the cloak of the public weal and the pretext of liberty. They threaten with unremitting persistence and malignity to overthrow all existing governments.'

Capo d'Istrias asked plaintively why the Spaniards and the Neapolitans did not have institutions calculated to ensure their tranquillity. At the same time he made his dislike of Metternich obvious by alleging that Austria had asked for a blank cheque from the other Powers to lay down the law at Naples and, in the name of her allies, to dominate Italy.

Alexander's proposal of a congress was tepidly received. Metternich's reluctance to initiate a lengthy meeting was influenced by Castlereagh's declaration that, in any event, Great Britain's domestic preoccupations would prevent her taking an active part in any reunion. All that Metternich was prepared to admit was a ministerial conference.

This did not please the Czar who then suggested that he and Francis meet alone. He had now transferred to the Emperor the admiration once felt for Napoleon. Alexander was ready for any sacrifice to achieve complete, intimate and cordial agreement with Francis of whose wisdom and integrity he was wholly convinced. To be in opposition to him on any matter whatsoever was intolerable.

Castlereagh, unaware that father complex rather than political affinity dictated Alexander's feeling, had little patience with his hyperbole. Whatever his own continued respect and attachment for the system Castlereagh no longer felt the same eagerness as in 1818 for further reunions of the Powers. He harped always on his dislike of discussions on abstract principles which required material backing to be effective. Above all, when the danger arose not from infraction of treaties but from the internal disorders of independent states, he failed to see the necessity for a sovereigns' reunion.

Stewart was the recipient of Castlereagh's final thoughts on the question of congress or no congress. Austria was justified in collecting her allies' views but her actions must be independent; she must, moreover, satisfy them that she intended no territorial aggrandizement in Italy. Stewart was not to encourage Metternich to hope for British participation in any reunion. He would have Castlereagh's moral support if he broke off diplomatic relations with Naples, but the only contribution Britain could make towards helping Austria was to send a man o'war to Naples to protect the royal family.

Metternich could now be in no doubt of Castlereagh's opposition to a full-scale congress. Stewart, however, needed no reminder that for British entry into a hostile league of the Five Powers, which might decide to use force against the *de facto* government of Naples, Parliamentary consent was necessary and most unlikely to be given.

'The objections to such a system in a government such as ours are insuperable', was Castlereagh's superfluous rider to his instructions to Stewart. A league of such a nature was wholly incompatible with the principle of neutrality towards Naples already declared by Great Britain. The British Minister was not withdrawn; diplomatic relations were maintained with the *de facto* government.

Castlereagh's arguments carried little weight with Alexander, determined now not only to have a congress but also to associate the Spanish with the Neapolitan question. As Metternich continued to hang back and repeat that a congress was useless and impracticable stalemate seemed to have been reached while the revolution continued unchecked in Naples. Alexander now persuaded Louis XVIII to pull his chestnuts out of the fire for him.

The King's dynastic links with the Bourbons in Spain and Naples made him particularly qualified to insist on measures being taken to preserve their thrones intact. The French government condemned the revolution as a criminal enterprise, inadmissible by all principles of right and public morality and a most sinister example for all states.

Louis pressed for a meeting of the Five Powers to concert action and issue a joint declaration in accordance with the undertakings entered into at Aix-la-Chapelle. This was stretching those undertakings rather far since the final Protocol of the Congress specifically stated that:

'In the case of meetings having for their object affairs specially connected with the interests of the other States of Europe, they shall only take place in pursuance of a formal invitation on the part of such of those States as the said affairs may concern, and under the express reservation of their right of direct participation therein, either directly or by their Plenipotentiaries.'

When the King of France declared that a congress alone could endow the decisions which might there be made with the necessary weight he was only partially influenced by the need to steady uneasy French public opinion. By carrying out Alexander's wishes he hoped to restore some at least of the Czar's confidence in France which, since de Berri's assassination, had been considerably undermined.

At this delicate stage of international negotiation when views between cabinets and their embassies abroad were very freely expressed the interception of confidential documents was particularly irritating. The British Minister in Milan complained that Sir William à Court had sent him despatches under flying seal 'for the purpose no doubt of enabling me to make the Austrian authorities here aware generally of the scenes which are passing round them without the delay of going first to Vienna'.

Stewart had his own method of circumventing the black cabinet which opened all letters in the Viennese chancery. When, for lack of an English courier, he was obliged to use a Russian or an Austrian for his despatches he divided them up so that there was no continuity in the text. Reports from secret agents for transmission to London must wait on the arrival or passing of an English courier.

Similar complaints went from St Petersburg to Paris. In Russia the French needed particular care in their choice of communications as here also letters were opened by the secret police. Although several cyphers were in use these were changed frequently to ensure absolute security. As an additional precaution the Baron de Boislecomte had been sent to St Petersburg to take charge of all secret documents.

Those who used these illicit means of discovering diplomatic secrets put them to good advantage. Metternich had long been employing all his arts to wean Alexander from addiction to those liberal ideas which Gentz said had become synonymous with licence, with revolt and all the disorders sapping the foundations of society.

In the events at Naples and Madrid, in plots and secret societies, Metternich had found the ideal source of bogies to frighten the Czar into resisting the march of free institutions. The Prince, however, realized that, while Capo d'Istrias remained so closely attached to Alexander, his chances of success were slender. Nevertheless, although the Czar had by no means abandoned his large ideas his confidence had been shaken by the disturbances in Europe. He still had faith in the benefits of constitutional government but not in the forcible manner in which they had been introduced into Spain and Naples.

To Lebzeltern, the Austrian ambassador to St Petersburg, Alexander summed up his political credo:

The Chevalier Friedrich von Gentz,
Secretary of the Congresses

Counts Nesselrode, Capo d'Istrias and Pozzo di Borgo,
Russian Secretaries of State and Russian ambassador to France

'As a human being I should like to make the whole world happy and content. As a sovereign I have the additional duty of rigorously maintaining order and discipline, without which no good and even society itself could not exist. A measure of restraint must be imposed on each concession to prevent abuse. That is how I govern this country.'

In reality the Czar was far less concerned with the internal government of Russia than with foreign affairs. Only twice in the year following the Congress of Aix-la-Chapelle had he attended to general political business and he was still absorbed in religion. Towards the end of 1819 a Marseillais mystic, Madame Bouche, arrived at St Petersburg and succeeded in gaining over Alexander the ascendancy once enjoyed by Madame de Krüdener. The death in January 1819 of the Grand Duchess Catherine deprived Alexander of the one person in the world to whom he was deeply attached. More than ever he found his sole consolation in religious mysticism.

His emotional isolation made the Czar concentrate on preserving the Quadruple Alliance, the constant object of his cares and ambitions, the foundation stone of the political edifice constructed in 1813–1815 and further cemented at Aix-la-Chapelle. Of anything which might compromise that alliance the Czar had a profound horror. He now saw the triumph of his wishes.

Throughout the month of September the notion of a congress was still being discountenanced at Vienna and Metternich was still hoping that a ministerial conference would suffice, followed perhaps by a meeting of the two Emperors. Since Alexander was insistent that there should be a congress of sovereigns and nothing but a congress Metternich was forced to give way. Castlereagh's announcement that he himself would not attend was nothing more than a setback; it would not affect the decision to hold the congress.

In face of Castlereagh's determination the French government took several paces backwards, despite the fact that France herself had been instrumental in demanding the congress. Although Franco-British relations were not cordial Richelieu did not want to be in too great contradiction to Great Britain. The Duc seriously displeased the Czar when he also decided neither to be present at the congress himself nor to send his Foreign Minister, Baron Pasquier.

Gentz sneered at the 'political pruderies' of the constitutional governments who were simply afraid of compromising themselves with their parliaments and opposition parties by adopting too

7

boldly the same line and language as the Continental Courts. Alexander agreed that the British cabinet's decision not to give its full co-operation to the sovereigns' meeting in no wise modified the engagements contracted by the other Powers whose dearest interests, in his opinion, demanded their punctilious fulfilment. Since there was no real change in either the outlook or principles of France and Great Britain the general attitude was unlikely to be affected.

Of primary importance was to avoid any suspicion of a schism in the Great Alliance. While Castlereagh harped on Parliament the others continued to stress moral and political unity among the five cabinets. Only this consideration influenced the sovereigns of Austria, Prussia and Russia to temper their conduct and decisions in order not to differ publicly from their *constitutional* allies.

No one showed greater impatience than Pozzo di Borgo with the hesitations and dependence on their parliaments of the constitutional governments which only reinforced Continental antipathy to their régimes; the Powers' first object should be to make common cause against the common enemy. Nesselrode demanded to know why France should take an independent stance when her own safety imperatively required fidelity to an alliance which had twice restored her political life and liberty. Richelieu must be warned of the perils involved in not supporting the Alliance.

Great Britain was severely judged abroad for washing the royal linen in public. In his mingled fury and anxiety George IV had provoked a scandal affecting his own country in a deplorable way. The ineffectual and cowardly cabinet in imminent peril of dismissal was no longer a support but only a nuisance to the Alliance. By admitting the Queen's trial it had lost its point; its sole object now must be to avoid being engulfed in the slime into which it had slipped.

These were Pozzo's strictures but Austria also received the sharp end of his pen. Her vacillations and reluctance to act without universal approbation showed her to be lacking both in moderation and force.

Metternich had, in fact, vacillated so long that he had lost the initiative but, once obliged to consent to the sovereigns' reunion, he intended to reap the maximum benefit therefrom. The Prince made strenuous efforts to get Alexander to agree that the meeting should take place in Vienna but he refused to hear of it; the isolation of a small town was infinitely more favourable than the bustle of a city to the weighty deliberations of a congress. Even Aix-la-Chapelle had proved too distracting. To Alexander's credit he had another motive for objecting to Vienna; he did not wish Francis to incur the expense of yet another congress in his capital.

Francis chose the small town of Troppau (now Opava) on the borders of Russia, Prussia and Austria where, nearly four months after revolution had broken out in Naples, it was at last agreed that the sovereigns should meet on 20 October. The choice of venue was not at all pleasing to Metternich. He calculated that couriers would need eighteen days to reach Paris and twenty for London. This lapse of time would make it almost impossible for any useful directives from the French and British cabinets to reach the representatives they would send to the congress. The question was who they would be and with how much authority they would be endowed.

For the first time in her life Caroline of Brunswick had an important influence on international affairs. In spite of all his disclaimers Castlereagh might perhaps have been persuaded to go in person to Troppau but during the 'awful trial' of the Queen it was impossible for him to leave London. The Duke of Wellington was under the same necessity of staying at home although Alexander would have welcomed his presence and the Duke himself would have liked to go. Sadly Gentz deplored the absence of the only two British ministers whose presence at Troppau could have been really useful. He himself would naturally accompany the Emperor and Metternich as secretary and protocollist of the meeting.

Great Britain would be represented only by Lord Stewart, her ambassador in Vienna, supported by a secondary diplomat, in the event Robert Gordon, secretary of the embassy. Sarcastically Alexander hoped that the advantage of meeting in a small town rather than in Vienna would allay the British fear of being compromised by Lord Stewart's obligation to make a public journey to Troppau.

Frederick William, who had been noticeably silent during the long drawn-out discussions on congress or no congress, would send the Crown Prince ahead of him to Troppau, accompanied by his Foreign Minister, Count Bernstorff.

Richelieu pleaded that he must remain in Paris during the partial elections but he was thought to be influenced by the possibility that Decazes would intrigue against him during his absence as he had done while the Duc was at Aix-la-Chapelle. He may not have liked his office but he did not intend to be jockeyed out of it.

France would be represented at Troppau by the Marquis de Caraman, her ambassador to Vienna, and Comte Auguste de la Ferronays, Minister to St Petersburg. Caraman, Metternich's satellite, was warned to behave with the greatest circumspection and under no pretext whatsoever to become an obstacle to the negotiations. Although junior to Caraman La Ferronays was confidentially informed to regard himself as head of the mission; this was in accordance with Alexander's wishes. When told that France was to be represented at Troppau at ambassadorial level only he asked that her chief delegate should be La Ferronays. The Comte's instructions were to act in concert with the Russian cabinet, a course he had been following since his arrival at St Petersburg in July 1819.

La Ferronays had set out with a distinct advantage. Out of three names submitted to Alexander to select the French minister to Russia the Czar unhesitatingly chose the Comte. In so doing he was fulfilling a promise made on the eve of the battle of Leipzig in October 1813.

As a youth of seventeen Auguste de la Ferronays emigrated from France to eat out his heart for twenty-five years in longing for his country, first in the army of the Prince de Condé and then in England as gentleman in waiting to the Duc de Berri.* From the soul-destroying inertia of the life of a poor exile in London he escaped whenever possible to undertake missions for Louis XVIII, always hazardous and generally hopeless, but at least offering some activity.

When La Ferronays arrived at Leipzig, without a passport or uniform, ill, discouraged, almost penniless, he found all doors closed to him. Finally, through Nesselrode's intervention, he succeeded in seeing the Czar who received him 'with that graciousness and nobility coupled with the simplicity and kindness which make him so beloved'. Nevertheless, La Ferronays' mission was a failure; Alexander could not accede to Louis XVIII's requests but his emissary made a most favourable impression. Later the Czar told Nesselrode that, should the King ever be in a position to send him an ambassador, he hoped it would be La Ferronays. Beyond his wildest expectations in 1819 La Ferronays found himself as Minister of France to St Petersburg.

La Ferronays was an émigré with a difference; he had forgotten

---

* For the early history of Auguste de la Ferronays see *The French Exiles 1789–1815* by Margery Weiner.

what the diehards so tenaciously remembered and learnt much to which they had turned a deaf ear. He was acutely aware of the émigrés' faulty judgment of everything outside themselves and had taken to heart the advice given him in Sweden during one of his foreign missions.

'If ever you do go back to France, you will have to shed your antiquated ideas and your prejudices—the only reform that there is to be made is of yourselves.'

La Ferronays' character had been formed by twenty-five years of precarious living. His ideas were liberal, his principles firm, his integrity unquestioned. Passionate devotion to the Bourbons had not blinded him to their mistakes. In some ways La Ferronays was unfitted for a diplomatic career because he had never learned to dissimulate nor could he shake off his émigré complexes, excessive diffidence and doubts of his own capacity, which was in fact considerable.

In appearance La Ferronays was handsome and he possessed a great deal of quiet charm. His greatest weakness was the *galanterie* which he shared with Alexander although the Czar now said that he had done with 'all that'. Unlike Metternich, Alexander had neither looked for nor found a soul-mate at Aix-la-Chapelle nor was he now known to have any sentimental attachment.

In 1817 a petty quarrel with the Duc de Berri resulted in La Ferronays being sent as French Minister to Denmark where he remained until appointed to St Petersburg. The same personal misfortunes which had dogged him all his life pursued him here. He himself described his novitiate at Petersburg as disagreeable; it was perhaps an understatement. All his goods and chattels were lost on their way to Russia when the ship carrying them was wrecked and a large number of his servants perished. Shortly after his arrival a fire destroyed the Consulate General and the chancery, although the confidential papers were saved. With no private fortune but only debts La Ferronays was obliged to support a large family and a huge mansion on a salary he feared would be inadequate since his daily expense exceeded that of his predecessors.

All anxieties were forgotten when Alexander received La Ferronays as an old friend. The Minister early succeeded in getting on terms with the Czar, despite the deafness which made confidential talks in public difficult.

That her Minister should be favourably regarded by the Czar was a matter of supreme importance to France since La Ferronays' instructions were quite simply to revive the *entente cordiale* previously existing between the two countries. For La Ferronays' benefit his instructions incorporated the French view of the European situation as a whole.

French entry into a quintuple alliance as an equal partner had not caused her to relinquish her hope of breaking up the Quadruple Alliance directed against her. As integral parts of the Quintuple Alliance both the Czar and Louis XVIII wished to preserve it, but Alexander was also deeply attached to the Quadruple Alliance. So long as any doubt existed in his mind about the stability of the Bourbon régime *this* Alliance would remain in suspense but would not be abolished. La Ferronays must use all his persuasion to combat the Quadruple Alliance which compromised French security and he must be on the watch for the enemies of France in St Petersburg.

The Minister's first step must be to woo the Czar back to his former friendship to France for which the climate seemed favourable. Personal warmth between the sovereigns of Russia and Prussia had not prevented official coolness between their countries. Prussia now seemed resigned to playing a secondary role to Austria but she was no longer essential as a counterweight to maintain the system of equilibrium.

Alexander was not now specially attached to any of the Great Powers but his increasing influence might well upset all Europe in the future, largely because of the rivalry between London and St Petersburg. Sooner or later these two Powers would clash head on particularly in those areas where their interests were most in conflict, Asia, Turkey and Persia. By drawing closer to England, perhaps in the hope of forming an alliance with her and Prussia, Austria was trying to insure herself against a possible Russian menace.

Although with a bias in favour of Russia France was in a completely independent position. Quite rightly Alexander, in view of all he had done for France, counted on the nation's gratitude and a kind of deference to his advice. Richelieu's resignation had, however, alarmed the Czar whose instructions to his political agents had immediately changed their character to reveal anxieties and possibly unfavourable dispositions.

Latterly Alexander's feelings towards France appeared to have softened so that the prospects of bringing him back to his former degree of intimacy with her looked brighter. The friendliness he had shown La Ferronays personally should simplify his task and make it more agreeable.

Finally, La Ferronays was to assure the Czar that, so far as possible internal troubles were concerned, France was a dying volcano. Alexander, whose judgment was sane and whose intentions were honest, could not fail to be impressed by all these arguments when adroitly presented to him.

La Ferronays found his task not quite as easy as his home government had so optimistically decided. In the year between his arrival at St Petersburg and the Neapolitan revolution he had many interviews with Alexander who was perfectly frank with him: the Czar was still attached to France although he continued to be worried by her internal state. Anyone who tried to disrupt the indissoluble union created at Aix must be regarded as an enemy to world peace—should France try to isolate herself it would for her be a great misfortune.

La Ferronays countered by assuring the Czar that nothing could either break the union to which he adhered so unwaveringly, nor lead to the supposition that France desired to disturb the peace of Europe. Alexander was still not convinced. Until his confidence in her administration was restored he could not renew his friendship. Pozzo di Borgo was, in fact, inciting Alexander to use his influence to end the Decazes' ministry. On his side La Ferronays informed his government that it would not be difficult to obtain Pozzo's recall should they desire it.

Alexander then spoke of civilian anarchists. Via La Ferronays the Foreign Minister, Baron Pasquier, retorted that France supported any measure which would quench the revolutionary spirit, but nothing was more unjust than the renewal of the Quadruple Alliance which isolated France and threw her back on herself.

Inevitably, given his temperament, La Ferronays was discouraged that he seemed to be making no headway but Capo d'Istrias begged him to be patient and assured him that the Czar had never been better disposed to France, to the King and to himself personally. Then the assassination of the Duc de Berri set La Ferronays' work back because all Alexander's fears about French stability revived with even greater force.

To La Ferronays he showed great personal kindness, sending his condolences by Capo d'Istrias to one inconsolable at the death of

the man who had been 'the support and benefactor of his whole life'.
Long years of shared poverty and exile had forged a friendship which
withstood a temporary disagreement. On his deathbed de Berri
begged that the cross of his own Legion of Honour should be sent
to La Ferronays.

The Minister had to set his grief aside to carry out Pasquier's
urgent exhortation to work to restore the sadly damaged confidence
between Russia and France.

In a country like Russia where there was little distraction, news
from abroad and their own relationships were of paramount importance to the *corps diplomatique*. La Ferronays felt keenly the
burden of an embassy of major importance to France. News from
home, the latest brochures and pamphlets, were essential if he were
not made to seem ridiculous by being unable to deny authoritatively
absurd or disastrous rumours. His crying need was for couriers to
make him independent of foreigners and *infidels*.

Apart from his official difficulties La Ferronays found less unity
among the diplomatists accredited to a great than a small Court like
that of Denmark. The Prussian Minister was rarely seen; his personal
and his country's credit were much reduced. Of his colleagues La
Ferronays liked best the United States ambassador, George
Washington Campbell. Lebzeltern, the Austrian, was out of favour
with the Czar but tried to ingratiate himself with La Ferronays, an
effort which met with no success. He did, however, exercise a certain
amount of influence on Nesselrode, who was inclined to follow the
Austrian line of severe repression of liberalism in opposition to
Capo d'Istrias. La Ferronays was in a minority among his colleagues
in thinking well of the Greek.

While La Ferronays' requests and complaints may have been
tiresome to the French Foreign Ministry, his reports were invaluable,
particularly those about Alexander himself.

La Ferronays had quickly realized the Czar's chief faults, his
liability to mistrust, his tendency to anxiety and suspicion, his
clinging to prejudices and allowing personal considerations to have
a dangerous influence on his decisions. At times La Ferronays
seemed to have borrowed Castlereagh's pen. While it was reassuring
to know that Alexander had no warlike or ambitious intention
anxiety was caused by 'the ardour with which his imagination
seizes and embraces ideas he finds pleasing and the invincible
obstinacy with which to gain his ends he overthrows all obstacles

and braves all the consequences'. Because he was omnipotent he mistook force and violence for a wise and good administration.

Lord Cathcart, brought up in Russia, might claim a better knowledge of the country and its people, but La Ferronays had been formed in a school where the most important lesson had been to learn to survive. His understanding of men was born of necessity since in the past to know one's man had meant for him life or death. To form a just idea of Alexander's character was not easy; no one who judged him could recognize him today:

'His deep dissimulation is less studied and less a defect than the necessary sequel and, so to speak, a consequence of the inconsequences of his character. He talks about the rights of man, of nations, of the duties of a sovereign, as the pupil of a philosopher should and ought to do, but at the same time his most arbitrary wishes are carried out with greater despotism and rigour than Paul I would have done.

'He seizes enthusiastically on an idea which pleases him; he pursues it vigorously, he supports it by all the means of limitless authority, but this idea can itself give place to another to whose realization everything must again be sacrificed and it is this which is alarming in this Prince's character. . . .'

What, asked La Ferronays pertinently, would happen when his religious absorption should make him realize the chimerical nature of his ideas? Would he then not want to make use of the million men he had still under arms, a question which would one day be decided either by a whim or bad advice.

Like Lord Cathcart, La Ferronays issued a warning, again not without contemporary significance, but one which went unheeded because at the time it seemed to lack validity:

'And if,' said La Ferronays, 'with no preparation, no education, without, so to speak, any ideas of civilization, this nation, still brutalized by ignorance and serfdom, should suddenly conceive the idea of liberty and feel a need for it, can one calculate without terror what the consequences could be for this country and perhaps for Europe with the excesses to which this nation of forty million people, still half savage, would be brought when it throws off its chains in the pursuit of independence and liberty of which they have no understanding?'

For the moment the future must take care of itself. Now, on the

7

very eve of the Neapolitan revolution, La Ferronays had come to the conclusion that the Holy Alliance existed only in name. Any weakening of Alexander's links with the world at large was all to the advantage of France which, as Gentz had foreseen, waited only for the opportunity of choosing her own allies and supporters. A Franco-Russian alliance was in the natural order of things and France must arrange her affairs in such a way as to be the power in which Russia put the most confidence.

La Ferronays' task would now be the easier because the hostility once focused exclusively on France was now directed at Russia. His great opportunity would come when the Allied representatives got together round the green table at Troppau, particularly since he himself had observed that the Czar's aversion to Metternich was more pronounced than ever. Carefully fostered by Capo d'Istrias it seemed almost to be hatred.

When La Ferronays set out for Troppau from Warsaw he did so in a comfort unknown in the days when he was obliged to disguise himself as a servant to escape Napoleon's police or, penniless, had walked from one post to another, but now as then his constant travelling companion was anxiety. He feared that the Czar would be extremely displeased that France would be represented by Caraman who was regarded at St Petersburg as Metternich's creature. La Ferronays was equally concerned by public reaction, especially liberal reaction, to two émigrés being entrusted with the interests of France. With some sinking of the heart he wrote to Pasquier:

'However moderate our political opinions may be, whatever the good faith with which M. de Caraman and I have accepted and sworn to maintain the institutions which govern us today, it is none the less true that our long emigration, the principles we professed, the kind of service even that we were able to give to the King's cause, give us in the eyes of a party always ready to suspect intentions, the colour of another party largely accused of being the friend of absolute and arbitrary power.'

Nothing, however, could have been more erroneous than to suspect Auguste de la Ferronays of being an ultra-royalist in spite of his close association with the Duc de Berri and the Comte d'Artois. He himself was mistaken in believing that the Czar was dissatisfied that he should be the French representative at Troppau. On the contrary, although Alexander was displeased that Richelieu himself was not to be there, the possible alternative would have angered him more. To La Ferronays he said,

'I think I ought to tell you, my dear Count, that I do not imagine that, should France decide to send a third plenipotentiary, they would think of M. de Talleyrand. You know that it is impossible for us to understand each other, to agree, or even to get near to each other.'

According to Gentz French anxieties were superfluous. He did not think the French, or indeed the British, delegates would play a very active part in the congress; they were in a perfect state of nullity. In London things were going from bad to worse and the ministers were struggling in painful agony.

In the two short years which had followed the Congress of Aix-la-Chapelle the congress system had suffered a rude shock. Even before the sovereigns and statesmen assembled at Troppau the absence of any senior British and French representation robbed the congress of much of its weight and authority. However brave a face the other Powers put on it, it was already apparent that the congress would be an anticlimax.

CHAPTER XII

The Congress of Troppau

EVERYTHING at Troppau, the scene, the weather, the faces, differed from Aix-la-Chapelle. Here were no spies, no intriguers, no amatory indiscretions, no petitioners, no interruptions to business; no one not concerned with the congress cared to venture into this remote part of Moravia in an autumn verging on winter.

The ancient and compact little town was both clean and bright and the environs pleasant even though the roads, both for walking and driving, were bad. Lodgings were dear but comfortable and unexpectedly suitable for housing so many distinguished guests; physical discomfort would not cause the diplomatists to cut short their stay.

Although the echoes were not as clear as at Aix-la-Chapelle the Troppauers were proud of the noise their town was making in the world; they were as much surprised by their fame as Metternich to find himself at Troppau.

The Prince had once remarked that a congress should always be held in a town where boredom forced one to attend to business. Initially he was sure of having no time to be bored and even hoped to enjoy his stay but Troppau exceeded even his desiderata. It was lacking in any distractions whatsoever; everyone was thrown back on their own resources.

Metternich's early enthusiasm for Troppau was shared by Gentz; he regretted only that the Congress of Aix-la-Chapelle had not been held in such peace and quiet, an almost rural atmosphere ideal for a political gathering. Had his arm not hurt so much he would have felt himself in heaven—happily the pain of his rheumatism was greatly relieved by drinking porter.

With no ceremonies or military parades, no balls or concerts to chronicle, many pages of Baron de Boislecomte's diary of the private lives of the sovereigns at Troppau remained blank. Once he had recorded Alexander's arrival—in Austrian uniform—greeted by a guard of honour from the local garrison, the statutory salute of 101 guns and illumination of the town, the Baron found little to add. Two public events only demanded his taking up his pen—a dinner of fifty covers given by the Emperor of Austria to his august friends and the whole diplomatic corps, and a service with glorious music on All Souls Day in the beautifully illuminated church. On this occasion alone did everyone don their gala uniforms and sport all their orders and decorations.

For the remainder of the time the Emperor of Austria lived in almost invisible domesticity with his current Empress. Frederick William, a late arrival, moped, nursing his unrequited passion for young Georgina Dillon whom he wanted to make his morganatic Duchess of Brandenburg. Alexander, who professed himself never to have been happier, absorbed the little limelight available.

When the Congress assembled on 20 October the weather was all that could be desired, but soon heavy and prolonged rain darkened the sky to the colour of a raven's wing. The streets melted into a sea of mud, soft and greasy like butter, over which, to ensure a safe passage, an ingenious municipality laid down a system of duck boards. This worked very well for one-way traffic but less so when a lady and gentleman met head on, as chivalry demanded that the gentleman step down into the morass to give the lady the right of way. Should one come face to face with the Czar out walking the problem was delicate. A gentleman obviously let him pass but, unless a lady anticipated the Czar by sacrificing to majesty the cleanliness of her skirts, Alexander himself leaped down into the mud.

These encounters would provide admirable material for Mr Cruikshank's caricatures, decided Metternich, until he fell into a pensive vein to deplore the fact that the most virtuous people were constantly plunged in mud. Castlereagh was sunk deep in the mud of the Queen's trial, 'one of the most fatal catastrophes of the times'. Never, sighed the Prince, since the creation had there been such a struggle between duty and repugnance as between politics and mud.

However general the displeasure caused by Castlereagh's attitude to the congress, his absence left a feeling of uneasiness. The delegates were rather in the position of schoolboys left by their master to act on their own initiative. Although exhilarated by their independence they were fearful of his disapproval.

The men of the second order who took the place of the giants,

Castlereagh, Wellington and Richelieu, were no substitutes for their ability and authority—Stewart and Gordon, La Ferronays and Caraman, Lebzeltern, and Krusemark and Golovkine, respectively Prussian and Russian Ministers to Vienna. Caraman especially illustrated the dangers of using local ambassadors as plenipotentiaries. Long residence in a foreign capital tended to make them identify themselves with the policies of the country to which they were accredited rather than the country they represented.

The only members of the old guard present at Troppau were Metternich, Capo d'Istrias, Nesselrode and Bernstorff. For much of the time Bernstorff was housebound by a severe attack of gout and old Hardenberg had to be brought in to second him—but Prussia had ceased to count for much in European councils. Politically speaking Austria and Prussia formed two great divisions of one body. In any event Metternich intended the Congress of Troppau to be his congress where the affairs of Naples were virtually subordinated to his determination to achieve the conquest of Alexander and the destruction of Capo d'Istrias.

Gentz was irritated that the congress had loaded itself up with the unnecessary ballast of the French and British, particularly as the powers of their representatives were not great. Stewart's instructions were to take everything *ad referendum*—to refer everything to the cabinet—and La Ferronays' to give his vote only when the four other Powers were in agreement. Since Stewart decided nothing without reference to London La Ferronays could in effect make little positive contribution to the congress.

As if to gratify Gentz, Stewart was absent more often than he was present at Troppau; in October and November he was rarely there for more than four or five days at a time and away for nearly the whole of December. His scuttling back and forth on the four-day return journey to Vienna at the imperious bidding of his wife, whom he had married in 1819, coupled with his nervous and tormented state, made him the object of mingled pity and mirth. Gentz thought Stewart half and Lady Stewart wholly mad thus to let him drive himself to death. On one occasion, as his carriage was twice overturned, this was almost literally true. Great Britain's influence at the green table, was Gentz' stern verdict, should not be subordinated to Lady Stewart's whims and Lord Stewart's uxoriousness although his presence or absence could have no real bearing on the congress's ultimate decisions.

Stewart's lame excuse for his frequent absences from Troppau was that most of his time was spent in galling idleness since he was excluded from the many conferences in which only Russia, Austria and Prussia took part; it was immaterial, therefore, whether or not he went up and down to Vienna. In fact he never left Troppau without a previous understanding with Metternich. All that he failed to do was possibly 'not giving an impression as to the politicks of Great Britain which, for Metternich's own game, he would rather had been made out'.

Stewart was burking the issue. He knew as well as anyone that as much was achieved by talks outside as inside the conference room. His presence at Troppau was intended as a conciliatory gesture on Britain's part to soften the effect on her allies of her aloofness from this negotiation. His absences and inconsequential behaviour weakened rather than strengthened the cabinet's intention.

La Ferronays, in the same position as Stewart, felt differently. While continuing to deplore his own inexperience in important and complex negotiations his regret was focused on the neutral and passive part he was obliged to play, which accorded ill with the dignity of the Power he represented. Paris, however, continued to ignore his appeal that a third plenipotentiary be sent to Troppau, better qualified and with greater authority.

At the opening plenary session of the congress on 23 October both British and French delegates were present. Metternich made some introductory remarks on the aims and objects of the meeting before opening the discussion to questions of procedure; his own preference was for a simple journal to detail the subjects treated at each meeting, the documents read and communicated and any further explanatory matter the delegates wished inserted in the text. His reason for choosing a journal rather than a protocol was that, under present circumstances, the usual form of recording proceedings might embarrass some of the delegates.

The Prussians concurred; the French took it *ad referendum* with provisional acceptance of the journal; Capo d'Istrias said his Court would prefer a protocol but, in view of the Prince's remarks, agreed to a journal; Stewart opted for the least solemn form.

Metternich's proposal was adopted and Gentz instructed to draft the conference journal in the agreed form, to be read at the following conference and, when approved, signed by him alone as Secretary of the congress. A certified copy would then be delivered to each member delegation.

The congress continued to linger on procedural matters safer, in spite of its apparent accord on principles, than debating the practical measures to be taken with regard to Naples. Its hesitation had been anticipated by Capo d'Istrias. Before they set out from St Petersburg he confided to La Ferronays that he augured no happy result from this congress because the Powers were submitting to public discussion and an uncertain issue questions which had not, as at Aix-la-Chapelle, been thoroughly aired in advance. The Powers primarily wished to affirm to the world at large their own close union but, so far from demonstrating unity, they were calling Europe's attention to the fragility of the chain of the Holy Alliance.

At his first long audience of Metternich Alexander outlined his own point of departure in a vague and theoretical generalization of the kind so much disliked by Castlereagh.

'We have met once again,' said the Czar, 'not as heretofore to combat a positive and known evil, but to examine and oppose overwhelming mischief which cannot be specifically named, but which is undermining all the governments of Europe.'

Metternich saw no change in Alexander's manners, as polite as ever; he looked no older, only a little fatter. What astounded the Prince was the Czar's hair shirt.

'You do not understand,' he told Metternich, 'why I am no longer the same. In 1820 I would under no consideration do what I did in 1813—seven years have gone by since then and for me they seem as long as a century. It is not you who have changed but I. You have nothing of which to repent. I cannot say the same.'

Metternich was not as ignorant as the Czar implied of the causes which had altered Alexander's outlook. Conspiracies in Belgium and elsewhere, the plot to kidnap him, the assassination attempt on Wellington, the murder of Kotzebue, disorders in England and Germany, revolutions in Spain, Naples and Portugal, the stormy Diet he had just attended in Warsaw, had all combined to dissipate, if not yet wholly to dissolve, Alexander's vision of a better order of things. In Gentz' view all these cruel experiences revealed to the Czar the enormous danger with which the social edifice of Europe was threatened, a danger overriding all geographical limits.

Most shattering of all to Alexander was the action of a 'perverted generation' in St Petersburg itself, which made him more responsive to Metternich's insistence that revolts everywhere must be crushed. News was brought him of a mutiny in his favourite Semenovsky regiment, whose green uniform he habitually wore. The colonel's severity was in fact responsible for the disciplinary breach but Alexander saw it as the work of radicals. Metternich did not agree; the actual importance of the mutiny was far less than that lent it by the public but, since no major policy matter was involved, the Prince was ready to pander to the Czar's belief in the interest of improving their personal relations.

La Ferronays had borne witness to the state of hostility towards Metternich in which Alexander arrived at Troppau. The Czar left it with charitable feelings towards the Prince, another of his famous *volte-faces*. That he was not entirely Metternich's dupe he made clear to the French ambassador when he talked about the Prince's 'intrigue' and 'the farrago of words in which he often shrouds his ideas'. Admittedly pompous speeches and solemn declarations had an infinite attraction for Alexander but he was too shrewd always to be taken in by them.

Modifying his antipathy to the Prince was essential as the Czar was ready to embrace enthusiastically any plan presented him by Francis, 'the only man who is never mistaken', and reach conclusions worthy of the important era in which they were living. In his many conversations with the Emperor at Troppau Alexander reached an unprecedented pitch of intimacy but, in the talking marathon, it was Metternich who took the palm.

As the weeks slipped by the boredom imposed on the British and French delegations infected their colleagues until Troppau became one vast yawn. Talking was the main and the most dangerous occupation. Everyone, Gentz told Pilat, wrote and talked too much; in such chaos no great thoughts could come to fruition. Nevertheless, apparently artless and idle talk could achieve much.

Nights of raging storm when heavy rain beat against the windows seemed expressly designed for the intimate conversation which made Alexander more pliable in Metternich's expert hands. Now it was the Prince's turn to say that, had Alexander in 1815 been what he was in 1813, then there would have been no 1820. As the Czar continued to beat his breast his chastened mood made their intercourse as easy as possible. They talked for hours not only without disagreement but frequently in perfect harmony.

'One could say', Metternich wrote to his wife, 'that only today has the Czar made his entry into the world and opened his eyes. He is now at the point at which I arrived thirty years ago . . . Those placed so high can have no accurate ideas of objects they haven't seen at close quarters.'

Metternich attributed this unexpected accord to the beneficial effects of tea. At long evening sessions when their conversations ranged over the widest horizons 'a capital proof of reciprocal friendly feelings' was furnished by tea. When they drank tea *tête à tête* they understood each other perfectly; if they were not friendly there was no tea. Thanks to tea, said Metternich, he felt able to say much to Alexander that would otherwise have been left unsaid.

This typical frivolity was only half the truth. Sympathy as well as tea drew the two men closer together. Alexander was an adoring brother, Metternich a devoted and adoring father. Since their last meeting the Czar had suffered the loss of his beloved sister, the Grand Duchess Catherine, Metternich in May of this year his sixteen-year-old daughter, Clementine, and so lately as July his darling, Marie Esterhazy, had died at the age of twenty-three.

The only personal plane on which monarch and minister had hitherto met was in the rival love affairs responsible for much of their dislike. When each dropped his public mask to reveal his private face he was surprised to discover the other's underlying humanity. Into those 'aromatic' cups of tea many tears must have fallen as the Czar of All the Russias and the Austrian Chancellor became only two sorrowing men whose mutual acrimony dissolved in grief.

Acrimony between Metternich and Capo d'Istrias could not be liquefied in the same way. With Capo the Prince was first and foremost a politician; destruction of the Greek's influence over Alexander was vital if Austria was to regain that control over international affairs usurped by the Czar.

Metternich's attacks on Capo d'Istrias varied as tactics demanded, at times in the open, at others under cover. At his first interview with the Greek at Troppau Metternich was taken aback to find that he had fallen from his seventh heaven to earth, naked as the truth, and in a mood almost as docile and self-condemnatory as his master's. Was the Greek perhaps wilier than Metternich and was his apparent change of heart merely an attempt to delude the Prince? Here was the tug of war.

Metternich, whose own conceit was unbounding, accused Capo of inordinate vanity and bewailed the fact that such a man—not bad, simply utterly and completely mad—should occupy so great a position. For good measure the Prince sneered at Capo's attempts to prove his intelligence by wit, but he had enough sense of humour to admit that no doubt Capo had the same feelings about him—in which case only a jury could decide between them.

Under the influence of tea Metternich unburdened himself to Alexander about Capo d'Istrias, whose good relationship with the Czar he failed to understand. He insinuated that it was unfortunate that Capo's intelligence was not matched by common sense— nothing confirmed the Prince's confidence in his own superior intelligence more than Capo d'Istrias' pathological analysis of politics.

So far as Gentz was concerned the Congress of Troppau resolved itself less into a meeting to contain the Neapolitan and Spanish revolutions than a personal duel between Metternich and Capo d'Istrias. What could Caraman, La Ferronays, Stewart or Gordon do to help or hinder the Austrians in their task which was called Capo d'Istrias? The Austrian problem was to discover which was the more powerful, Alexander or his minister.

Unlike his colleague, Nesselrode always kept to the same line; he was less complex, more timid than Capo, but still he knew the ways of the world better. Since regrettably Nesselrode effaced himself so much Metternich impatiently regarded him as morally dead; he might not exist, perhaps an inaccurate judgment. Nesselrode, shrewdly perceiving that Capo d'Istrias was heading for disaster, might wisely prefer to wait in the shadows to pick up the mantle he would drop.

With the passing of weeks a kind of paralysis stole over the congress, satiated with talk. Only Gentz was fully stretched; with less clerical assistance than at previous congresses he must divide his time between work and Metternich. He spent all day with the Prince, dined with him and his satellites and stayed on in his salon in the evening for tea—and cards when the boredom became unbearable. This close association had its compensations; never before had Metternich treated him with so much confidence nor taken him so fully into his inmost thoughts.

For any sustained social life at Troppau ladies were far too thin on the ground. The only resident was the Gräfin Urban, apparently so charming that for Gentz at least, despite his gruelling work, she made Troppau a paradise. A long visit paid by the Czar's sister-in-law and a shorter one by Metternich's sister, the Duchess of Württemberg, were welcome additions to Troppau's small society. Metternich sniggered that the Duchess's visit might have provoked a second edition of the English royal law suit because the Czar called on her daily. Hopefully her landlord rented out a skylight overlooking her rooms, but his clients parted with their money for nothing. These interviews were perfectly innocent. Alexander, who had done with 'all that', was merely delighted to have someone with whom to talk while his ministers were conferring.

At the daily conferences which filled up the empty hours for the plenipotentiaries, British and French appearances were rare. In the two months they spent at Troppau only eight plenary meetings of the congress were called and, even then, 'plenary' was a misnomer as Stewart and La Ferronays were politely but firmly pushed into the background. Neither appreciated the insignificance thrust upon them but the French were in a particularly irritating and anomalous position since the congress had assembled on Louis XVIII's initiative.

Gentz saw no point in inviting the British or French to confer on matters already decided by their governments; they were merely external ornaments to a congress where everything must be decided by Russia and the German states alone. This separation of Powers fundamentally of the same mind but sent by their varying positions along different paths was a great evil for Europe.

Metternich was determined that the present régime in Naples must end. From the congress he wanted approval for the despatch of an Austrian army to restore the King's authority. Once Ferdinand was freed from the trammels of the constitution imposed on him he should, with the aid of the Powers, decide how his kingdom should be governed.

France wanted the Naples affair to be solved by mediation either by herself or Russia. Capo d'Istrias would prefer to see the King of Naples reconciled to his people in accordance with their wishes. Castlereagh was sympathetic to Austria's desire to suppress the revolution provided she acted alone without involving the Alliance. Metternich succeeded in overcoming Capo's opposition to reach a confidential understanding with Russia and Prussia, tantamount to approval of the course he wished adopted.

The three Central Powers continued their daily meetings despite the strong representations made by Stewart and La Ferronays about the unconventional and perhaps impolitic course of the congress. Metternich blandly pretexted the need to prepare their work, smooth out difficulties and simplify discussions. In any event were not the British and French debarred by their instructions from any useful contributions to the talks? How justified was Gentz in observing that this conference bore little or no resemblance to its predecessors!

The substance of the talks in which they took no part was communicated to the British and French with a kindness bordering on condescension. All documents were made available to them— the obligatory memoirs submitted by each delegation which vied with the others for appropriate adjectives to express their horror at the iniquity of the Neapolitan revolution. The Prussians, anxious perhaps to assert themselves, asked two pertinent questions in their memoir. Were the Powers justified in intervention in Naples? Was Austria right in taking her precautionary measures? Not content with one of Capo d'Istrias' dreaded memoirs Russia submitted also Notes and explanations of Notes.

Only when the Three Powers had discussed, approved and signed their first important resolution were the others informed; no opportunity was given them for preliminary study, still less of making alterations or modifications. The resolution was presented to them as the fruit of mature deliberations and already invested with the imposing approbation of the sovereigns. Once their approval had been given there could be no going back. No wonder Pasquier thought that the sovereigns' presence was frequently as great an embarrassment as an advantage.

This resolution, in the form of a Preliminary Protocol, issued on 19 November, opened a breach in the Quintuple Alliance. The Protocol demanded the temporary exclusion of any state, hitherto part of the European alliance, should insurrectionary movement lead to changes in its system imperilling the well-being of other states; if necessary force might be used to bring the offending member back into the fold. This Protocol clearly sanctioned the principle of an Austrian occupation of Naples.

A further decision embodied in the Protocol was to send an invitation to the King of Naples to join the congress which would be adjourned to Laybach, the last German city in the Austrian province of Carniola. Metternich did not feel justified in asking his allies to penetrate further into Italy in its disturbed state.

Stewart and La Ferronays were profoundly dissatisfied with the Prince's casual explanation of this extraordinary démarche on which hung the fate of Naples. The dangers of the 'principle' were especially apparent to La Ferronays. France could be subjected to a military occupation should the Powers decide that their own safety was threatened by any disturbance which might arise there. Both plenipotentiaries found themselves forced into the position either of assenting to measures of doubtful success, or should they refuse, exposing themselves to the dangers of isolation and jeopardizing the union of the Five Powers.

In reality only two Powers had any decisive voice, Austria and Russia. Little time had been needed for Metternich to whittle the triumvirate down to a duumvirate by elbowing Prussia out of the discussions—an oblique revenge on the British government's detachment from the congress and the only slightly less firm posture of the French.

While Stewart's mind was divided between his domestic affairs and his mission La Ferronays was wholly devoted to carrying out his instruction to instil into Alexander's mind the idea of mediation in Naples. All La Ferronays' problems were connected with his duties; he had to overcome his diffidence, his sense of frustration and his anxiety about his ignorance of diplomatic forms and procedure. The ambassador had neither the vaguest notion of the required style should he be obliged to submit an official Note, nor whether anyone on Caraman's staff could draft one. He begged Pasquier for the good of the service to send some qualified person to Troppau so that the French delegation should not find itself at a disadvantage when faced with Gentz' expertise.

A further disadvantage suffered by La Ferronays was being as starved of news as at St Petersburg. Gentz suggested that the mere trickle which came from Paris was because the French government was either totally absorbed in the elections or, not knowing what to say, it preferred to say nothing. Whatever the reason for the silence, few French couriers arrived at Troppau compared with those of other Powers. The distance separating the French from the source of their instructions and the time taken for their own despatches to reach Paris were handicaps whose gravity was insufficiently understood at home, but whose extent was keenly felt by the men on the spot.

Stewart suffered in the same way, but he had an additional cause of complaint; he suspected that Metternich was stopping his correspondence sent by Austrian couriers to Sir William à Court at Naples.

'You will admit,' he wrote to Castlereagh, 'that he acts sometimes more in the *Bonapartean* than in the European diplomacy.'

Castlereagh who at Vienna had some experience of the activities of the black cabinet could scarcely have been surprised.

Pasquier did little about couriers but he did send La Ferronays a Foreign Office official named Prévost to assist him on the technical side and to encourage him with verbal instructions to persevere on the lines laid down for him. La Ferronays may have been ignorant of diplomatic usage but he was no innocent abroad where knowledge of men was involved. He had not been long at Troppau before writing to Pasquier:

'I am convinced that frankness and the kind of cordiality displayed are only superficial, and that my own temperament by no means fits me to unravel everyone's real intentions from all the intrigues and dissensions. Everything I see and hear is for me so novel, these intrigues seen close at hand have in them something so astonishing that I frankly confess I am acting at random, not knowing at any moment whether I shall not fall into some trap like the one in which M. de Caraman fell.'

Caraman had, in fact, been so foolish as to reveal to Metternich the content of his instructions, an indiscretion which earned him a well-merited reprimand.

La Ferronays continued in the same despatch:

'M. de Metternich and M. de Lebzeltern, who do me the honour of considering me as head of the opposition, would be very pleased to see me make a serious mistake—I hope I shall not give them the satisfaction for which they are looking.'

La Ferronays was able or lucky enough to avoid open conflict with Metternich, but it was impossible for him to maintain friendly relations with Caraman, with whom he was quite simply at loggerheads. He admitted to Alexander that his opinions were totally opposed to Caraman's, a fact well known to Pasquier who sighed,

'Decidedly, we have two Frances at Troppau.'

Each man had his own virtues and each his supporter. Caraman's integrity was not in doubt but too often his over-confidence and naïveté made him unreliable. La Ferronays, enlightened and of unquestioned loyalty, was paralysed by circumstances impossible to foresee when he was seconded to Troppau. He himself believed that it was to the Austrians' attempts to blacken him in the Czar's eyes that he owed the redoubling of the kindness and confidence with which Alexander deigned to honour him during their stay at Troppau. Nevertheless, however cordial the relationship between the Czar and the French Minister, it did not approach the intimacy and confidence existing between Alexander and Richelieu.

At Troppau where the three Central Powers were represented at summit level by their sovereigns and first Ministers, the British, like the French, limped along on one leg. No one could replace Castlereagh; Stewart lacked his experience, his authority and his faculty for conciliation. Instead of concentrating exclusively on the Czar Metternich might have used some of his persuasive powers on his friend to get him to come to Troppau.

Since Castlereagh believed that the Czar stood in awe of nothing so much as the British character in Europe, then he was at fault in absenting himself from the congress, or at the least in not obtaining its postponement until he was able to be present. He still showed no disposition to join his colleagues when in November the government majority was so small on the Third Reading of the Bill of Pains and Penalties to deprive Queen Caroline of her title and dissolve her marriage that Liverpool dropped the Bill.

No one was surprised that Castlereagh did not come to Troppau; nothing now could be expected from England. With the bit between his teeth Metternich had some justification for his conviction that Russia and Austria were the only Powers which counted in Europe. In this belief he was assured of Alexander's concurrence.

At Stewart's first statutory interview with the Czar he was received, as on previous occasions, with great personal kindness. Less acceptable was Alexander's reproof that, although he religiously respected Great Britain's determination to take no active part in the Naples affair, she should at least not impede the steps being taken by others. He gave Stewart no hint as to whether he would be content to confine the reunion at Troppau within the prudent limits proposed by the Emperor of Austria, as Castlereagh hoped, or whether once again he was going to run amok, hazarding those general declarations so much deplored by the Foreign Secretary as being incapable of redemption.

Castlereagh continued in his despatches to repeat what he had so often said before—interference in other states could never *a priori* be made the subject matter of an alliance among the Great Powers.

So far as Stewart was concerned he knew that, whatever form this proposal took, his own must be a negative response, mortifying to anyone of his temperament. Torn between the desire to be in Vienna with his wife who was expecting their first child, and the necessity of being in Troppau, even if only as a fly on the wall, Stewart's impetuosity got the better of him. In debate with Metternich he crossed swords so fiercely that a literal crossing of swords was expected. Rumours that a duel had actually taken place were 'infamous, absurd and without foundation'. Stewart himself hotly denied that there had been a *fracas*. Gentz took up the cudgels for Metternich, the Prince treated Stewart with kid gloves because his situation inspired pity rather than anger.

Stewart also managed to antagonize Gentz, who had got on his nerves in much the same way as at Aix-la-Chapelle. Nothing at Troppau could be concealed. La Ferronays reported to Pasquier that at Bernstorff's Lord Stewart had said,

'Gentz is an ass and I told him so yesterday. He refuses to understand the difference between signing and not signing. I'm quite capable of doing something silly, but I would not want to tell you I had done it, still less to write about it.'

The inspissated monotony of Troppau, the worsening of the weather and the hard frost which made the duckboards useless was finally getting on everyone's nerves. Troppau, they decided, was too tranquil a place to make decisions on the tranquillity of Europe; there was no sense of urgency about the place, in fact it was quite unsuitable for a congress. Why, there was not even an atlas in the whole town!

Even Metternich felt that Troppau had exhausted its usefulness.

'The worst part of a congress,' he moaned to his wife, 'is first of all the labour to be done, then the stay in this little town, then the bad weather. The masters of the world do not notice such small details. I find I am worth less in a disagreeable place—I need space —I can't bear to be cooped up.'

Alexander, however, showed no disposition to return to Russia or even to leave Troppau. He categorically refused the suggestion that the conference be transferred to Vienna; he was determined that the Russian public should not think him capable at this moment of looking only for amusement. So long as the Czar wished to remain everyone else must remain and suffer their *ennui* as best they could.

The arrival of Pozzo di Borgo at least provided a fresh face. His own satisfaction at the compliment of being invited to Troppau was tempered by regret. He was reluctant to leave Paris to make a winter journey half way across Europe—age and gout were beginning to tell, he wrote to Nesselrode. He also severely criticized Metternich's delays—had the Prince acted with greater frankness his battle would already have been won. Perhaps no one more than Pozzo himself would have been surprised that he was adopting Castlereagh's tone when he said that Metternich, by preferring clever combinations and subtle ideas, had both alarmed Italy to an unconceivable point and made a particularly unfavourable impression in France.

About the deplorable delay there could be no argument. Six months after revolution had broken out in Naples and six weeks after the assembly of the congress nothing practical or positive had been achieved; only of talk had there been a plethora. Metternich blamed the sluggishness on Capo d'Istrias. Capo, Capo *da capo* was the Prince's refrain—to do anything with him was a labour of Hercules; his alterations to Metternich's memoirs made them unrecognizable to their author; could the Prince but bend him to his own will speed and success would be assured; Alexander was an obstacle only because of his minister. Without Capo d'Istrias everything could be settled in a day.

La Ferronays did not belong to the anti-Capo d'Istrias league; on the contrary, he found him most co-operative. The ambassador warned Pasquier not to lose sight of the fact that, of all those in close contact with Alexander, Capo d'Istrias was the *only* one who let him hear the language of moderation, though La Ferronays himself spoke out forthrightly when occasion demanded.

Alexander had expressed his displeasure at French dependence on England in her attitude to the congress. He was *ashamed* and embarrassed, he told La Ferronays, to see France attach herself voluntarily to the reins of a government willing to indicate neither its policy line nor its intentions.

La Ferronays never lacked courage and, where French interests were involved, he was a lion. France was entitled to her independence. 'Everyone agrees,' he told the Czar bluntly, 'that the repose of

Europe depends on the tranquillity of France but, to be tranquil, Sire, we must be strong, and this strength we cannot hope to obtain so long as we have not actually recovered the rank and the attitude France ought to have.'

Happily the news of France brought by Pozzo di Borgo considerably mollified Alexander. The spectre of revolution, Pozzo said, was disappearing so rapidly that the whole physiognomy of France seemed changed and she offered the prospect of great welfare and a long peace.

However welcome this information was to La Ferronays he was still uneasy because he suspected that the duumvirate was now not debating Naples alone—the only matter of concern to France—but the far more controversial question of suppressing revolution everywhere. He did not know how 'our very odd congress will end' but, despite his doubts as to whether he had justified the confidence the government had honoured him with or whether he had earned its disapproval, he was not going to yield the French position without a struggle.

France, Gentz declared, was infected by the bad British example; the British government, once the strongest and most intrepid in Europe, was reduced to a position so unhappy that its anxieties, fears and alarms seemed to have redoubled. When La Ferronays made known his instructions Gentz' opinion was confirmed. France would not agree to the march of an Austrian army to Naples unless an expedient was previously sought of giving the King and his government the chance of reaching an amicable agreement. If no attempt at conciliation was made and Metternich insisted on sending the army now massing on the Po then La Ferronays was to inform the Prince that France reserved the right to act in accordance with circumstances. Gordon reinforced La Ferronays in this move with far greater emphasis than Stewart would have done.

Francis' and Alexander's letters of invitation to Ferdinand were supported by one from Louis XVIII urging his acceptance. Metternich himself intended that, if Ferdinand did go to Laybach, he would there be persuaded to summon the people of Naples to abandon their constitution under threat of invasion. On this procedure the advice of the British and French was not asked; they were merely informed of a proposal obviously distasteful to them. Both constitutional governments wished to preserve some kind of representative régime in Naples.

Any constitutional government in Naples would be a bad example to Austria's Italian states which would inevitably demand the same kind of régime for themselves. Alexander, who had not yet relinquished all his liberal ideas, still hankered for a constitutional government in Naples. Although Metternich and the Czar were agreed in principle Alexander had to be weaned from his own to the Prince's point of view.

Metternich succeeded so well by raising the spectre of his phantom drummer that he persuaded Alexander never to recognize the Spanish constitution in Naples. He next obtained his agreement and that of Prussia to a Circular addressed to their respective missions at foreign Courts concerning the affairs of Spain, Portugal and Naples. This Circular, dated 8 December 1820, to be communicated confidentially to the Courts to which the Ministers were accredited, was couched in more moderate terms than the Preliminary Protocol.

The object of the Circular was to suppress the 'malevolent and false rumours' spread abroad on the aims and results of the Conferences of Troppau. Arising from the great anxiety and sorrow caused by the events in Spain and Naples to all those persons obliged to watch over the tranquillity of States, the congress had assembled to deliberate on means of preventing all the evils threatening to fall upon Europe, 'to curb the tyrannical and detestable force of revolution and crime, a motive so honourable and salutary, that the goodwill of all right-minded men would no doubt follow the Allied Courts in the noble arena in which they had entered'.

This rhodomontade was followed by the claim put forward by the Powers to their undeniable right to concert together upon means of safety against those states where the overthrow of a government by revolution could be considered only as a dangerous example resulting in a hostile attitude to all legitimate government.

A slightly defiant note could be heard in the Three Powers' assertion that the system they followed was not an innovation. Their invitation to the King of Naples—a step undertaken to deliver his will from all external restraint—rested upon the same maxims as those which served as bases of the Treaties upon which the Alliance of the European states was founded.

Somewhat anxiously the Central Powers hoped that Britain and France would not 'refuse to give their assent, the principle upon which the invitation to the King of Naples is founded being in perfect harmony with the Treaties which they have previously agreed to, and offering besides a guarantee of resolutions of the most pacific and equitable'.

Metternich had no grounds for imagining that Castlereagh would subscribe to sentiments so directly contrary to the *spirit* of previous agreements and to his reiterated statements on British policy. The time lag in communications prevented Castlereagh's answer to the Circular arriving at Troppau before the congress broke up but his reaction to the Preliminary Protocol was submitted by Stewart on 16 December in a memorandum diamond clear in its language and equally cutting.

The British government could never join such a concert, whatever form or principle it took; it did not lie within its power to establish a system incompatible with the constitution of England. Could it be supposed that all the other states of Europe would choose to accede to such a system and, if not, what was to be the position of the non-acceding states?

Castlereagh wished to take no further part in discussions to which such a proposition would give rise. He protested against any attempt to consider it under *any imaginable* circumstances as being applied to the British dominions.

Since Naples had ceased to be a purely Austrian matter as, by linking it with a wider plan, the cabinets had made it a European question, the Court of London had no other course open to it but that of strictest *neutrality*. Finally Castlereagh urged the Three Powers to abandon a project which would of necessity separate England from an alliance to which, up till now, she had attached so great a price.

Gentz might rage that, if the Troppau discussions ultimately proved abortive, the British government would be responsible to posterity. His reproach was tinged with a slight sense of guilt— 'if we had dealt only with Naples perhaps finally England would have given her moral support and not wholly separated herself from her allies'.

Metternich was not going to be held responsible for any British retreat from the alliance although, in his reply to Castlereagh, he uneasily acknowledged that he had manœuvred the texts of existing treaties to suit his book. He asserted that, as the texts offered no remedy against the 'greatest danger which had ever menaced Europe, they must be completed by new stipulations'.

Having bitten a certain amount of dust Metternich turned to the attack. If England found insuperable obstacles to agreement with these stipulations, she should not act the dog in the manger. The other Powers with the enemy, so to speak, at their gates could not, to save British scruples, neglect what they owed to their own security. The Central Powers were nevertheless in an awkward position. Should France and Great Britain abstain from representation at Laybach then the schism in the alliance they all hoped to avoid would be apparent to the whole world.

Even Capo had told Richelieu that the general alliance was becoming a perilous abstraction, the more dangerous because of the complacency which led the Central Powers to see themselves as the armed guardians of all thrones. As such—in the concluding words of the Troppau Circular—they hoped 'as a reward for their efforts and their case, for the unanimous approval of the world'.

Meanwhile at Troppau a long stage wait ensued until an answer was received from the King of Naples. The sad fact was that Ferdinand of Naples was not himself worth saving at the expense of the alliance. From the beginning his conduct had been a tissue of weakness and duplicity; every overt act of his had been accompanied by secret protests addressed to Francis, Louis or even à Court that he was acting under duress. The King was too much a coward either to accept the revolution or to resist it.

During the period of waiting Metternich fell to philosophizing. Until he knew whether or not Ferdinand would go to Laybach many days must still be lost in that shoreless sea called time. 'I reach the end of every day,' he sighed, 'as I shall one day reach the end of my life, that is to say without having lived.'

Happily, to save the Prince from falling into total despair, there was always Capo d'Istrias; if the results the congress was now reaching were not at the high level for which Metternich had hoped, the fault was Capo's. Eighty-five per cent of the victory would belong to Metternich but, with the remainder, 'Capo would lose the world its peace, reason its authority and good sense the honour it deserved.' In his elegiac mood the Prince mourned the new sad proof of the primitiveness of the wretched century which did not know how to recompense virtue, and of whose virtue but his own could he be thinking?

Utter stagnation was kept at bay by prolonged discussion on general measures to arrest the progress of the revolutionary spirit.

Everyone thought in terms of controlling it from above, no one of investigating it at the level at which it flourished. Alexander persisted in his belief that the greatest deterrent was the universal act of guarantee he had first mooted at Aix but, as at Aix, the British rejected this thesis as wholly impracticable. Admitting the Quintuple Alliance was as far as Castlereagh was prepared to go. Any possibility that he might venture a little nearer European unity was dashed by his profound shock that the Powers confused European federation with a European police force.

In the interest of preserving the unity which still existed Castlereagh relented sufficiently to announce that both Stewart and à Court go to Laybach if, as protocol required, Francis invited the one and Ferdinand the other. They would, however, attend conferences only when requested to do so. Neither was to allow his own judgment to be contaminated by the generalities so beloved of the Czar, Metternich and Capo d'Istrias.

Finally, on Christmas Eve, after everyone had been running in all directions for news, the arrival of a courier from Naples relieved their suspense; the King of Naples would join the congress at Laybach. His reply had come in the nick of time; nothing more was left to say, to write or to do. Gentz marvelled that everyone clung to Troppau as if they did not want to leave. He himself was ready to go, his only personal regret the Gräfin Urban. For his journey back to Vienna he was well supplied with reading matter, including a belated copy of Lady Caroline Lamb's *Glenarvon*.

Gentz' departure on Christmas Eve itself was followed by Metternich's on Christmas Day, Francis' the following day and Alexander's on 27 December. All were making for Laybach, pausing only briefly at Vienna.

Metternich could congratulate himself on one achievement at Troppau; his wooing of Alexander had been so successful that he was confident at Laybach of leading him to a sacrificial altar, there to immolate the remains of his liberalism. Capo d'Istrias had been pushed so far into a corner that he had little room left in which to manœuvre. Not much more effort would be needed to flatten him completely.

Nevertheless the Congress of Troppau had by no means been the pretty little Congress of Aix-la-Chapelle. The closer association established among the Central Powers had been offset by the alienation of Great Britain and France resulting from the Preliminary Protocol and Circular. Already Troppau was apparent as a watershed—down one side of a steep incline rushed the torrent of reaction, while on the other the British stream wound sluggishly towards social and political reform. Where Great Britain and Austria had once co-operated wholeheartedly in the conferences and treaties in which, since 1814, they had been involved together, now they stood aloof 'like rocks which had been rent asunder'. Then Great Britain had been willing to associate herself with Europe; now her total withdrawal loomed threateningly over the alliance.

While Metternich preened himself on his own ascendancy he could not avoid a feeling of unease. Had he sacrificed the valuable asset of British co-operation in Europe for the doubtful benefit of an Austrian army marching to Naples to bring a rebellious people to heel?

Time alone would answer Metternich. Now as he posted towards Laybach he might be thankful that at least the congress system still survived.

Comte Auguste de la Ferronays,
French ambassador to Russia

Charles, Lord Stewart,
British ambassador to Vienna

The Roman amphitheatre at Verona at the time of the Congress, 1822

CHAPTER XIII

Metternich's Congress

SINCE the tabling in February 1822 of the Troppau Circular and Castlereagh's answering State Paper of January His Majesty's government was under fire from the Opposition benches for its 'most reprehensible conduct'. The radical Sir James Mackintosh coupled 'the self-constituted, usurping, tyrannical and insolent tribunal at Laybach' with the principles contained in the Circular of the Allied Sovereigns. Not only were they inconsistent with the independence of nations but they would permit the landing of Cossacks in England to restrain her from adopting a line of conduct disagreeable to the Russian Autocrat.

Studied moderation was the keynote of Castlereagh's reply to this fanciful flight. He informed the House that at Troppau Stewart's instructions were not to commit his government by any acts or opinions of his own. Castlereagh himself had not wished to engage in a war of State Papers, but he had felt obliged so to do to correct any mistaken impressions left by the Troppau Circular on British missions abroad.

The State Paper was divided into two heads; the establishment of certain general principles for the regulation of the future political conduct of the Allies, and the proposed method of dealing with the existing affairs of Naples under these principles.

The British government abstained from intervening in Naples for fear of establishing a precedent for more frequent and extensive interference in the internal affairs of other nations. By arrogating this freedom to themselves the Allies were assuming a supremacy incompatible with the rights of other states. Any attempt to introduce a federative system into Europe was to be deplored, not only as 'unwieldy and ineffectual to its objects but leading to many most serious inconveniences'.

Having, to his own satisfaction at least, removed any possible misconceptions from the Troppau Circular, Castlereagh admitted the right of states to interfere in the internal affairs of other countries where their own immediate security or essential interests were seriously endangered, but he stressed that such a right could never apply generally and indiscriminately against all revolutionary movements.

The State Paper concluded by paying lip service in the usual formula to 'the purity of the Allies' intention' and the assurance that 'the difference of sentiment prevailing could make no alteration in the cordiality and harmony of the alliance on any other subject, or abate their common zeal in giving the most complete effect to all their existing engagements'.

The Commons was quick to seize on the apparent inconsistencies of Castlereagh's review of the affairs of Naples. Great Britain both publicly disapproved of the procedure by which revolution in Naples had been effected and of any interference with the existing Neapolitan government. At the same time the cabinet disclaimed the right to impede the course adopted by any other country which felt itself threatened by the Neapolitan revolution since this would constitute interference in the internal policies of another nation.

Liverpool appeared to clinch the matter in the House of Lords when he asked the pertinent question,

'Have we any right to prescribe a rule of conduct to Austria?'

When reports of the parliamentary debates reached Laybach the 'odious news' sent Gentz into a fury as great as that of the House of Commons. Once again the incompatibility of absolute and constitutional monarchies had been demonstrated but Gentz was aware that, as yet, insufficient weapons were available to fight an enemy like Parliament.

Alexander, continuing to show his misunderstanding of Parliamentary temper and procedure, congratulated Robert Gordon whom he met on the promenade on the government's success. Gordon found some difficulty in persuading both the Czar and Metternich that victory in Parliament neither indicated nor permitted any change in British policy towards Naples.

By now the congress was firmly under way. All eyes were fixed on what Edward Ward in Lisbon described as 'the Constellation of Laybach destined to guide Europe's movements under the domination of that great planetary body'. He might as well have substituted Metternich for his constellation since the Prince presided unchallenged over the firmament.

Metternich had been the first to arrive at Laybach, by-passing a dress ball given in Vienna by Stewart for a few days of solitude until the 'sad avalanche of statesmen' descended. The town was not as awful as he had feared, his lodgings comfortable and spacious nor need Madame de Lieven fear a rival in his landlady, ugly as the seven capital sins.

To take the winter journey over the mountain passes which he dreaded Gentz had fortified himself with a new carriage and a magnificent fur coat. He was, however, a little out of temper, disliking the freezing cold, Bignon's obnoxious book, the *Congrès de Troppau*, and the eternal conferences which succeeded one another in rapid succession.

Next to arrive were the sovereigns and their ministers. The only additions to those present at Troppau were Baron Vincent from Paris, the Duc de Blacas, French ambassador to Rome and brother-in-law of Auguste de la Ferronays, and the Italian ministers in attendance on the King of Naples.

Although Stewart had duly received his invitation to be present from Francis he obtained Castlereagh's permission to remain in Vienna, his place at Laybach taken by Robert Gordon. Nevertheless Stewart thought it advisable to put in an appearance at the end of January to give his brother the benefit of his personal views.

Between life at Troppau and life at Laybach there was little to choose; the pattern was identical although the superior natural setting of Laybach promised that the town would prove much pleasanter when the weather improved. Everyone hoped, however, to be gone before the spring. Living in one's trunks, away from home and family and normal avocations was beginning to pall; the last few years had indeed for the cabinets of Europe been 'diplomacy of the highway'.

Gentz summed up his far from brilliant existence at Laybach as '*gearbeitet, gegessen, gelesen*'—worked, ate, read. The Russians had wanted to revert to the formal usage of recording proceedings by protocol but, as a great conciliatory gesture to the British, debarred from signing a protocol, the system of a journal as used at Troppau was again adopted. Gentz disclaimed the sterile honour of being sole signatory of the journal but, although he pressed for the formal protocol, he was overridden.

While no argument existed that the Neapolitan revolution must be suppressed the congress took an unconscionable time in reconciling the infinite shades of opinion among the Austrian, Russian and French ministers, their discussions so prolonged that even Metternich grew weary of them.

'Is there anything in the world today but ink, pens, conference chambers with green tables and miserable fools designated to hold meetings there?' was his cry.

The most obvious fool was Ferdinand of Naples, who regarded a throne as an armchair in which to take his ease, who was incapable of reading more than one page of a despatch, who veered from imprudence to fear and from fear to pot-valiant temerity. Everyone commiserated with everyone else at the ally Providence had given them and whose interests they had to preserve.

Alexander, ranking now as Metternich's satellite, could not therefore merit his epithet. Two months' propinquity at Troppau, followed by the intimacy of Laybach, had consolidated a perfect entente between the Russian Autocrat and the Austrian Chancellor, incredible to anyone unable to comprehend that tea was capable of working miracles.

An additional cause of self-satisfaction to Metternich was that Capo d'Istrias' star was definitely on the wane; wriggling about like the devil in holy water, he was unlikely to be able to rise from the depths to which he had sunk. The abyss separating Alexander from his minister was daily growing deeper because the Czar had proved the stronger of the two and good sense had prevailed in the subterranean diplomatic campaign waged by Metternich. Capo had got the worst of it and would now pay the piper; if all turned out well in Naples he would have lost, if it turned out ill he would be saved. Metternich, however, had no doubts as to the happy outcome at Naples which would inevitably lead to Capo's retirement.

The Prince, slightly surprised to discover that Nesselrode liked him, now decided that he was a good man with the right ideas, a change of heart no doubt also dictated by Nesselrode's standing in high favour with the Czar between whom and Metternich he acted as intermediary.

Capo d'Istrias' position was pitiable; he complained that everyone had abandoned him but, despite his personal ambition, he was moved less by the decline of his own prestige than by Alexander's subordination to Metternich. By throwing in his lot so irrevocably with Austria the Czar was forfeiting his claim to be hailed as the general dispenser of justice. This, not tagging along behind the Prince, was the *beau rôle*.

Robert Gordon, too, was distressed by the Czar's new allegiance; he was so entangled in Metternich's toils that the Prince could not speak with greater decision than if Russia had actually been transformed into a province of the Austrian empire.

The three-pronged contest, Alexander *v.* Capo d'Istrias *v.* Metternich was watched with some cynicism by all the European Courts. While Lamb from Frankfort wrote to Castlereagh, quoting a letter from Laybach, saying that Capo was completely lacking in influence and Alexander totally in the hands of Metternich, Bagot in St Petersburg insisted that Capo's sway might yet suffice to thwart at least some of Metternich's schemes and that power he would certainly not fail to use.

To send or not to send an Austrian army to Naples was the main subject of discussion at Laybach. Capo d'Istrias believed that, if Britain held firm to her neutrality, the Austrians might have second thoughts about sending an expedition. Although Prussia showed unusual initiative in hanging back, with Russia's enthusiastic support Austria paid no heed to British opposition but determined both to send her army to Naples and thereafter to occupy the kingdom for three years.

This decision threw liberals everywhere into a state of fury against Austria. From Pisa Shelley wrote on 15 February,

'We are now in the crisis and point of expectation in Italy. The Neapolitan and Austrian armies are rapidly approaching each other and every day news of a battle may be expected.'

Shelley was justifiably afraid of the slight chance stood by the new and undisciplined levies of Naples against a superior force of veteran troops. He forgot what the undisciplined levies of France achieved against superior force in 1792, but then the French had fire in their bellies; the Neapolitans were as flaccid as cold spaghetti. Against all evidence to the contrary the poet continued to hope because 'The birth of liberty in nations abounds in reversals of the ordinary laws of calculation; the defeat of the Austrians would be the signal of insurrection throughout Italy.'

Since, when the Neapolitans met the Austrians on 7 March at Rieti, they fled incontinently, the laws of calculation were neither reversed nor was any signal given except the warning that any general insurrection in Italy would be immediately suppressed.

At Laybach debate had continued around the green table until every subject was exhausted. The congress, therefore, had its formal closure on 26 February although the Austrians decided to remain where they were until their army occupied the city of Naples—a thirty-day march from the Po. In fact the delegates lingered on—no one quite knew why—until 12 May when the Final Declaration of the congress was issued. Metternich, the first in the field, was the last out of it on 22 May.

Stewart made his first appearance at Laybach at the plenary session of 26 January. On the following day in a most secret and confidential 'separate' he outlined the existing situation for Castlereagh. Metternich, wrote Stewart, doubting whether Austrian power was sufficient to strike an immediate blow at Naples, to bear its odium or risk its failure, originally intended to ask for Russian aid. The Prince had succeeded so well in 'sounding the tocsin of military revolt and occult sects' in the Czar's ears that, despite his deafness, he swam into Metternich's pond. Stewart laid the blame for this easy victory on the failure of the Czar's entourage to keep him on his normal cautious and tortuous course.

Subsequently Metternich, having weighed up the physical strength of the three Central Powers, decided to forfeit Russian co-operation and let Austria take the initiative alone, always preferring, as Castlereagh himself had observed, 'more complicated than direct proceedings'. All that Metternich now needed was to bring France into line with the Central Powers in their *immediate measures* with regard to Naples.

Stewart himself considered that France was continually vacillating between ranging herself in appearance with the Three Courts and not alienating herself from Britain. The rejection at Troppau of the French proposal of mediation had caused a certain amount of damage to Franco-Austrian relations, but now Metternich needed France. Her support, valuable in itself, would also leave Britain lying out on a solitary limb, from which she might then be persuaded to climb down.

Blacas played into Metternich's hands. Unlike La Ferronays he was an émigré who had not profited by his emigration. His only qualification for the post he held was Louis XVIII's favouritism but his ultra-royalism had proved too dyed-in-the-wool even for the most ultra of royalists to stomach and the King had been forced to send him into honourable exile as ambassador to Rome.

Given the ultra-royalists' eagerness that Bourbon prestige in Europe should be raised and the encouragement they had received in the partial elections which had kept Richelieu from Troppau, Metternich was confident of meeting little difficulty in bringing Blacas round to his point of view.

Stewart was too shrewd to be Metternich's dupe. He knew how much France wished to raise herself up in the alliance, a desire which grew in proportion as her government and institutions gained strength but, in addition, Metternich was able to play, in the person of M. de Blacas, 'on the vanity belonging to all Frenchmen'.

The extent of the Prince's success was confided to Stewart by Blacas himself. He had found it virtually impossible to make any suggestions because the three Central cabinets were deaf to any opposition to their fixed plans. Therefore, in the overriding interest of unity, Blacas determined to co-operate in their measures with regard to Naples. On his own responsibility he sent a message to the French *chargé d'affaires* at Naples, bidding him act in concert with his Austrian, Russian and Prussian colleagues.

'We must, therefore,' Stewart sadly concluded his despatch, 'no longer conceal from ourselves that we stand alone in our position and that Austria has embarked the other three Powers under her banner in her present purpose.'

Decidedly this was Metternich's congress. First he had enslaved the Czar, then he had taken the French in tow. How much more glorious would be his triumph if he could attach Great Britain to his chariot wheels, bearing aloft the slogan, 'unanimity and *solidarité*'.

In seeking to realize his objective the Prince made every effort to spare Britain embarrassment but Stewart resisted his seduction; in his own mind as well as by virtue of his instructions he was determined not to embroil his government in any general declarations. Frustrated of making any headway with Stewart Metternich tried his arts on Gordon who reported to Castlereagh,

'I have been expressly assured that the first wish of the Three Powers is to shew every disposition to listen to the voice of Great Britain, and to adopt the line of conduct most likely to suit her convenience.'

This was patently untrue. 'The overbearing preponderance of

the three cabinets determined them to pursue their own plans and modes of expression.' Stewart's last word from Laybach was,

'Metternich's immediate pursuit is irrevocably fixing the Czar Alexander and marching *de front* with his ministers, for which purpose he perhaps has sacrificed, as at Aix-la-Chapelle, all the management of the *boutique*.'

This despatch Stewart was careful to put into the safe hands of Lord Clanwilliam since couriers and communications from Laybach were as much a thorn in the flesh as elsewhere. Particularly distressing was the leakage of Stewart's despatches to à Court in Naples as Metternich extracted from them anything he wanted to while an additional irritant was the delays to and from Naples when the Mediterranean was turbulent.

Stewart put his trust neither in cyphering nor in Austrian or French couriers. Perhaps he had some justification for distrusting French couriers since the behaviour of one of them opened the whole system to suspicion.

On his way from Laybach to Goritz a French courier, Maconnois, spent two unauthorized hours at an inn where the Duc de Gallo, the Neapolitan minister, was lodging. Worse still, Maconnois had been closeted for one hour with de Gallo, ostensibly to receive despatches the minister wanted taken to Paris. This breach of the regulations was reported by the postmaster at Goritz to Metternich who in turn informed Blacas.

The ambassador took a sufficiently serious view of the case to write to Pasquier; if the courier had delivered M. de Gallo's despatches to the Foreign Minister his only fault was to have stopped on his way at a stranger's request. Should Maconnois make a mystery of his conduct he would be highly guilty and Pasquier would no doubt consider that the courier deserved a severe reprimand.

The early departure from Laybach of Stewart and the King of Naples was a welcome relief. Stewart's presence at conferences was embarrassing because of a certain ambivalence in the British attitude. While Britain stood voluntarily apart from her allies, she seemed at the same time to resent her exclusion from something in which she did not want to be involved A parallel. could be found in British behaviour towards the Treaty of Rome in 1957 and subsequent blowing hot and cold on the European Economic Community.

In 1822 personalities counted more perhaps than they do today.

Such was Metternich's suavity and charm that, despite the *fracas* at Troppau, Stewart could write,

'Although you may be hurt by his *légèreté* and inconsequence, you never can be really angry with him from his personal amiability and kind manners.'

No one regretted the King of Naples when that wily monarch, instead of returning to his palace to be dictated to by the Austrians, departed to hunt near Vienna. Like a later King of Saxony, his farewell message to Laybach might have been,

'Clear up your own mess.'

Rid now of Ferdinand's tiresome and Stewart's troubling presence, the Three Courts turned their attention to planning the reconstruction of the Neapolitan government when the revolution was finally suppressed. From these talks the French as well as the British were excluded despite Blacas' and Caraman's submission to Metternich's views.

Chateaubriand from his embassy in Berlin scoffed at the Austrian occupation of Naples and asked the pertinent question what she would substitute for the constitution she did not want. Men? Where were they? A liberal priest and two hundred soldiers were enough to start the revolution all over again. Chateaubriand argued strongly in favour of a constitutional government which would respect all social liberties but he had little confidence of being heard.

Laybach, Metternich observed with some satisfaction, was now beginning to empty. Vincent and Blacas, with the Neapolitan Prince Ruffo and Pozzo di Borgo, were leaving to join the Austrian army in Naples, followed by the remaining Italians. La Ferronays' departure for Paris en route for St Petersburg was preceded by an encomium from Capo d'Istrias who wrote to Richelieu:

'While respecting what is to be respected in your present mission to the congress, I can with complete sincerity assure you that it is the Count alone who has rendered essential service.'

Little alteration to the social life of Laybach was caused by these departures. Although restricted it was livelier than at Troppau despite the order of the Austrian police that no strangers might reside at Laybach during the 'convocation of crowned heads'. Both for the Russian New Year and the Emperor of Austria's birthday the town was very prettily illuminated but two public masked balls were pitiful. A beautiful country did not automatically produce

8*

beautiful women, was Metternich's sad reflection. At one ball the only pretty woman was a Russian cook who created great havoc among the couriers but the Prince, not being a courier, left after fifteen minutes. The second ball was disastrous—forty-five men and one woman who fell asleep in a corner of the room.

A more successful ball on a larger scale was offered by the town to its distinguished guests in the Redoutensaal—were congresses perhaps no more than a progression from one Redoutensaal to another? To Gentz these entertainments were of no interest. When he was not sitting up at his work till all hours of the night he played écarté at Metternich's.

During his stay at Laybach Gentz suffered a severe financial loss in the death of Prince Stoutzo, the Hospodar of Wallachia who was his principal source of income. The removal of the burden on his rheumatic arm was small compensation for the emptiness of his pocket but the prospect of an early end to the congress held out the hope of gratifications.

The final protocols were drafted, everyone began to relax, the two Emperors, in perfect harmony with each other, planned to visit the Roman antiquities at Pola while Metternich gave himself up to an unprecedented orgy of narcissism.

Everything at Laybach had so far gone the Prince's way. Convinced that the Neapolitans would welcome the Austrians as friends and liberators he gloated in advance at the howls of the liberals because he liked the abuse of people on whose toes he trod. He rejoiced that Capo's character and mischievous politics had now been revealed to the world. He gloried in the change he had wrought in Alexander. He even invoked the future as witness to his own merit; he fancied that a thousand years hence someone would unearth his name to reveal that in the distant past there had been a man of outlook less limited than a number of his contemporaries, so fatuous as to believe that they had reached the apogee of civilization. Undoubtedly Metternich had reached the apogee of his own fatuity.

After being cooped up so long in the conference room the Prince waxed lyrical about the space and beauty of the countryside, the glorious sunshine and the temperature in the seventies. The green tables had done their duty and could be set aside.

In thus discarding the essential furniture of congresses Metternich was somewhat premature. Even while he was congratulating himself that any honest man could unblushingly accept the paternity of

Laybach's progeny he was horrified to find them hideous and hydra-headed.

The Neapolitan revolution had barely been suppressed when to everyone's fury Jacobinism raised its head again in Piedmont and the Austrian army was called in to extinguish the flames of revolt. Chateaubriand, anxious in common with other ultra-royalists that France should play a more active role in Europe, thought the moment opportune for her to occupy Savoy and cast longing eyes on Spain. At the same time the Greeks in the Danubian principalities rose against their Turkish overlords. Although by the end of March Metternich was able to say that two revolutions had been suppressed about the third he entertained serious fears.

Such was the Prince's complacency that he easily shook off his disappointment that popular movements refused to submit to force by dwelling on his victory over Alexander, a perspective as wonderful to contemplate as the view from the mountains around Laybach. No one in the world was intelligent and wide awake enough even to hazard the nature of their conversation. If anyone had changed from black to white it was Alexander.

Was it in the course of this particular conversation that Metternich concluded the arrangement of which he later spoke to Stewart with perhaps calculated indescretion ? So secret was the understanding reached by him with the Czar on the present state of Turkey that Metternich had written it out with his own hand. He himself had taken the copy for the Emperor of Austria while Alexander preserved the original; no trace of the document existed in any archive.

Shuttling self-importantly between the two Emperors, whose complete confidence he enjoyed, Metternich was loath now to leave Laybach, alleging that here he could do in a minimum of time what would take months by courier, but at last there seemed no possible justification for prolonging the stay. Even Alexander felt that after some nine months' absence from Russia he ought to return.

A *Te Deum* was sung in the cathedral in honour of the 'victory' in Naples, the Emperor and Empress of Austria, watched from his window by Alexander, walked in the Easter Resurrection procession, a ball given by the nobility and a final supper and concert by Metternich heralded the end of the congress. As usual Metternich fell into a pensive mood; he now decided that Laybach's greatness, like the greatness of all things, was passing. Happily, to relieve his gloom the opera staged some good performances of Rossini's works which the Prince particularly admired. *Edoardo e Cristina* he considered one of his best operas and there was an enjoyable revival with better singers of *La Cenerentola*.

With greater eagerness even than usual Gentz set about collecting his 'gifts'—a fairly satisfactory conversation with Caraman about the French *douceur* was followed by a more cheering interview with Nesselrode and a gift of a thousand ducats with the hint of a pension. Most gratifying, in view of his previous neglect, was the promise of a testimonial from Francis together with a thousand ducats and a suggestion that suitable emoluments might be forthcoming in the future. The loss of Gentz' correspondence with the Hospodars would be less keenly felt.

At last came the final conference, the farewell visits of many Laybachers and on 12 May the 'Final Declaration of the Allied Sovereigns of Austria, Prussia and Russia on the breaking up of the Conferences of Laybach after the Suppressions of the Revolutions in the Two Sicilies and Sardinia'.

Gordon was much relieved to have it in his power to forward these last Allied *travaux* which had been brewing for ten days because he had been left in 'such perfect ignorance of the nature of them during their concoction'. Chief cook of the declaration was Pozzo di Borgo with language even more florid than Gentz' who now with a sigh of relief shut up his 'kitchen'.

The Declaration made up in length what it lacked in substance. The Allied Sovereigns, who had discovered the betrayal of throne and state by the Piedmontese conspirators, now happily announced that 'crime had disappeared before the sword of justice'. Under the guidance of Providence the Allied forces had come to the assistance of subdued peoples, not as an attack on their independence, but in support of their liberty, 'striking terror into guilty consciences'.

'All friends of right will see and will constantly find in their union a guarantee against the attempts of disturbers of the peace', trumpeted the Allied Sovereigns as, in the concluding paragraph of the Declaration, they 'proclaimed to the world the principles which guided them, from which they had decided never to depart.'

The tale of signatures to these high-sounding sentiments had shrunken considerably from that of Aix-la-Chapelle—for Austria only Metternich and Vincent, Krusemark alone for Prussia and the three stalwarts for Russia, Capo d'Istrias, Nesselrode and Pozzo di Borgo.

Four months had been idled away at Laybach to reach the only political decision of the congress, to send an army to Naples, which could easily have been taken at Troppau. Suppression of the revolt in Piedmont was a natural sequel to suppression of revolt in Naples but, if Metternich believed that the spirit of revolt could be quenched with the same ease as an uprising, he found he was mistaken.

The real success of the congress was the dominion gained by Metternich over Alexander, if the Czar were not again dissembling. So pleased was the Prince with himself that he even spared a little pity for Alexander's difficult position; he admitted that it was not easy suddenly to change the road one has taken all one's life. The Czar would need to show a great deal of strength to resist his entourage but in his moral dilemma he could fall back on the Austrian Chancellor.

With ill-concealed delight Metternich wrote to his wife,

'In Russia and among all the Russian diplomatists abroad there are two parties, openly called by the names of Metternich and Capo d'Istrias—Alexander is a Metternich.'

Stewart's reaction to the Final Declaration was immediate and angry. Great Britain's position was no longer the same with Austria as before the revolution in Italy.

'This Court and that of Russia so entirely play their game together when they formerly were so suspicious of each other that we are not looked upon as a feature of the same importance', Stewart wrote to Castlereagh.

Gentz had certainly not overstated the case when he said that Britain must be in the front rank, that a secondary role did not suit her. Clearly Stewart resented that the future policy of Austria and Russia would be to keep Britain from a close understanding with France.

'The decline of our importance in Italy and on the Continent in general will be approved of by Russia, for it has long been the secret aim of M. Capo d'Istrias and it will not now be opposed by Austria as she is not playing her cards now with us and we shall find her acting with France rather than England in Italian politicks.'

Perhaps it was alarm at the increasing isolation of Britain, not on the terms she had wanted but on those on which the Continental

Powers had decided, that caused Castlereagh to avail himself of the privilege he had used rarely of direct communication with the Czar. Two months after the closure of the congress at Laybach Castlereagh wrote to Alexander, reaffirming his belief in the unity of the existing system: whatever the late divergence of opinion on abstract theories of international law and the line of neutrality adopted with respect to Italian affairs 'there happily has hardly occurred an instance, since the auspicious period which gave birth to the existing Alliance, of any point of grave, practical, political difference between Your Imperial Majesty's councils and those of my August Master'.

Castlereagh was deeply convinced that the present European system would long continue to subsist for the safety and repose of Europe. In the interest of maintaining the Quadruple Alliance Castlereagh was anxious not to add any fuel to the flames of the Greek revolt, however great the outcry of liberals all over Europe.

> 'Turkey', he told the Czar, 'is an excrescence in Europe, scarcely to be looked on as forming any part of its healthful organization. What risks does Russia run of being disturbed by the insurrection propagating itself in its direction? What may Russian servants and subjects suffer in Turkey?'

Castlereagh urged Alexander to exercise forbearance and magnanimity to Turkey. Thus with the Italian situation in order, whether or no he approved the means taken to achieve it, Europe might be said to have settled down into a state of tranquillity, uneasy to be sure, but still tranquillity.

Nothing more than an event, not known in London until July, showed the difference in the preoccupations of the Congress of Aix-la-Chapelle and that of Laybach. At Aix the name of Napoleon Bonaparte figured on the agenda and his great shadow hung over the congress. Now, his death at St Helena on 5 May 1821, while the Congress of Laybach was in progress, obtained only a passing glance. The Annual Register for that year had no more to say than, 'The interest in England is chiefly as enabling a diminishing of expenditure by the reduction of the establishment at St Helena'—a nation of shopkeepers indeed. 'In France it has produced no sensible effect on the funds.' Byron for one saw Napoleon's death in its right perspective,

'. . . the fetter'd eagle breaks his chain
And higher worlds than this are his again!'

Before the Congress of Laybach had its formal closure in February
the decision was reached to call another congress in September of
the following year. September being a month which would not
interfere with Parliamentary business it was hoped that on this
occasion Castlereagh could be prevailed upon to attend.

'Since the Congresses of Vienna and Aix-la-Chapelle,' sneered
Chateaubriand, 'the princes of Europe have their heads turned by
congresses where one enjoys oneself and parcels out a few peoples.
Scarcely had the congress ended, begun at Troppau and continued
at Laybach, than they were thinking of summoning another at
Vienna, Ferrara or Verona.'

Before that congress took place Castlereagh and Metternich met
at Hanover in October 1821. As Prince Regent George IV felt
constitutionally inhibited from meeting the sovereigns of Europe.
No such delicacy was necessary now that he was king. He had toyed
with the idea of going to Vienna but perhaps was loath to drag his
bulk such a distance; instead he took the shorter journey to his
German kingdom of Hanover with his Foreign Secretary in attendance.

Since Castlereagh and Metternich had last met in 1818 Castlereagh
had changed his style and title when in 1821 he succeeded to his
father's marquessate of Londonderry but there was no alteration in
his affectionate regard for the Prince. The Turkish question was
the main subject of their friendly conversations, for once regarded
by Castlereagh as a practical not a theoretical matter. Their future
policy in this area was settled to their satisfaction and, when they
parted, Metternich took with him Castlereagh's promise to attend
the next congress to review the general situation. Verona was settled
on as the venue—perhaps everyone was now bored with the boredom of small towns.

At Laybach Metternich had resisted the discussion of Spanish
affairs pressed on him by the Czar. Now, when civil war broke out
in Spain in June, this discussion became imperative. The confidence
of the Three Courts that their intervention in Naples and Piedmont
had ensured the tranquillity of Europe was shaken. Once again their
councils were needed to arrest the tide of revolution.

CHAPTER XIV

The Gentlemen of Verona

'But lo! a Congress! What! that hallow'd name
Which freed the Atlantic! May we hope the same
For outworn Europe?. . . .

Pure rhetoric on Byron's part; neither he nor any other liberal
expected from the Congress anything but further repression, but
it was too useful a target for satire to neglect.

'But *who* compose this senate of the few
That should redeem the many? *Who* renew
This consecrated name, till now assign'd
To councils held to benefit mankind?
Who now assemble at the holy call?
The blest Alliance, which says three are all!'

The arithmetic was at fault; the Congress of Verona was a plenary
conference of the Quintuple Alliance and the gods themselves had
taken a hand in deciding who should be present in addition to 'the
earthly trinity'.

Richelieu would not be there. His ministry fell in December
1821, victim of the Comte d'Artois' bad faith, the contemptuous
indifference of Louis XVIII and the ultra-royalists' venom. In May
1822 Richelieu died, sincerely mourned by Alexander as 'the only
friend who made me listen to the truth' and for his great serivces
to Russia.

La Ferronays shared the Czar's regrets. Both felt keenly that
France failed to value Richelieu and what he had done for her and
that never again would Louis XVIII find such disinterested attachment. La Ferronays reflected sadly that the Duc was too diffident to

appreciate the confidence he inspired and the great ascendancy he might have gained over France. The Comte could only trust that the worth of this paladin, 'the model, henceforth lost, of a true French gentleman', would now be recognized.

Europe had barely recovered from the shock of Richelieu's death than it was appalled by an even greater calamity. The Duc died at the age of fifty-six from natural causes. On 12 August 1822 Castlereagh, three years younger, died by his own hand a few days before his planned departure for Verona.

Each man in his own way had fallen a victim to contumely and injustice which, preying upon sensitive natures hidden beneath a mask of indifference, undermined their nervous systems. Years of stress and overwork had exhausted Castlereagh until the worn tissues of his brain could not resist the final straw of a fancied threat of blackmail.

Castlereagh's bravery, imperturbable sang-froid, apparent disdain of men and things, instinct for despotism and secret scorn for constitutional liberties, said Chateaubriand, now French ambassador in London, made him detested but also feared. His faults, to Chateaubriand at least, were virtues fitting him to battle successfully against the propensities of the age.

Whatever the validity of this judgment and whatever the rejoicing of his enemies at home, Castlereagh's death caused consternation among his European colleagues and plunged the cabinet into a terrible dilemma. A British plenipotentiary had been promised for Verona where in the interests of unity it was vital that an authoritative British voice should be heard, but who could fill Castlereagh's place at the green table?

He alone in the cabinet had a genuine interest in and understanding of European affairs. He alone since 1813 was the constant factor in British foreign policy. No other British statesman was so intimately acquainted with the sovereigns and their ministers, no one else had fathomed their policies, their ambitions and their *weltanschauung*. Castlereagh was an irreparable loss to Europe.

Although since Troppau British policy had not wavered, hope persisted that in conference Castlereagh might have been persuaded to modify his views. Certainly his own moderating influence and the prestige of his presence would be badly missed at Verona. Whom would Britain send to the congress?

One man alone had a status in European councils as commanding as Castlereagh's, had comparable experience of negotiating with the European statesmen and enjoyed their confidence,

> 'Proud Wellington, with eagle beak so curl'd
> That nose, the hook where he suspends the world.'

Personal considerations were never allowed to impinge on the Duke of Wellington's sense of duty but understandably at this moment he was in a bad temper. He had just endured a painful operation to improve his hearing but it had been a disastrous failure, his balance was affected and he felt ill. Now he must be dragged out of bed to take the wearisome journey to Vienna and then participate in the delicate negotiations at Verona. The Duke was slightly cheered when George IV consented to the appointment as Foreign Secretary of George Canning whom Wellington supported. He was further mollified by a gracious letter from the King who placed his reliance in the forthcoming discussions on his 'friend'.

When, on 29 September, the Duke arrived at Vienna to find everyone on the point of departure for Verona he became decidedly tetchy again. Should he accompany the sovereigns or await their return at Vienna? In view of the cabinet's unalterable determination not to intervene in Italian affairs he feared his presence at Verona might be misconstrued. On the other hand he felt that the absence of a British plenipotentiary could only damage Britain's influence on her allies. Metternich succeeded in soothing both Wellington's fears and his temper and the Duke proceeded to Italy.

His mission was joined by Joseph Planta, despite the awkwardness of leaving the Foreign Office with a new Foreign Secretary who had not yet played himself in. The other members were Lord Clanwilliam, Lords Strangford and Burghersh, respectively ambassadors to the Sublime Porte and Tuscany, and Lord Stewart from Vienna.

When Stewart succeeded to his brother's honours as third Marquess of Londonderry he decided to leave the diplomatic service to look after his inheritance and his wife's vast fortune but not to ask for his letters of recall until the congress ended. A journey to Italy where she could take the baths at Venice and near Verona, would benefit his wife's health, always to the doting husband a matter of concern as vital as the destinies of Europe. Metternich was, therefore, asked to recommend Stewart's courier, Adamberger, and a great favourite with him and Castlereagh, to the Austrian quartermaster to find a suitable lodging.

Briefly the sovereigns were flattered by the expectation that for the first time the King of England would lend his countenance to a congress but, as his current mistress was reluctant to take the long journey, George IV decided to stay at home under the shelter of the umbrella of the British constitution.

Among the galaxy of sovereigns which made the Congress of Verona a close second to the Congress of Vienna the King of England's presence could be regretted but not missed. Francis of Austria brought his Empress and a large suite, Alexander a smaller entourage than at Aix-la-Chapelle, Frederick William the largest following of all, making up in numbers his own deficiencies. Bernstorff would lead the Prussian delegation; Hardenberg was another of the old guard who would not be at Verona. He was dying quietly at Genoa.

The King of Naples was persuaded to abandon for Verona the charms of hunting in the Vienna woods, preferable in any event to returning to a kingdom still occupied by the Austrian army. And every Grand Duke and Duchess from the minor states of Italy helped to fill the palazzi of which here there was no shortage.

Absent were the rag-tag and bobtail of Vienna and Aix-la-Chapelle. While those congresses were a free-for-all at Verona uncommon secrecy prevailed. Two hundred police from Venice and two hundred from Milan were drafted into the city where 'every precaution was taken to baffle prying curiosity; no stranger was allowed to remain without a most satisfactory explanation to the Austrian authorities, nor was permission even to pass through the town easy to obtain'.

Naturally this *cordon sanitaire* was relaxed to permit the passage of the Rothschilds, involved now in an Austrian loan, and Angelica Catalini. Somehow London journalists slipped through the net without passports 'to spy on history to catch it in flight'—the phrase is Chateaubriand's.

Boislecomte, again engaged in recording the private lives of the sovereigns, was a little wide of the mark in declaring that they generally regretted the peaceful and retired life of Laybach. They lived as informally at Verona as at other congresses but in an atmosphere of far greater interest and beauty.

Verona, with some 50,000 inhabitants, set in the fertile and luminous plain of the Po at the base of the olive-clad Alpine foothills

which rose in the distance to mountains topped with snow, was
cut in two by the noisy torrent of the Adige. An ancient castle
dominated the city's crenellated walls, its 12th-century Romanesque
cathedral, the Roman theatre and amphitheatre untouched by time
but damaged by an earthquake in 1814. Verona and its environs were
almost exaggeratedly rich in associations—Juliet's tomb, the castles
of Montagu and Capulet, Sirmione with its memories of Catullus,
Mantua and Vergil, Brescia and Bayard, the Brenta with its fabulous
Palladian villas and Venice crumbling and deserted.

The modern associations were less pleasing to the present visitors;
nearly every place name near Verona recalled a Bonaparte victory.
Many had given titles to his marshals and ministers—Treviso,
Padua, Rivoli, Castiglione, Conegliono, Montebello, Istria, Belluno,
Ragusa, whose Marshal-Duke, Marmont, handed Paris over to the
Allies in 1814, and Vicenza, dukedom of Caulaincourt, the negotiator
of Châtillon—names now best forgotten together with that of
Napoleon himself lying beneath the willows in Geranium Valley on
St Helena.

One person at least of all those at Verona found it easy to forget
the very name of the Emperor—his widow, Marie Louise, Duchess
of Parma. Heavily pregnant, she had eyes and thoughts only for
her *chevalier d'honneur*, Count Neipperg, father of her three bastards;
her recollection of the son of her marriage to the Emperor was vague.

Metternich's choice of Verona in preference to Florence as the site
of the congress was to impress his allies with the essential solidarity
of Italy and Austria as the city had a history of devotion to the
Imperial house and memories of the terrible vengeance exacted in
1799 by the French. The Prince was mistaken; perversely to all but
the French the Veronese gave a cold reception.

The indifference of the Veronese counted little to Metternich
against the built-in advantage he had again secured for himself with
a congress in his master's domains; naturally the presidency fell to
him. This was no empty honour since it gave him the initiative in
calling conferences, choosing his moment for attack or adjourning
meetings when conversations took an unfavourable turn.

Crowning Metternich's euphoria was the eclipse of Capo d'Istrias,
in which he believed he had played the major part. In fact what had
finally caused Alexander's revolt against Capo was his warm espousal
of the Greek cause. Robert Gordon reported the Czar's exasperation
with his ministers.

'All or the major part of the people I employ', he complained, 'are either Greeks or liberals. What is one to do with such people?'

What Alexander did was to dismiss Capo d'Istrias under the pretext of prolonged leave of absence in Switzerland. Russia knew no more 'the sinister element of eternal divisions'.

Because of *his* language and conduct on the Greek question and as a member of the Capo d'Istrias faction Pozzo di Borgo also stood in danger of utter disgrace. Before the congress party left Vienna for Verona the Czar scarcely tossed him a word but, in his strenuous efforts to reinstate himself in Alexander's good graces, Nesselrode stood Pozzo's warm friend. Since Nesselrode's patience and self-effacement had been rewarded with Capo's place he could afford to be generous.

No one, Metternich believed, stood as high as himself in the Czar's esteem; their personal relationship was as wholly intimate as the world demanded.

'He believes in me,' the Prince wrote to his wife, 'as much as does my August Master, and affairs benefit from this confidence more than they could by any other combination.'

The picture was far too rose-coloured. Wellington told Canning a different story.

'Since Prince Metternich has removed M. Capo d'Istrias from the Czar's presence, he has become in great degree himself His Imperial Majesty's principal adviser but, in order to maintain the influence he has acquired over H.I.M.'s counsels, he is obliged to bend his own opinions and to guide the conduct of the Austrian government in a great degree according to the views of Russia.'

Gentz might say that 'in the opinion of all the Courts and the world Metternich is justly regarded as the central point and the real moderator of European politics'; Chateaubriand would not agree. Since Metternich, while feigning to be Russian, detested Russia, he was caught in a noose of his own making.

As the congress proceeded Chateaubriand had ample opportunity of forming his own judgments of Alexander. Although Stewart still spoke, with echoes of Castlereagh's voice, of 'the mad notions and pretension of the Czar of Russia, whom it is necessary to calm and bring down from impolitic and impossible fancies', Alexander was no longer the ebullient personality he had been. His health was failing, his deafness an increasing handicap. He fell readily into melancholy, inescapable to the religious exaltation fatal to Russian sovereigns. The Archimandrite Photius was Alexander's Rasputin.

As they strolled together along the banks of the Adige when Alexander dwelt nostalgically on the beauties of St Petersburg in a dusk neither day nor moonlight, his elegiac mood harmonized with that of the archetypal romantic figure of René, Chateaubriand's self-portrait. Particularly were René's religious feelings the Czar's own.

'Solitude is evil to him who does not inhabit it with God . . . Whoever is endowed with strength should dedicate it to the service of his fellows: neglect to do so is punished first by secret misery and sooner or later heaven will inflict on him a terrible punishment.'

For the man whose *Génie du Christianisme* had influenced Napoleon to restore Catholicism in France the Czar could have nothing but respect, while under the influence of Chateaubriand's own charm he was disabused of the warnings he had received against him.

Another link between the two men was their earlier admiration for Napoleon. As a young man Chateaubriand vacillated between adherence to the Bourbon cause, which prompted his emigration to years of privation in England, and enthusiasm for the Emperor. From a great romantic anxious also to cut a figure in the diplomatic world consistency could not be awaited. Chateaubriand, drawn back into the Bourbon fold, was now afire to restore to the white cockade its pristine purity.

Mathieu de Montmorency, the French Foreign Minister and chief plenipotentiary to the congress, had tried to exclude Chateaubriand now ambassador in London but failed in face of his insistence on being present and his friendship with the Comte de Villèle, Richelieu's successor.

For as long as possible Montmorency kept Chateaubriand in the background as one of the crowd of French ambassadors, among them La Ferronays and Caraman but, when Montmorency returned to Paris, Chateaubriand was able to play the great game it was rumoured that he intended to do. For whatever slights he endured Chateaubriand was able to take a unique revenge. In his *Congrès de Vérone* he damned with superlative style if not always with truth everyone's house but his own with vigour exceeding Mercutio's.

Given Chateaubriand's obsessions—horror of the Treaties of Vienna, iron determination to give the Bourbons an army capable of defending their throne and freeing France from her dependence on her allies—his chief *bête noire* was the Duke of Wellington. The Duke had injured the Bourbon régime by giving it Fouché as minister and the nation by the crime of winning the battle of Waterloo.

Boislecomte's assessment of the Duke in his official résumé was more parliamentary. He, too, regretted the Duke's connection with Waterloo but felt it was now superseded by his character, his appreciation of Europe's general interests, his high personal understanding of and superiority to national rivalries. While Boislecomte predicted that the Duke's loftiness of mind would prove an obstacle to his entering into the prolonged dissimulation of political intrigue, Chateaubriand thought it merely a waste of time to attempt to influence Wellington to reverse his country's policy.

The French were more clear-sighted than Metternich, who fell into the error of overestimating the Duke's abilities as a negotiator because of his earlier successes, but Wellington had not yet encountered the difficulties he met at Verona. According to which side of the fence one sat on Wellington was either too inflexible or too lacking in subtlety to cope either with Metternich's complexities or Chateaubriand's romantic ardour.

The Duke moved on a higher plane at Verona than that of 'the thousand petty hatreds, jealousies and calumnies which met head on, the mutual detestation cloaked under a veil of liking, neighbours whose praises were sung on the staircase and torn to pieces behind closed doors—the old way of the world'.

After the preliminary skirmishing at Vienna the Congress of Verona was inaugurated by a ceremonial dinner at Metternich's lodging, the Casa Castellani. Did any significance attach to the Czar's being housed at the Palazzo Canossa? Would he at Verona as at Troppau continue to play the repentant Emperor to Metternich's Pope? And ought not the name of Alexander to have been substituted for that of the Greek hero in *The Ascent of Hercules to the Temple of Fame*, Tiepolo's fresco which adorned the walls of the *piano nobile* at the Palazzo Canossa?

The formal opening of the congress took place on 20 October and then followed the established routine—sittings as and when each Court produced a communication to be read and copies circulated to the other plenipotentiaries who generally replied by a Note then annexed to the *procès-verbal*.

Metternich was certain that the Congress of Verona was the most important held since 1814 but Gentz augured nothing good of it and was uneasy about its different 'feel' from its predecessors. While Alexander was still insistent on the preservation of unity among the Powers nothing could lead anyone to suppose that the divergences of Troppau could be reconciled.

The Czar was still singing the same tune; as once he had saved Europe from Napoleon's despotism so he was continuing to defend civilization from anarchy. His duty was to show himself convinced of the principles upon which he had founded the Alliance—and to the idea that it was his own creation Alexander stuck like a limpet. What embittered him was the antagonism aroused by his attachment to collective security.

'What has not been done to shatter the Alliance?' he burst out to Chateaubriand. 'They have in turn tried to prejudice me and to wound my *amour propre*; they have insulted me openly. They do not know me well if they think my principles are based on vanity alone and would yield to resentment. No, I shall never divorce myself from the monarchs with whom I am united. Kings should be permitted public alliances to defend themselves against secret societies.'

At Verona only two of the five main questions on the agenda of the congress were calculated to stir Alexander, his own dispute with Turkey and the dangers of the Spanish revolution for Europe and especially for France. Of lesser concern were piracy in the Atlantic, the Spanish colonies, the position of Italy and the perennial problem of the slave trade.

The quarrel between Russia and Turkey was dealt with at ambassadorial level by the representatives of Great Britain, Russia, Prussia and Austria. On this matter the British were allowed to shape their own course on the spot, referring home if need be, but under no circumstances to admit anything in the nature of a guarantee.

A congress within a congress, composed of representatives of all the interested parties, examined the question of Italy. Here Britain withdrew completely. So scrupulous was Wellington about British non-intervention in Italian affairs that he wished to leave Verona before the subject came under discussion. Britain had nothing to add to or subtract from the line taken in 1820 and 1821 at Troppau and Laybach.

Canning, snatched at the eleventh hour from his preparations for departure to India as Governor-General, and who had not even kissed hands on his appointment as Foreign Secretary before Wellington left for the Continent, had no time to formulate his instructions for the congress. Castlereagh had, however, written his own which were now Wellington's brief.

The policy laid down by Castlereagh was definite, immutable and, to the other Powers, foreboding. With regard to Spain Britain's attitude would be the same as to Naples—solicitude for the safety of the royal family but rigid abstinence from interference in Spanish internal affairs. Her attitude to the Spanish colonies promised to be more flexible. The British plenipotentiary must endeavour to persuade the Allies to adopt a common course while reserving the right of independent discretion according to circumstances. Although in April Castlereagh had told Chateaubriand that 'the English were not at all inclined to recognize the revolutionary governments in the Spanish colonies' it was now generally believed that in the interests of their commerce they would shortly do so.

On metropolitan Spain no compromises were possible. From London Canning warned Wellington that the Allied sovereigns contemplated some joint public declaration on her affairs, had even determined a project of interference by force or menace. So useless, so dangerous, so objectionable in principle and so utterly impracticable in execution was this course that Wellington must frankly and peremptorily declare that, come what might, His Majesty would not be a party to any such interference.

The Duke's inability to swim with the undercurrents of the congress led him to the comfortable conclusion that 'although he had never yet been witness to so much difficulty and embarrassment as in the discussion of the Spanish question', he felt the upshot would probably be to leave Spain to herself. At the end of October he reported that he thought all notion of what was called a European army or any offensive against Spain was at an end. The only battle to be fought would be at the green table with himself and the French in the thick of the fight while Metternich and Bernstorff would stay on the touchlines.

In fact Prussia put forward the sensible opinion that foreign Courts could not judge which institutions best suited the character, customs and real needs of the Spanish nation. Their future attitude towards Spain must naturally be guided by the possible effects upon themselves of the events there in progress.

Wellington's false optimism was based on his conversations in Paris with Villèle; he had formed the opinion that the French Prime Minister was disinclined to commit his country to war in Spain. The army of 100,000 men in southern France was to act as a *cordon sanitaire* against the yellow fever rampant in Spain. Villèle discounted the idea of any *moral* contagion for France from the Spanish revolution although he now felt that the army's role should be that of an observation corps to maintain the integrity of the frontier.

Chateaubriand deplored Villèle's moderation, that he was blind to the glaring evidence that legitimacy in France was dying for want of the victories to which Napoleon had accustomed the nation; glory was an idea more natural to the French even than liberty. An observation corps could not assuage the nation's thirst for glory.

To turn from the complex question of the Spanish revolution to the abolition of the slave trade was almost light relief although the congress raised a collective eyebrow at British insistence on discussing a matter so remote from the urgent affairs under consideration. Such perseverance was admirable but misplaced.

Hope of 'extirpating the scandal of the civilized world' had, in fact, been damped during the Duke of Wellington's conversations on the subject with Villèle. If only to avoid angry discussion with Britain the French government was anxious to end the traffic, but abolition was too unpopular in France to expect success. Since abolition was pressed on Louis XVIII by the British, submission would be a national disgrace.

Canning had feared that any moral pressure Wellington tried to bring to bear would be ineffective because Europe no longer felt the same enthusiasm for humanitarian causes as in 1815; he was also aware that other colonial powers accused Britain of cloaking self-interest under the mask of humanity.

The French justified their unco-operative attitude in their answer to the memoir on the slave trade submitted by Wellington. They fulfilled Canning's suspicion that they would block the adoption of any effectual resolution by the Allies or, if one were adopted, frustrate its operation.

For posterity Chateaubriand recorded the excoriating opinion which diplomacy made it impolitic for him to air at the congress. He sneered at the Tories who for thirty years resisted Wilberforce's exertions for the slaves but now, while continuing to oppose the liberty of the whites, were fanatical about liberty for the blacks. The secret of these contradictions lay in the private interests and mercantile genius of England, afraid lest the trade she regretfully abandoned benefit her commercial rivals. This fear must be appreciated in order not to become the dupe of a zealous but tardy philanthropy. Finally Chateaubriand asked why the British should hope for concessions on a matter affecting them deeply when they refused any compromise on subjects of equal concern to their Continental colleagues.

Not all Chateaubriand's leisure hours at the Palazzo Lorenzi were spent in compiling his future history of the Congress of Verona. The choice of entertainment was almost as wide as at Aix-la-Chapelle—the inevitable balloon ascent, riderless horse races, excursions to the lakes and mountains, drives up and down the Corso on Sundays, *soirées musicales* at the Duke of Wellington's and Metternich's, concerts and theatrical performances at the two theatres. In fact the professional actors were up-staged by the two amateurs—Metternich in narcissistic admiration of his own performances and Chateaubriand who dramatized himself and his actions.

Metternich was fortunate in having his own *claque* at Verona in the person of Dorothea Lieven, with whom he spent his evenings, claiming that she was his sole resource for society. The Prince need fear no rival in Chateaubriand who detested the 'dowager of Congresses' and regarded Madame de Lieven as a vulgar, arid woman who represented the diplomatic puerilities of the past, hiding the paucity of her ideas under an abundance of words and clothing her nullity with a superior air of *ennui* as if she had the right to be bored.

Chateaubriand still had some vitriol to spare for Marie Louise. While her father continued his simple and well-regulated existence his daughter made a parade of herself which in her equivocal position was almost indecent. She showed no hesitation in going into dinner on the 'right arm, yet red from Waterloo' of the Duke of Wellington, was eager to have Chateaubriand to dinner and blandly played cards for stakes in *napoléons*, apparently oblivious of any incongruity in her behaviour.

Gentz' reaction to Marie Louise was naturally different; to him she was the daughter of the Emperor of Austria, not a faithless wife. He was flattered to be received by her, to make a grand 'toilette' to have dinner with her, and found her charming and kindly. His audience with Alexander offered him another kind of satisfaction.

The Czar, with no reviews or regiments to inspect, filled his empty hours with his second love, conversation. Verona presented him with little other opportunity of drawing attention to himself, still less of attracting the personal acclaim which meant so much to him.

These pleasant meetings were only an interlude for Gentz in the arduous work of a congress bedevilled by the Spanish question which seemed incapable of solution. By now it was apparent that for all the positive contribution the British plenipotentiary was going to make in clarifying this intractable problem he might as well have stayed away. The invidious task would fall upon the Four Powers—if they could reach agreement.

Metternich opposed the idea that in Spain France should act as Austria had acted in Naples but, like the Prince at Troppau, Montmorency wanted to make peace or war a wholly European question. Villèle's contention that it was a matter for France alone had Chateaubriand's ardent suport.

What Gentz had already foreseen in 1818 was now coming to pass, that for France the alliance was a burden rather than a benefit and that five or six years hence she would find means of going her own way. His timing was accurate. The Spanish revolution was the means, dangerous but glorious, of simultaneously restoring French political power and military force and detaching France from the alliance.

Chateaubriand gloated that unconsciously both Canning and Wellington played into his hands. The Duke, conducting himself at Verona as if still commanding at Waterloo, was insistent that, if France entered the Peninsula, she would be lost. What greater satisfaction, therefore, to the French royalists than equalling Wellington's triumphs in Spain, that an impotent old king without an army should succeed where Napoleon failed? Had not the Duke said, moreover, that it was madness to contemplate military intervention in a country as impervious to attack and as unconquerable as Russia? French success in Spain would provide a glorious opportunity for avenging Waterloo and humbling the Duke of Wellington.

No one else should share France's glory. When Alexander, with a gesture as romantic as any made by Chateaubriand himself, told the Ambassador that his sword was at the service of France, the offer was gracefully but hastily declined. France, Chateaubriand answered, should by her own efforts regain the place of which the Treaties of Vienna had deprived her; when her dignities were restored she would be a more useful and honourable ally for Russia.

What Chateaubriand refrained from saying was that nothing on earth would persuade the French government to permit a Russian army to march through France. Alexander's offer was not inspired by chivalry alone. Repeatedly he had attempted to get his army adopted as the army of Europe and on each occasion he had met Castlereagh's strenuous opposition. Metternich also would not countenance the idea. Whatever the affection and understanding between him and the Czar of Russia, the Prince told Stewart, he would never submit to a Russian army being forced on France. He flattered himself that with management and Austro-French agreement on this point, he had discovered the means of 'paralysing the Czar of Russia's eagerness, without offending that chivalrous and moral spirit and action which it is so much all our interests to preserve'.

Frustrated again of using the Russian army as a European police force, Alexander was now pressing for a joint declaration of the congress similar to that issued from Troppau but he was obliged to pause when Wellington declared Britain's readiness to quit the alliance rather than consent to a démarche which would inevitably lead to war.

While Villèle still hoped to keep the peace, in France agitation was growing for war against Spain. Although he wished France to act alone, if war was inevitable, Villèle was still anxious to know what assistance she might expect in case of need from her allies. The three Central Powers agreed that their ambassadors in Madrid should make representations to the government demanding a change in the Constitution, a move strongly deprecated by Wellington. The Duke favoured mediation—were Great Britian invited to mediate; she would not propose it herself.

No argument could persuade the British that Spain in revolt constituted any threat to Europe, an attitude which clashed head on with that of the French and in the following year brought the two countries to the verge of war. By then Chateaubriand had succeeded Montmorency as Foreign Minister and achieved 'his war' with Spain and 'all the argument about it and about' had proved in vain.

On this unsatisfactory note the congress was drawing to its close although still striving to maintain at least the appearance of the *solidarité* so dear to Metternich and Alexander. The harmony lacking in conference Metternich sought to achieve in other ways. For the congress the Prince had invited Rossini to compose and conduct some ceremonial pieces, rather for his own delectation than for that of others. Rossini's frequent appearances and solos at Metternich's salon produced the groan from Gentz, 'That's all we needed.' Frederick William was another who would endure rather than enjoy Rossini's music. In Berlin he had confided to Chateaubriand how much he detested it and how much he loved Gluck. The King dwelt gloomily on the decadence of art and particularly the destruction of dramatic singing by the gargling of notes.

By borrowing from some of his own compositions Rossini hastily put together four cantatas with libretti by Gaetano Rossi. Their titles flattered the congress—*Il vero omaggio*, *L'augurio felice*, *Il Bardo* and *La Santa Aleanza*. The greatest honour fell to *La Santa Aleanza* which was performed on 24 November in the amphitheatre with a scratch orchestra made up of local musicians and military bands. To add to the enjoyment of the sovereigns and a vast audience there was dancing, mime and a lottery with prizes.

This occasion which Gentz found splendid and unforgettable was quite differently regarded by Boislecomte. The imposing sight of 50,000 spectators ranged on the rows of the amphitheatre diminished the majesty of the sovereigns. The presence of the multitude underlined its power and the danger of permitting it thus to demonstrate its latent force. It was, said the historiographer, a mistake the sovereigns were not tempted to repeat.

Whether or not the monarchs shared Boislecomte's fears the season was now too advanced for further out-of-door entertainments. Rossini's next cantata, *Il vero omaggio*, was sung before the sovereigns at the Teatro Filarmonico. Of the performance of *Il Bardo* and *L'augurio felice* no record exists, perhaps because the auguries were far from auspicious.

Although at the last moment Britain's attitude appeared to be softening and she showed herself less opposed to the interests of Continental Europe, the time for any démarche from her had passed, if it had ever been practicable. From the moment the Four Powers reached agreement they became more indifferent about Britain.

Chateaubriand heaved a sigh of relief that the congress was dying; had it died before it was born it would have saved great embarrassment. He hoped that this congress would be the last, a hope that was realized. The Congress of Verona was the last of the series of congresses begun at Aix-la-Chapelle and continued at Troppau and

Laybach. Europe was not alone responsible—the growing importance of the United States substituted a global for a purely European outlook.

Had the Congress of Verona reached any definite conclusions the Powers might have been tempted to prolong the congress system but the only achievement to which the final Circular, issued on 14 December, could point was the settlement of Italy. The plenipotentiaries were obliged to admit openly that no such agreement had been reached with regard to Spain. The congress had eluded rather than resolved difficulties, adjourned rather than concluded decisions.

Perhaps Castlereagh could have produced a more conciliatory attitude, discovered a more satisfactory formula to patch up the alliance. Canning was only too eager to strike out a line of his own, to implement the views on international meetings he had expressed in 1818. Unexpectedly he had achieved the office of which he had despaired, so long held by his rival. Perhaps it was only human that he should seek to upset Castlereagh's policies.

In 1823 Canning denied to the House of Commons that he knew that Spain would be the main topic of discussion at Verona and withheld from the House the documents which gave him the lie. Boislecomte attributed Wellington's inflexibility to the bitter passions of the people around him which modified his general conciliatory dispositions. He did not mention Canning whose duplicity allowed the blame for the failure of Verona to fall on Castlereagh; it was at least shared.

Not all Canning's contemporaries were his dupe. Hazlitt met Canning with wit for wit and even greater pungency.

'When a monstrous claim that threatens the liberty and existence of the civilized world is openly set up and acted upon, and a word from Mr Canning would arrest its progress in the direction in which it is moving with obscene, ghastly, bloodstained strides, he courageously reminds his hearers . . . that the epithet quixotic would be eminently applicable to the conduct of Great Britain if she interfered in the affairs of the Continent at the present juncture . . . One moment he is all for liberty, and the next for slavery. First we are to hold the balance of Europe, and to dictate and domineer over the whole world; and then we are to creep into our shells and draw in our horns.'

Now the Congress of Verona was at an end. More Orders and decorations if fewer ducats for Gentz. More Rossini for Metternich as in Venice he gorged himself on his music at the Fenice and the Court concerts the composer gave for Alexander and Francis, pausing at Venice on their homeward way. To Wellington Metternich wrote enthusiastically about a new *piano forte* invented by a Venetian; he strongly recommended the Duke, such an amateur of singing accompanied by a piano, to commission the new invention for himself. And then the music lover gave way once more to the statesman, to congratulate himself on the uncommon *tour de force* he had accomplished with Alexander,

'I am on the best possible terms with him and have no fear of this state of affairs ending.'

Metternich forgot mortality.

The Vicomte François-René de Chateaubriand,
French ambassador to the Court of St. James's

Cartoon of 1823 entitled

CHAPTER XV

The Unconscious Europeans

SOME ten years after the congress Chateaubriand passed through Verona on his way to Rome. The city, so lively in 1822 in the presence of the sovereigns of Europe, had reverted to silence. Through its now solitary streets the Congress of Verona, like the Court of the Scaligers and the Senate of the Romans, had flitted and, like them, the place thereof knew it no more.

Wandering alone along the banks of the Adige, where once he had walked with Alexander, Chateaubriand mused upon the men who had directed what dramas, dreamed of what futures, explored and weighed what national destinies. When last he had strolled here with the Czar he had a presentiment as he took his hand in farewell that they would never meet again, that soon Alexander, still so young, so strong, so handsome, would be looked for in vain.

In the deserted amphitheatre, where once the brilliant personalities of the congress had listened to Rossini conducting *La Santa Aleanza*, Chateaubriand called the roll of the pursuivants of dreams. He opened the book of the *dies irae* to summon up the past.

'Monarchs! Princes! Ministers! Here is your ambassador, here your colleague returning to his post; where are you? Answer!' And round that vast enclosure ran the echo, 'Dead'.

Dead, Alexander, Byron's 'coxcomb Czar, The autocrat of waltzes and of war, As eager for a plaudit as a realm'. The plaudits so frequently denied Alexander in his lifetime were now eagerly offered him in the tomb. To Stewart, who at Aix-la-Chapelle had thought so lightly of the Czar, his death was an event disastrous for Europe; he was persuaded that no sovereign ever had brilliant qualities nor any private individual more estimable attributes. Stewart looked back with nostalgia to 'the memorable transactions . . . which formed a union of amity and bond of confidence which ensured peace'.

9

Wellington, a just man, agreed that in England especially Alexander's value was not sufficiently appreciated.

Dead, Alexander? Dead, the Czar, 'too strong to be a despot, too weak to establish liberty'? Then what was the real identity of the hermit who made a sudden appearance in Siberia ten years after the Czar's death, whose resemblance to him was so pronounced, who had such powerful protectors and so intimate a knowledge of the Russian royal family? Dead, Alexander? Then why, when his coffin was opened years later, was it found to be empty?

Many people have thought that the solution to the possible mystery lay hidden in the papers of that Lord Cathcart who was ambassador to St Petersburg in Alexander's lifetime. They were mistaken; the papers have nothing to tell. That theory must now be abandoned. If it was the wish of the Czar of All the Russias to feign his death so that Alexander Romanoff could seek salvation in a life devoted to prayer then the hermit, Fyodor Kuzmich, should be allowed to keep his secrets and the body of Alexander, wherever it may lie, to rest in peace.

In the amphitheatre Chateaubriand continued his apostrophe to the relentless echo. Dead, Louis XVIII, and Wellington's prediction at last fulfilled; the descendants of Louis XV no longer reigned in France. Dead, Ferdinand of Naples, dead Ferdinand of Spain, the two effete monarchs whose failure to come to grips with the spirit of the age was responsible for the calling of the Congresses of Troppau, Laybach and Verona.

Dead, George Canning, never a congress man but one whose opposition effectively destroyed the congress system. Dead George IV and Bernstorff and Neipperg whose place in Marie Louise's bed was already filled.

Dead, Capo d'Istrias, not a Verona ghost but one which haunted the sites of previous congresses. In the end it was Capo who triumphed; until struck down by an assassin he had fulfilled his cherished dream that Greece might still be free and died as first President of the Ionian Republic.

Gentz had outlived the glorious congress years, to lose Metternich's confidence, to see himself rejected by the world, forced, after the July Revolution, to concede that the spirit of the age was more powerful than the spirit of tradition. No one now came to offer him the flattery to which he was so susceptible. Surrounded only by cases of the Orders and decorations which once had meant so much to him to win, only his autumnal passion for the young dancer, Fanny Elssler, brought a little sunshine into those abandoned years.

So many great figures now vanished from the European scene that the cry must be *qui vive*? Francis of Austria lived on, wax in the hands of Metternich, himself ever more self-satisfied, ever unwilling to credit the nations with any aspirations other than eternal devotion to their hereditary sovereigns. Metternich was the perpetual Mrs Partington of Europe, trying with the ineffectual brooms of police and censorship to stem the rising tide of nationalism and revolution until in 1848 they swept him away. In the end he returned from exile to Vienna, to the villa on the Rennweg whence he had gloriously manipulated the Congress of Vienna. There in 1859 he died, a monument to a vanished age.

Qui vive? The Duke of Wellington lived on until 1852, just before the nephew of his enemy proclaimed himself Emperor of the French as Napoleon III. The Duke was never a congress man in the same way as his colleagues. He could organize the British squares to victory but he lacked Castlereagh's gift of charging through the massed ranks of intrigue and ambition to the heart of the matter.

And Frederick William survived until 1840; he had never counted for much at the congresses and now did not count at all, but his second son, William, first Emperor of the united Germany, changed the face of Europe until his grandson, the second William, changed the face of the world. Under the direction of Bismarck, the man of blood and iron, more powerful than Hardenberg, Prussia became the threat to Europe foreseen by Talleyrand.

Qui vive? Pozzo di Borgo and Sir Charles Stuart, now Lord Stuart de Rothesay, continued their careers, one as Russian ambassador in London until shortly before his death in 1842, the other as British ambassador to St Petersburg. Stuart had the last word in their perpetual debate; he survived Pozzo by three years.

And then, of the congress men, only Nesselrode lived on. At Troppau Metternich sneered that Nesselrode was morally dead but he practised the art of survival with such success that he signed yet another Peace of Paris, the peace which in 1856 ended the Crimean War when, for all the strenuous efforts Richelieu had made to unite them, France and Russia were on opposite sides.

After his death in 1862 Nesselrode's diplomatic fame melted away, fragile as the confection of ice cream and chestnut purée created by Carême and in the diplomatist's honour called *Bombe Nesselrode*.

And Chateaubriand himself? Today he yawned his life away in poverty and eclipse when all that remained to him was his pen and his unquenchable ardour for lost causes. In that superb piece of egotism, the *Congrès de Vérone*, he re-lived the days of his power and glory, confiding the misfortunes as well as the splendours of his life to his massive posthumous memoirs, *Mémoires d'Outre-Tombe*.

As his greatest glory Chateaubriand counted 'his' war with Spain in 1823, the war which almost succeeded in precipitating war between England and France and which earned him the sharpest digs of Canning's pen.

'You have united the opinions of this whole nation, as if it were one man, against France. You have excited against the present sovereign of that kingdom the feelings which were directed against the usurper of France and Spain in 1808.'

Canning's sneer, however, was vain—'You have, you say, a million soldiers at your call; I doubt it not and it is double the number or thereabouts, that Buonaparte buried in Spain.' France won her puny war against the Spaniards and her troops remained to occupy the country until 1828.

One Foreign Minister spoke to another when Canning thus addressed Chateaubriand. On his return from Verona Chateaubriand succeeded Montmorency, but his tenure of office was brief. He had his revenge for his dismissal in helping to bring down Villèle's ministry and then boxed and coxed as ambassador in Rome with Auguste de la Ferronays, himself briefly Foreign Minister in 1828. Then the Bourbons, for whose cause both men had made such sacrifices, were turned out of France in the July Revolution. For La Ferronays once again a voluntary exile and for Chateaubriand a bravura part in the Duchesse de Berri's mad enterprise in the Vendée to win the throne back for her son.

Chateaubriand needs neither chefs' compliments nor a Spanish war nor the holding of high office on which to rest his fame. The great romantic, who shaped his own life in the mould he created for his heroes, influenced a century of writers and keeps an unassailable position in the literature of the world.

Time now to leave Verona and its memories; here there was no more to do.

'Hence, my Muse, from the green oases,
Gather the tent, begone!'

No one came again to trouble Verona's ghosts; the congress system
did not long survive its two architects, Castlereagh and Alexander. The
Congress of Verona in 1822 was the last of the congresses miscalled
'of the Holy Alliance'; they were never that. The Congress of Aix-
la-Chapelle assembled under the auspices of the Quadruple Alliance.
Troppau, Laybach and Verona, although dominated by the three
Central Powers, were ostensibly under the aegis of the Quintuple
Alliance although only Verona, where Britain and France had full
plenipotentiary representation, really merited the name of a congress
of the Five Powers.

A few half-hearted attempts were made in the eighteen-twenties
to hold further congresses, but the same ties no longer held the
nations together. Their common enemy was no longer a man,
Napoleon Bonaparte, but a spirit, the spirit of the age, about which
there was no unanimity of views. Liverpool and Canning, securely
seated in Castlereagh's chair of Foreign Secretary, could now with
impunity ignore Article VI of the Quadruple Alliance. Without fear
of contradiction Canning could revive the arguments used in 1818
to convince Castlereagh of the inadvisability of holding periodical
reunions of sovereigns or statesmen.

Alexander's congress at St Petersburg in 1824 to discuss the
Graeco-Turkish question was in reality only a conference at ambassadorial level nor was Great Britain represented. No conclusions
were reached; its sole achievement was to open a rift between Austria
and Prussia, demonstrating the actual tenuousness of Metternich's
vaunted ascendancy over Alexander. Nicholas I, Alexander's
successor, was not amenable to Metternich's seduction.

The congress system did not die *sine prole*. Although Alexander's
death in 1825 deprived it of its conductor and one by one the
member states, like the players in Haydn's *Farewell Symphony*,
silently blew out their candles and stole off the rostrum, they left
behind their scores with their chords and discords to be picked up
by other players with different instruments.

Eldest child of the congress system was the system of conferences which, throughout the 19th century and into the 20th,
followed its seniors in attempting to regulate international disputes
by getting together round a green table. These conferences were

bound by no treaties or ideologies like those of the Quadruple, Quintuple or Holy Alliances; no one put forward doctrines like Alexander
at Aix-la-Chapelle. The diplomatists dealt with those matters which
were the *raison d'être* of their meeting and went their ways.

Lacking the pomp and panache of the sovereigns' presence, their
personal role increasingly on the decline, the conferences could not
in distinction rival the congresses. Only two by their scope challenged
comparison with the Congresses of 1818–1822—the Congress of
Berlin in 1878 and the Conference of Berlin in 1884, both summoned
by Bismarck on whom Metternich's mantle had fallen. The mere
choice of venue showed how the balance of power in Europe had
shifted.

An earlier generation of statesmen might well have tried as did
the Berlin Congress to achieve a balance in south-western Europe,
but not even Canning could have foreseen that in 1884 the partition
of central Africa among the European Powers should be debated
at any level. During the congress years the only extra-European
problems occupying the statesmen were the slave trade and the
Spanish and Portuguese colonies nor was President Monroe's
doctrine given to the world until a year after the Congress of Verona.
The men of the congresses would now have found themselves
on familiar ground only with the eternal problem of the slave
trade.

Europe was no longer the axis around which the world revolved.
Now she was only one of five continents, progressively losing her
ascendancy to the American. True, that vast empire with which
Napoleon had kindled Alexander's imagination at Tilsit was daily
growing in size and strength, but the British Empire, on which the
sun never set, ruled unchallenged over east and west alike.

The chief reproach now levelled at the congress statesmen is their
neglect of the rising tide of nationalism, yet to this accusation there
is a very simple retort. With rare exceptions they had no nationalistic
feelings because they did not serve the countries of their birth.

Metternich, the great Austrian chancellor, was a Rhinelander.
Hardenberg, one of Prussia's most distinguished statesmen, a
Hanoverian. In common with most of the Russian ambassadors
abroad Alexander's chief advisers on foreign affairs were non-
Russians, La Harpe a Swiss, Czartoryski a Pole, Nesselrode a
German born in Portugal. Capo d'Istrias a Corfiote Greek and
Pozzo di Borgo a Corsican Frenchman. Castlereagh and Wellington

were Irishmen who grew up in the sister kingdom before the Act of Union, while Planta was of Swiss origin and Clancarty, Clanwilliam and Cathcart Scots or Irish. Significantly only France, long a united nation, was represented by Frenchmen born and bred.

All these men would strenuously have denied that they were the mercenaries of diplomacy although many of them, voluntary or involuntary émigrés like Pozzo di Borgo, were happy enough to find a haven for their bodies, an outlet for their talents and a means of livelihood in foreign countries. Of them all only La Harpe, Czartoryski, Pozzo di Borgo and Capo d'Istrias continued to hold their native lands in their minds and hearts, and of the quartet only two were congress men. Try as Pozzo might to be a Russian he succeeded only in remaining a Frenchman. Capo d'Istrias controlled his Greek patriotism better but, when opportunity presented itself, he gladly abandoned Russia for Greece.

In thus wedding their destinies to countries other than those of their birth the congress statesmen became not only unconscious Europeans but even unconscious internationals, although only Gentz, a Prussian in the service of Austria, had some title to be considered the first international servant outside the Roman Catholic church. All of them would have stoutly rebutted the title of European; none of them would have admitted the internationalism which was the dream Alexander confided at Verona to Chateaubriand,

'In the civilized world there must be no more English, French, Russian or Austrian policies, but only a general policy which, for the salvation of all, must be recognized both by peoples and by monarchs.'

At St Helena Napoleon, embroidering his past in the cause of his legend, asserted that he had intended to weld the great nations of Europe into a confederation united by the same codes, principles, opinions, feelings and interests. This project may have been the product of *esprit de l'escalier* but the nucleus of such a confederation existed already in the French Empire. When with time the steel bonds of French domination loosened, as they must have done, it is not perhaps too fanciful to imagine that a real European federation might have evolved under a *pax Gallicana*.

Did not the Congress of Vienna give its blessing to the Confederation of Germany, an amalgam of autonomous states under federal suzerainty, based it is true on geographical and linguistic rather than national principles? That this Confederation could develop into the German Empire was proof of the evolutionary possibilities of any federation of states.

Any attempt to contain 'Jacobinism' on a European scale died with the congress system but, whatever the inherent weakness and deficiencies of that system, its influence succeeded in steering the nations away from general war for almost precisely one hundred years after Waterloo. Gentz had no confidence in a perpetual peace but it is at least arguable that a continuing congress system might ultimately have succeeded in total elimination of war. The gods saw otherwise.

When the Great War ended on 11 November 1918 not only battle scars had changed the face of Europe; an epidemic of revolutions had swept away princes and kingdoms. The vast areas of empires broke up into ethnic groups, mainly of the shattered Austro-Hungarian empire, which clamoured now for the national entity that had eluded them during the congress years. Curiously, or perhaps because the new nations realized that autonomy was not identical with strength, with nationalism came a desire for internationalism or what Alexander had called *solidarité*.

Before his election as President of the United States Woodrow Wilson was an academic, certainly acquainted with all previous attempts to introduce to the world what was now his Fourteenth Point: 'Formation of a general association of nations to guarantee the political independence of all states'.

In 1919 this 'general association' became the League of Nations with a permanent home in Switzerland, whose perpetual neutrality had been guaranteed by the Congress of Vienna, with a permanent secretariat. As the world had grown immeasurably larger since Gentz' day the membership of this secretariat went far beyond the European bureau suggested in Paris in 1815 but the League's ideals and guiding principles remained substantially those of the men who struck the opening bars of the Concert of Europe.

Like the Final Act of the Congress of Vienna, the Peace of Paris and the Quadruple Alliance, the Covenant of the League of Nations was signed by the signatories of treaties of peace, known in this instance collectively as the Treaty of Versailles; like them the League was empowered to admit those who wished to join and who subscribed to its aims and objects as set out in the Preamble to the Covenant.

'The High Contracting Parties in order to promote international co-operation and achieve international peace and security agree to this Covenant of the League of Nations by the acceptance of obligations not to resort to war; by the prescription of open, just and honourable relations between nations; by the firm establishment of international law as the actual rule of conduct among governments and by the maintenance of justice and a scrupulous respect for all Treaty obligations in the dealings of organized peoples with one another.'

What essential difference is there between this manifesto of the League of Nations and all the proposals put forward by Alexander during the congress years, particularly the Russian memoir which at Aix-la-Chapelle so irritated Castlereagh? Muffled they may be in Capo d'Istrias' tortured phrases but Alexander's ideas on how to achieve the 'order which is the basis of human society' still emerge.

The Czar looked forward to the day when the moral force of the wider association of nations he advocated would be strengthened by time and experience, when the security both of governments and peoples would be protected by guarantees similar to those which protect individuals, when from the principle of mutual defence, publicly proclaimed and universally accepted, the liberties of peoples would be ensured.

No one in 1818, with the exception of Friedrich von Gentz, was ready to admit that wider association for which Alexander fought so passionately. An alliance of Five Powers was the limit to which they would go in their unwillingness to suspend disbelief to extract what was concrete in Alexander's abstractions. Castlereagh's narrow nationalistic doctrine prevailed and was pursued, after his death, more vigorously by Canning. Their posthumous influence succeeded in postponing for a hundred years the federation which, had it been given the Czar's 'time and experience', might have succeeded in establishing the tranquillity first of Europe and then of the world on an impregnable basis.

As Dr Chaim Weizmann said in another context,

'A great opportunity found a small generation.'

Yet all was not lost. The congress system established precedents which could not be ignored and was triumphantly vindicated by its direct descendant, the League of Nations.

Alexander could not understand why a nation should renounce its peaceful and honourable existence, expose itself to the horrors

9*

of revolution and war, if no suitable opportunities offered to tempt its ambitions.

> 'And who is the usurper or conqueror who would still dare to emerge with no nation to corrupt? How could he carry along with him a nation which saw disaster in following him and with Europe in arms forbidding him any territorial aggrandizement?'

The League of Nations failed precisely because such a conqueror did emerge in the person of Hitler. Where Alexander was always eager to commit his army of Europe to defend her from Jacobinism the League's reluctance to resort to war permitted Hitler to indulge his unjustifiable greed for territorial aggrandizement.

Once again after a global war the nations in 1945 made a fresh effort to curb their own turbulence, to find a formula for perpetual peace. The gentlemen of Verona would have been astounded to see the faces at the opening conference of United Nations, every degree of black, every shade of yellow almost dominating the white. They would have caught a familiar note, however, in the First Article of the First Chapter of the Purposes of United Nations.

> 'To maintain international peace and security, and to that end to take collective measures for the prevention and removal of threats to the peace and for the suppression of acts of aggression or other breaches of the peace, and to bring about by peaceful means, and in conformity with the principles of justice and international law, adjustment or settlement of international disputes or situations which might lead to a breach of the peace.'

Will United Nations endure and will it be more successful than its predecessors in keeping the peace? If, with all the nations of the world gathered under its roof and the world's resources at its disposal, it fails to do so then who can blame the congress system for disintegrating? The times alone are different, human aspirations are the same—nations wearied by prolonged and devastating wars seek, as they sought in the congress years, to ensure that there will be no repetition. All depends upon the men who make policies; policies do not make men.

United Nations acts as a vast and permanent congress to settle the world's affairs rationally and amicably but, within its framework, two Powers still struggle for supremacy, Russia and the United

States, as once the Russian and the Austrian empires competed with each other. To counteract their hegemony and to form a buffer between them has grown up the idea of a united Europe.

This idea of a united Europe is not an innovation; it merely revives in modern economic terms a very old ideal. Did Rousseau not see in federation the only hope for Europe, the idea Alexander caught on the wing to enmesh in his own ideology? Nor were these men alone in believing that union was the only guarantee of security. In 1800 another political thinker, the French Delisle de Sales, advocated a congress of all the European Powers, one neither intimidated by open force nor influenced by secret machinations. This congress should lay the foundation of an equilibrium, altering the elements of no throne or republic, but tracing the first lines of a diplomatic act which no Power would find it advantageous to violate. Every Power, not excepting San Marino, should send its plenipotentiary to the permanent home of this congress.

In reviewing Delisle de Sales' plan the *Anti-Jacobin* expressed a good deal of scepticism. English phlegm prevented its rising on the wings of French enthusiasm and viewing this promised land with any hopes of future possession.

'Imperfect materials can never produce a perfect work; and unless this projector can form men anew he will find that he has promised what human nature cannot attain.'

Are men, although capable of lofty aspirations, incapable of compassing them? Is the rule of reason, justice and humanity always to be unattainable? Perhaps Bignon, implacable enemy of the Holy Alliance though he was, gives the answer. He, too, foresaw a congress of the civilized nations, speaking the same language in twenty different idioms, as the only infallible tribune, but even this congress must yield to an authority greater than its own—the authority of time.

Select Bibliography

Archives des Affaires Etrangères, Paris
   Correspondance diplomatique, Mémoires et Documents
   Auguste de la Ferronays, Dossier personnel
Archives de l'Etat, Archives Diplomatiques des Pays Bas,
   Recueil Charles de Jonghe
Public Record Office
Stadtarchiv, Aachen
British Museum, Heytesbury Papers, Add. Mss. 41522, 41523
                        Liverpool Papers, Add. Mss. 38286, 38287
Durham County Record Office, The Londonderry Papers, D/LO/D
Archives du Ministère des Finances 1817–1824
Historical Manuscripts Commission, Bathurst Papers
Aix-la-Chapelle, Souvenir d', Anon, 1846
ALISON, SIR ARCHIBALD, *Lives of Lord Castlereagh and Sir
   Charles Stewart*, William Blackwood & Sons, Edinburgh & Lon-
   don, 1861
ARMSTRONG, WALTER, *Lawrence*, Methuen & Co., Ltd., 1913
BIGNON, L. P. E., *Les Cabinets et Les Peuples*, 1822 Paris Béchet Ainé
                        Du Congrès de Troppau, Paris, Firmin Didot, 1821
BOULART, *Mémoires de Baron*, Paris, A la Librairie Illustrée
BOURQIN, MAURICE, *Histoire de la Sainte Alliance*, Génève,
   Librairie de l'Université Georg et Cie, 1954
CARÊME, M. A., *Le Maître d'Hôtel Français*, Paris, Firmin Didot,
   1822
CASTLEREAGH, *Letters and Despatches and Other Papers*, John
   Murray, 1853
CHATEAUBRIAND, F. R. DE, *Congrès de Vérone*, Paris, Delloye 1838
                        Mémoires d'Outre-Tombe, Paris, Le
                        Livre de Poche, 1951

CHOISEUL-GOUFFIER, COMTESSE DE: *Mémoires historiques sur l'Empereur Alexandre 1er*, Paris, 1829

COX, CYNTHIA, *Talleyrand's Successor*, Arthur Barker, 1959

EMPAYTAZ, H. L., *Some Particulars relating to the late Emperor Alexander Previous to his Arrival and during his Stay in Paris in 1815*, with notes by the Rev. Lewis Way, Simpkin & Marshall, 1830

ENGEL, JOS-KRINS, *L'Etranger à Spa*

GENTZ, FRIEDRICH VON, *Briefe an Pilat*, Leipzig, Verlag von F. T. W. Vogel, 1868

Dépêches Inédites aux Hospodars de Valachie, Paris, E. Plon et Cie, 1876
Tagebücher, Leipzig, F. U. Brockhaus, 1873

GILBEY, SIR WALTER, *Modern Carriages*, Vinton & Co., 1905

GORCE, PIERRE DE LA, *La Restauration, Louis XVIII*, Paris, Librairie Plon, 1926

GREEN, J. E. S., *Castlereagh's Instructions for the Conferences at Vienna 1822*, Royal Historical Society Transactions, Third Series, Vol. VII, 1913

GRUNWALD, CONSTANTIN DE, *La Vie de Metternich*, Paris, Calmann-Lévy, 1938

HALL, HERBERT BYNG, *The Queen's Messengers*, Ward, Lock & Tyler, 1870

HAZLITT, WILLIAM, *The Spirit of the Age*, Grant Richards, 1904
The Plain Dealer, Everyman's Library, J. M. Dent & Sons, Ltd., 1928

HEARNSHAW, F. J. C., *European Coalitions, Alliances and Ententes since 1792*. Foreign Office Handbooks, No. 152, H.M.S.O., 1920

HERTSLET, SIR EDWARD, *Recollections of the Old Foreign Office*, 1901, John Murray

Map of Europe by Treaty, Vol. I 1814–1827 Butterworths, 1875

HOWARTH, M. E., *The Silver Greyhound*, Tinsley Brothers, 1880

HUYSKENS, ALBERT, *Festschrift des Aachener Geschichtvereins*, Aachen, 1922

GUEDALLA, PHILIP, *The Duke*, Hodder and Stoughton, 1949

LAS CASES, E. DE, *Mémorial de Ste Hélène*, Paris, Garnier Frères, 1822

LEY, FRANCIS, *Madame de Krüdener et son Temps*, Librairie Plon, 1962

MANN, GOLO, *Secretary of Europe*, The Life of Friedrich Gentz, Yale University Press, 1946

METTERNICH, *Mémoires, Documents et Ecrits Divers laissés par le Prince de*, publié par son fils le Prince Richard de Metternich, Paris, E. Plon et Cie, 1881

MEYER, KARL FRANZ, *Aachen der Monarchen-Kongress*, Aachen, 1819

MIKHAILOVITCH, GRAND DUKE NICHOLAS, *Scenes of Russian Court Life*, Jarrolds Ltd., 1917

MOORE, THOMAS, *Poems*

MÜNSTER, E. F. H., Count von, *Political Sketches of the State of Europe 1814-1867*, Edinburgh, 1868

NAMIER, L. B., *Basic Factors in 19th Century European History*, University of London, The Athlone Press, The Creighton Lecture, 1952.

NESSELRODE, *Lettres et Papiers du Chancelier Comte de Nesselrode, 1760-1850*, Paris, A. Lahure, 1908

NICOLSON, HAROLD, *The Congress of Vienna*, Methuen, 1961

ORDIONI, PIERRE, *Pozzo di Borgo, Diplomate de l'Europe Française*, Librairie Plon, 1935

PASQUIER, *Mémoires du Chancelier*, Paris, Librairie Plon, 1894

PIRENNE, JACQUES-HENRI, *La Sainte Alliance*, Editions de la Baconnière, Neuchâtel, 1946

POELLNITZ, CARL LUDWIG VON, *Les Amusemens de Spa*, London, 1737

PONCHEVILLE, R. MABILLE DE, *Scènes et Tableaux de la Restauration*, Paris, Gautier Languereau, 1935

POZZO DI BORGO, *Correspondance Diplomatique du Comte, et du Comte de Nesselrode*, Paris, Calmann Lévy, 1890

PRADT, ABBÉ DE, *L'Europe après le Congrès d'Aix-la-Chapelle*, Paris, Chez F. Béchet Ainé, 1819

Recueil de la Société Impériale d'Histoire de Russie, Vols. LIV, CXXIX, St. Petersburg, 1908

ROCHECHOUART, COMTE LÉON DE, *Souvenirs*, Paris, 1889

ROUGÉ, A. DE, *Le Marquis de Vérac et ses Amis, 1768-1858*, Librairie Plon, 1890

SATOW, SIR ERNEST, *International Congresses*, Foreign Office Handbooks, No. 151, H.M.S.O., 1920

SAVIGNY-VESCO, MARGUERITE, *Une Fresque Romantique, Les La Ferronays*, Editions Sésame

SKRINE, F. H., *The Expansion of Russia*, Cambridge, 1903

Spa, Les Bobelins ou La Vie aux Eaux de, en 172..., Spa, J. Goffin, 1875

Spa, *Liste des Seigneurs et Dames Venus aux Eaux Minérales de Spa de l'An 1818*

STIRLING, A. M. W., *The Ways of Yesterday*, Thornton Butterworth, Ltd. 1930

STRAKHOVSKY, LEONID, *Alexander I of Russia*, Williams & Norgate, 1949

TILLEY & GASELEE, *The Foreign Office*, London & New York, G. P. Putnam's Sons, 1933

VALLOTTON, HENRY, *Metternich*, Paris, Fayard, 1965

VANDAL, ALBERT, *Napoléon et Alexandre 1er*, Paris, Librairie Plon 1891

WARD, SIR A. W., *The Period of Congresses*, S.P.C.K., 1919

WAY, LEWIS, *Mémoires sur l'Etat des Israélites*, Paris, Firmin Didot, 1819

WEBSTER, SIR CHARLES, *The Congress of Vienna*, Thames & Hudson, 1965

WEINSTOCK, HERBERT, *Rossini*, Oxford University Press, 1968

WELLINGTON, DUKE OF, *Supplementary Despatches, Correspondence and Memoranda of F. M. Arthur*, John Murray, 1865

WILLIAMS, D. E., *The Life and Correspondence of Sir Thomas Lawrence*, Henry Colburn & Richard Bentley, 1831

WOLF, LUCIEN, *Notes on the Diplomatic History of the Jewish Question*, Jewish Historical Society, 1919

Index

Europe in 1815

KINGDO
NORWA

•Christia

DENMARK

Copenhagen

swig

LÜBECK MECKLEN-
BURG

ANOVER   U Bew
R   BRAN

SAXON STATES

BAVARIA

TTEM
RG

D

BARDY   VENETIA
ilan   Verona
RMA
MODE
STA
PA
TUSCANY   STA

Rome

PORTUGAL
Lisbon

S

Gibraltar

Pa